Wizards and Warriors: Massively Multiplayer Online Game Creation

Jason Darby

Course Technology PTR

A part of Cengage Learning

Australia • ... • ...apore • Spain • United Kingdom • United States

COURSE TECHNOLOGY
CENGAGE Learning

Wizards and Warriors: Massively Multiplayer Online Game Creation
Jason Darby

Publisher and General Manager, Course Technology PTR: Stacy L. Hiquet

Associate Director of Marketing: Sarah Panella

Manager of Editorial Services: Heather Talbot

Marketing Manager: Jordan Castellani

Acquisitions Editor: Heather Hurley

Project/Copy Editor: Kezia Endsley

Technical Reviewer: Joshua Smith

Interior Layout Tech: MPS Limited, a Macmillan Company

Cover Designer: Mike Tanamachi

Indexer: Kelly Talbot Editing Services

Proofreader: Kelly Talbot Editing Services

For product information and technology assistance, contact us at **Cengage Learning Customer & Sales Support, 1-800-354-9706**

For permission to use material from this text or product, submit all requests online at **www.cengage.com/permissions**
Further permissions questions can be emailed to
permissionrequest@cengage.com

All trademarks are the property of their respective owners.

All images © Cengage Learning unless otherwise noted.

Library of Congress Control Number: 2008935838

ISBN-13: 978-1-59863-851-6

ISBN-10: 1-59863-851-3

Course Technology, a part of Cengage Learning
20 Channel Center Street
Boston, MA 02210
USA

Cengage Learning is a leading provider of customized learning solutions with office locations around the globe, including Singapore, the United Kingdom, Australia, Mexico, Brazil, and Japan. Locate your local office at: **international.cengage.com/region**

Cengage Learning products are represented in Canada by Nelson Education, Ltd.

For your lifelong learning solutions, visit **courseptr.com**

Visit our corporate website at **cengage.com**

Printed in the United States of America
1 2 3 4 5 6 7 13 12 11

To my wonderful family, Alicia, Jared, Kimberley, and Lucas, for all their support.

ACKNOWLEDGMENTS

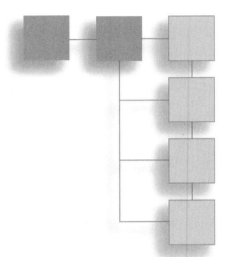

I would like to thank a number of people who have helped me and have been involved in the creation of the book. Without their help, this book would definitely not have been made.

To my wife, Alicia, and my children—Jared, Kimberley, and Lucas—who have supported me through this project.

To Jared Belkus from Solstar Games, who provided me with answers to the many questions that I had throughout the project.

To the professional and friendly staff at Cengage Learning—Heather Hurley and Kezia Endsley—who again have provided excellent support throughout the whole process.

ABOUT THE AUTHOR

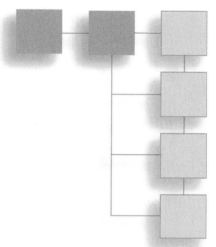

Jason Darby is currently working as an Experienced Game Designer for one of Europe's Leading Game Developers and Publishers, working on a leading AAA game title for the PS3 and Xbox platforms.

Jason is the author of a number of game creation books, including *Make Amazing Games in Minutes, Power Users Guide to Windows Development, Awesome Game Creation – Third Edition, Game Creation for Teens, Going to War: Creating Computer WarGames,* and *Picture Yourself Creating Video Games,* which have all been published by Cengage Learning.

He has also had a number of articles published in the UK press, including a number in *Retro Gamer* and *PC Format,* both leading magazines in their field.

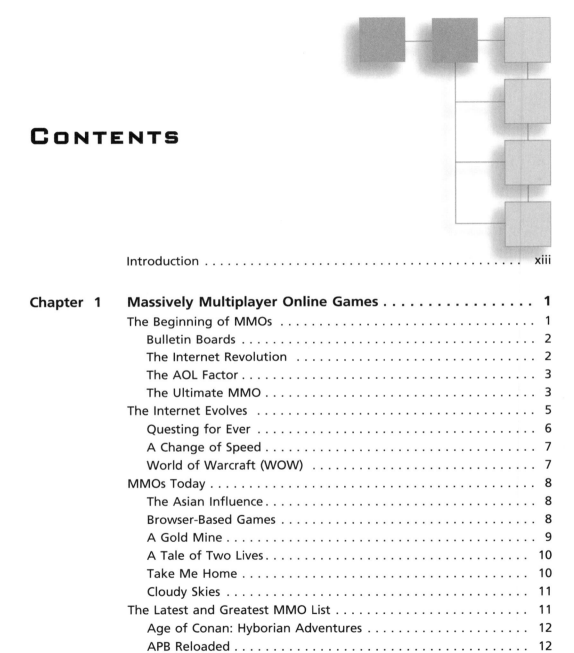

Contents

Introduction

Welcome to the book *Wizards and Warriors*. This book is aimed at anyone who wishes to make an MMO (Massively Multiplayer Online) game. This book will show you what an MMO is comprised of, how to design your game ideas, and give you an extensive tour of an MMO creation package called Realm Crafter.

By the end of the book, you'll be ready to start designing and creating your very own MMO games.

Audience

If you've purchased this book or are reading it in a bookstore, I can assume you're interested in making MMO games. You may be in school or college at the moment and want to make a fun game for your friends and family, create a game that you've always wanted to, create a project that can show off your game making skills, be an indie game maker, or just want to create a game for a bit of fun. As long as you are interested in MMOs and would like to know how to create one, you are in the right place.

Aim of the Book

The aim of the book is to allow anyone to learn what makes an MMO and learn the MMO game creation tool Realm Crafter.

Some of the things that are covered in this book are as follows:

- Understanding what an MMO is

- Considering MMO settings

- Setting up servers and clients for your game

- Using XP and leveling up

- Learning how to come up with your own MMO ideas

- Understanding what Realm Crafter is

- Touring Realm Crafter and learning how it works

- Creating your own terrains and landscapes

- Testing your MMO game

- Getting help

By the end of the book you should be comfortable with the Realm Crafter software and be ready to start on your own MMO creation adventure.

This book does not do any of the following:

- Teach more complex programming languages such as C# and isn't meant to. I do cover the basics of C# in Chapters 14 and 15, which will give you an idea of what you need to do to make your own scripts in Realm Crafter.

- Teach you how to be a graphic artist or music creator. Look at *Composing Music for Video Games* by Andrew Clark or *3D Graphics Tutorial Collection* by Shamms Mortier for such instruction.

- Show you how to become an indie developer or build a team (if you want more information on being an indie developer, read *The Indi Game Development Survival Guide* by David Michael).

- Assume you are an expert at game creation. This book is aimed at those with little or no knowledge of game creation and also at those who have an idea how things are put together but need more information.

Chapter Overview

This book runs in a simple yet effective order to allow you to get the most out of reading it. It is possible to skip certain chapters, but it is recommended that you read through every chapter in the order they appear in the book.

Chapter 1, "Massively Multiplayer Online Games": The book starts off with looking at what an MMO is and how it all began.

Chapter 2, "More About MMOs": A closer look at the key elements of an MMO that you can consider for your own games.

Chapter 3, "Cultivating Your MMO Ideas": How to go about creating your own ideas for your MMOs.

Chapter 4, "Realm Crafter": An introduction to the Realm Crafter software, including its system requirements, installation process, and running it for the first time.

Chapter 5, "The MMO Test": Testing a default project in Realm Crafter to ensure that everything is working correctly. In this chapter, you'll go through the main parts of Realm Crafter that you will need when you are ready to test your game.

Chapter 6, "Compiling Your MMO": The process needed to generate your MMO game so that you can give it to others to test.

Chapter 7, "Adding Media to Your Game": How to get your own media in the Realm Crafter software and how to use the Media tab.

Chapter 8, "The Actors of Your MMO": This chapter discusses the Actors tab in Realm Crafter, which deals with the characters in your game.

Chapter 9, "An Adventurer's Items": This chapter discusses the items that a character might have in an MMO, and also covers the Items tab.

Chapter 10, "World Tour": A tour around the World tab. The World tab is one of the key areas of the game where your characters will walk around.

Chapter 11, "Post Process, Emitters, and Help": The final tabs in the Realm Crafter software, which deal with graphical effects and getting Realm Crafter program help.

Chapter 12, "Creating and Editing Zones and Terrains": In this chapter, you will learn how to create your own MMO zones and terrains.

Chapter 13, "The Create Panel": The Create panel allows you to place various objects in your MMO world; this chapter discusses what those objects are.

Chapter 14, "Scripting Introduction": A basic introduction to the world of scripting.

Chapter 15, "Using the Script Editor": A tour of the Script Editor in Realm Crafter.

Chapter 16, "Putting It All Together": In this chapter, you look at all of the tasks involved in creating your MMO.

Chapter 17, "Game Design Ideas": This chapter contains story ideas that you can use as the basis for your own MMO ideas.

Chapter 18, "Resources": MMOs can require lots of content to make them interesting, so in this chapter you'll learn where you can find additional resources to help you make your game quicker and more efficiently.

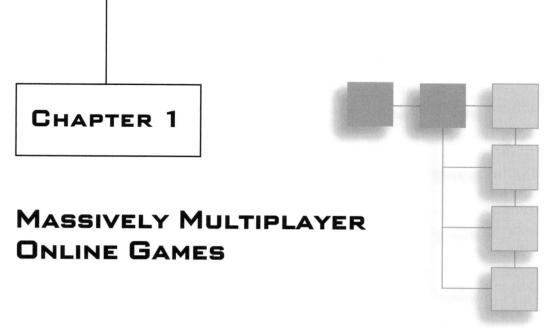

CHAPTER 1

MASSIVELY MULTIPLAYER ONLINE GAMES

You may have heard the term MMO or MMORPG used in gaming magazines or on the Internet. MMO is the abbreviation of Massively Multiplayer Online, whereas MMORPG is that of Massively Multiplayer Online Role Playing Game. These are games that are played over the Internet with other players, sometimes hundreds or even thousands of players working together (or against each other) in the same world (*realm*).

In this book, you will learn how to make your very own MMO game using Realm Crafter from www.realmcrafter.com. By the end of the book, you will be able to make your own exciting MMO games.

This chapter takes a look at the brief history of MMOs and the major events or technologies that have brought us to where we are today.

THE BEGINNING OF MMOS

The very first computer games were created on expensive computer systems called *mainframes;* the majority of these early games were made in universities as programming projects. This was before the home computer revolution took place. These mainframe systems were used to take information and generate results and were perfect for generating statistical information. Unfortunately they had very limited graphical output unlike today's computers and in many cases they would only display text-based characters.

As computer technology was still relatively new and was only being used in universities and businesses, the lack of amazing graphics was not a hindrance as it would be in today's modern games. The technology was as amazing to the people using it as the automobile or airplanes were at the start of the 20th century.

The initial games on these mainframe systems were text-based and text-based adventure games were a perfect fit for this technology. The university systems were networked and it wasn't long before these adventure games were given a basic level of multiplayer functionality. Many of these first adventure games were based on fantasy role-playing games such as *Dungeons and Dragons*. These computer games were named MUD, which is an abbreviation of multi-user dungeon. The multiplayer aspect of these games was basic by today's standards and was limited to sending email messages and chatting within the game.

Bulletin Boards

As computer systems began to improve and move from universities and enterprise businesses to the home, new technology began to appear that allowed home users to communicate with computer systems around the world. This technology was called the Modem (*modulator demodulator*), and by placing the phone receiver on a box (later on this was replaced by using a small box or internal PC card connected directly to the phone line), you were able to make the computer call and connect to another computer or server. Software was created to make it easier to connect to these remote computer systems called bulletin boards. Bulletin board software also provided additional features to download, upload, email, chat, and play online games, whereby the users could play a game remotely, usually in single player mode. Due to the slow download speeds of the early modems, these bulletin boards were generally text based.

The Internet Revolution

The process of connecting to, and communicating with, other machines over a telephone line was still problematic. Telephone call charges were expensive, modems were extremely slow (and expensive), and limited access to a particular machine/server meant redialing every time to get a different set of information/ site. A number of events took place that managed to take accessing remote computers from a specialist only activity to a wider ranging and more popular activity. First was the introduction of the World Wide Web (the Internet), allowing computers in various parts of the world to know where a particular computer (domain) exists and then quickly and easily connect to it using just its name. The second was the introduction of the graphical browser (rather than just text based). The graphical browser meant that information could be presented to the end user in a much more friendly and interesting way. Finally, the speeds of modems began to increase allowing for a much better online experience.

These advances led to a technology and services boom. A number of telephone and computer-based companies began offering easy access to the Internet.

The AOL Factor

One of the big winners from the Internet service providers was a company called America Online (AOL). Many of AOL's competitors provided a simple dial-up connection whereby the user would then use a browser to search the Internet for content. AOL created an exciting and graphically rich front end to the login process. Instead of the user needing to open up a browser and search for particular items, or download programs to help with chatting, AOL provided it all within the same program. AOL contained items such as websites, forum boards, chat rooms, and most importantly games.

In addition to giving the user the ability to access single player games, AOL is also accredited with releasing the first graphical MMO game called *Neverwinter Nights*. The game was first released in 1991.

There were still some serious issues with MMO-based games and the general technology available to the end users. Games were still graphically limited, the speed of modems was very limited, and the cost of Internet access was steep. The high Internet access fee was due to the cost of the actual phone call paid to the telecom provider and a cost per minute paid to AOL. Staying online for too many hours could result in a hefty phone and Internet provider's bill.

The Ultimate MMO

Ultima Online is considered the MMO game that started it all in terms of what users would come to expect from an MMO game. The game was released in 1997 and is still running today with thousands of users, who all pay a monthly subscription. The MMO is a fantasy game based in the lands of Britannia, which is ruled by Lord British. The game mixes fantasy creatures and a medieval-based world with magic and chivalry using 2D graphics.

Ultima also contained some very exciting game play mechanics that ensured that it would become the first MMO to gain large subscriber numbers. The game contained game play mechanics and concepts such as:

- **Horse travel:** As well as allowing players to walk and run over the landscape, players could also obtain mounts such as horses that meant travelling time was substantially reduced. This also allowed players to out-run any potential dangers.

- **Teleports:** Travelling across the world could still take a while on horseback so to allow players to get from one area to another there was a selection of teleports. Each teleport could send a player to various locations, which the player could identify by clicking on the teleport. Some teleports would transport the user to a city location, whereas others would transport the player to the middle of a forest.

- **Quick travel:** There was a third method for quickly moving to a particular location. By using runes and magic, players could inscribe a particular location into memory and then recall it to automatically go back to that location. This was the preferred method for moving quickly between locations players had been to previously.

- **Buying a house:** Sometimes players wanted a place to rest or a place to store their in-game loot. *Ultima Online* allowed the players to buy a house, a shop, and even a castle to use as a base of operations.

- **Owning a ship:** In *Ultima Online* there were a number of locations including islands. Though the players could get to them using a portal, they could also purchase a ship to sail across the seas.

- **In-game chat:** When chatting to other players in the world the typed-in text would appear in a speech bubble above the player's character.

- **Good and evil:** One of the key selling points was the ability to play a character however you wanted to. This could involve creating a small band of evil characters, hiding and waiting for people to walk by alone and then attacking them so players could steal their equipment. Players could pickpocket players and run off with their loot. If players were being pickpocketed and were in a town, they could call the computer AI guards to put the players in their place. Players could also join groups of other players that would hunt down the evil characters.

- **Skills and crafting:** Another key selling point that many of today's MMOs still haven't been able to replicate with success is the skills and crafting systems. *Ultima Online* had a wide ranging skills-based system, allowing the players to choose from a large selection of skills, ensuring that no two players are exactly the same. Perhaps your player will create magic, create traps, or be skilled at fishing. Along with the action-based skills is also a number of crafting skills, allowing the players to make a variety of objects to both use and sell. The players could make their own musical instruments and play them if they had the right skills (much to the annoyance of other players nearby).

- **In-game events:** MMO games should be taking place in evolving worlds, where the player feels that the game is a living entity. *Ultima* created in-game events such as invasions, quests, and player meetings to give the game a real-world feel.

Even with the high costs of Internet access and poor connection speeds, *Ultima* proved a major hit, especially when you take into account that people were paying a monthly subscription to access the game. With dial-up access it was common to find the connection dropping out at the most inappropriate times (for example, when in a battle with other characters). This would lead to finding your character dead, but the game had so much depth that these problems didn't put people off from playing it.

Note

You can find out more information about *Ultima Online* at http://www.uoherald.com/.

THE INTERNET EVOLVES

Not long after the release of *Ultima Online*, the popularity of the Internet and the growing competition in the telecom industry began to drive major changes to the pricing model. The first of these changes were the charges from the Internet providers, moving from per minute charges to a flat fee rate. These changes meant that people could begin to spend more time on the Internet without worrying about exorbitant charges.

Internet speeds were still extremely slow by today's standards, but did improve from 28Kbps and 33Kbps to 56Kbps. At 56Kbps, there were two competing modem formats called K56flex and X2; fortunately a simple firmware update allowed support for either.

Questing for Ever

Even though the Internet speeds people were obtaining were still only 56Kbps, computer technology and graphics cards had been advancing rapidly. The next major MMO to be released was called *EverQuest*, again following the fantasy swords and sorcery type game.

It didn't take long for the 3D aspect of the game to ensure its success and within a short space of time it had already surpassed the subscriptions that *Ultima Online* had achieved.

Players could select from a large set of character classes within the game. These classes provided the players with the basic building blocks and attributes that determined how the characters reacted within the world. These character classes have been reused by many other games since *EverQuest* was released, in games such as *World of Warcraft*. By selecting certain classes, the players might be good at healing themselves or other players, good at close combat, have strong defensive skills or be able to inflict heavy damage.

The interest in *EverQuest* and MMOs in general did increase with news stories, some positive and others negative. These news stories were about in-game marriages between players and people who met within the game starting relationships and in some cases getting married in real life. There were also cases of couples getting divorced due to spouses playing the game too much. You could say *EverQuest* was one of the first MMOs to get TV coverage for MMO addiction. The same issues are still talked about today; in fact the only difference is the name of the actual game.

N o t e

You can find out more information about *EverQuest* at http://eqplayers.station.sony.com/.

A Change of Speed

One of the biggest changes that benefited the world of MMOs is the speed at which computers connect to the Internet. As more and more people found getting access to information and email an important everyday task, this led telecom companies to invest large sums of money to provide faster Internet connections. The first big jump was the ability to move to a technology called ISDN, which used two lines connected at the same time. The users still had to pay per minute charges for Internet access on two lines, which wasn't cost-effective for the home user because telecom companies were starting to offer free weekend calls. The success of ISDN in the home environment was limited and the take up was mainly in businesses.

The advent of ADSL (Asymmetric Digital Subscriber Line) changed the gaming landscape. Unlike dial-up, ASDL allowed you to still use the telephone line while using the Internet. ADSL is commonly known as broadband and provided a massive leap forward in terms of data transfer speeds. Today, the speed of ADSL varies in cost and in features, but it is relatively cheap to get a low-speed ASDL, which is about 10 times the speed of dial-up.

Note

ADSL is also known as DSL in some countries.

As more and more people are using the Internet to watch TV and play online games, the technology will not be standing still. ADSL+ is already being used in some countries and can provide speeds up to 24Mbps; the fiber technology (using light sent down through flexible glass tubes) allows speeds up to 100Mbps. This will be very important for the future of MMOs as they become more complex and contain a larger number of players.

World of Warcraft (WOW)

There are many MMOs available today for the game player to choose from, including those based on TV, movies, and comics as well as the traditional fantasy-based games. The MMO that took the *EverQuest* crown for the largest number of subscribers was a game called *WOW* (*World of Warcraft*), based on a game called *Warcraft,* which originally was an RTS (Real Time Strategy) game.

The game was originally released in 2004/2005. Currently it has over 10 million subscribers who each pay around $14 per month. The success of WOW and the money it generates has led to an explosion in the number of MMO games being released or in development. All the major MMO creators are hoping to replicate the major success that WOW has achieved over the last few years, but for the moment, no one has been successful in replicating its success.

Note

> You can find out more information about potential subscriber numbers for MMOs at http://www. mmogchart.com. This list only runs up to 2008, but gives a good idea of some of the ups and downs an MMO might get in terms of subscriber numbers throughout its life.

MMOs Today

The MMO market is continually changing. This section takes a small look at some of the other influences, changes, and issues that have changed the way MMOs are designed, made, and marketed to the end users.

The Asian Influence

MMOs are extremely popular in Asia, and many of the Western-based MMOs are being translated to Korean and Chinese to increase their subscriber numbers. There have also been a number of Asian-based MMOs translated into English. Many MMOs seem to originate from Korea where there is a very strong gaming presence. In countries such as Korea, gaming Internet cafes are very popular and are seen very much as a social part to playing games. Gaming cafes have not been as successful in Western countries, where people are more inclined to play MMOs at home.

Korean MMOs have a reputation for being a "grind fest," whereby you repeat the same process many times, such as attacking creatures and collecting the items they drop.

Browser-Based Games

With the traditional MMO, you go to your local game store and purchase a boxed product, take it home and install it, and maybe download any updates that have taken place since the CD-ROM was manufactured. Some game companies decided that all this effort was a barrier to casual game players and their young audience. Rather than go direct to retail with a boxed product, which can be very costly, some game companies decided to follow the online game arcade model. If you browse the Internet, you can find many "Play Now" game arcades, using web technology such as Flash and Java. These types of sites allow you to quickly log online and play a game instantly without the hassle of the big budget MMO games. One such MMO that can be played in a browser is *RuneScape*; you only need the Java client software installed on your PC. Once that is installed you can get up and running quickly, as you don't need to install *RuneScape*. Browser online games such as *RuneScape* have been very successful, as they provide free games with a low monthly fee for additional features. It's a model that many companies are now following.

Note

> *RuneScape* also has a Windows client that users can download and use instead of the Java browser client.

Note

> Browsers are becoming increasingly relevant in today's MMO game market, and with the increasing number of changes that are taking place within an MMO game, browsers provide a cheaper, quicker, and easier method to get users playing your game online, especially in the casual market, where users don't want to wait for hours for the latest MMO patch to be installed.
>
> You can find out more information about *RuneScape* at http://www.runescape.com/.

A Gold Mine

Because MMO games have complex virtual economies where buying and selling have a profound effect on the world that people play in, it is no surprise that there are people who try to abuse this system to make money. *Gold farming* is the process of playing a game with the sole intent of obtaining gold and objects that can then be swapped for real money. Micro industries exist whereby players in poorer countries play for hours in order to earn in-game currency that they then try to sell to players who want to gain an advantage. According to some estimates, this industry has become big business and millions of dollars is exchanged each year. In many cases this type of activity is banned, but MMOs have been unable to stamp it out fully. In fact, if you log onto a game like WOW, it's likely that within a half hour you'll see a message from a gold seller.

Some games have decided not to charge a monthly subscription, but instead charge users for getting additional benefits. This does prevent some aspects of gold farming, although it is the case that many games do not allow the payment of money for gold, but usually in-game items.

In many cases, players can report other players to the administrators of the game. In most cases you can play MMOs and never have to use this feature. Some MMOs use these types of features for identifying problem users such as gold sellers. It is not uncommon to hear regular stories of MMO games banning thousands of users at a time. These are usually spam-type characters whose only role is to sell or advertise gold to other players.

A Tale of Two Lives

In addition to the traditional hack and slash (fighting)-based MMOs, there has also been a growth in social-based MMOs. These programs are about meeting other people, chatting, and socializing. There are social events and games that can be played such as chess. One particular MMO called *Second Life* has also included a financial aspect where you can buy land and items, but more importantly you can sell services to other users.

It has also become a tool for companies, religious organizations, and education establishments to market their products and services to the general public.

Note

You can find out more information about *Second Life* at www.secondlife.com.

In the section of MMOs listed later in this chapter, I also discuss a rise in a new form of MMO games, which one could call the Facebook MMO or social MMO. Multiplayer online games do not necessarily have to be about killing dragons, being a pirate, or flying spaceships; they can also be as simple as looking after your own farm, running a sandwich shop, or being a penguin.

Take Me Home

The current generation of consoles has been built to include advanced networking technology. They have login accounts and online stores where you can access games and, in some countries, video-based stores.

Sony, makers of the PS3 console, decided that part of its core strategy would include a social-based experience much like *Second Life*. The key difference being that it would be game-centric. PlayStation Home was released as beta at the end of 2008 and has grown to include areas for players to socialize related to games releases such as *Resident Evil* and *Uncharted 2*. Home is free to access and all that is required is a PS3 and a PlayStation Network Account. Within the virtual world you can also play chess, arcade machines, pool, and more. The world also includes micro transactions and the user can buy items for their virtual home and avatar.

Although Home has been derided by some users and has had mixed reviews, Sony has claimed that sales in just one month were one million dollars.

Cloudy Skies

This chapter has already covered how browsers are changing the way people access MMOs (and games in general). A new service that is beginning to appear is the cloud network. Rather than rely on the people's hardware to play games (for example when a new game is released it has to support many different hardware specifications), what if you could release a new game that runs on old computers? The concept is the same as what in some businesses is called "thin client". The way thin client (and the cloud) works is that you don't have to worry about changing the hardware every few years to support improvements in applications or even operating systems. All that is sent to and from the users is screen display data, and input information from the mouse and keyboard. A small client application is installed on the computer (PC/Mac) and small amounts of data are sent back and forth. At the moment there are a number of systems being launched. For smaller games these are perfect, although there is a Lag issue with first person shooters (and this would also be a problem in MMOs).

N o t e

Lag is the time delay in doing an action, such as moving a character and the time it takes to see that action take place. Lag is a major problem in MMOs, and can really affect a player's opinion of a game.

THE LATEST AND GREATEST MMO LIST

There is a growing list of popular MMOs available now. This section takes a whirlwind tour of some MMOs that are currently available or will be released soon (this list is correct as of this writing and some games may or may not be available at a later stage). This list isn't meant as an in-depth analysis of the MMOs listed as there would be too much to cover. The list should give you a taste of what the game is about and give you an idea if you should consider downloading the game to try.

Many MMOs contain similar ideas and concepts and it is useful to try out as many games as possible so you can see what might be good to add in your own MMO games. It is also a useful exercise to see how the game mechanics work, how the worlds and maps are designed, and how they integrate the main story within the game. You may be able to pick up a boxed product at reduced prices with a free 30-day access, or some games you can download off the MMO's website or access automatically through a web browser. There is such a wide range of MMO games that it would be expensive or time-consuming, so try to pick games that match the type of game you are thinking about making in Realm Crafter.

The following is a selection of the MMOs available or coming soon; I recommend you use the Internet and in particular game websites to find out about any others.

Age of Conan: Hyborian Adventures

Age of Conan is based on the books by Robert E. Howard. Or you might know about Conan from the 80s movies starring Arnold Schwarzenegger. *Age of Conan* is a mature MMO. On its release it obtained some excellent pre-order sales and it is said that over 700,000 copies were shipped to retailers.

As with many MMOs, *Age of Conan* is in an ever-changing landscape where new features and changes are made at an amazing pace, and so something that might not have worked six months ago might have been changed.

You can find out more information about *Age of Conan* at http://www. ageofconan.com.

APB Reloaded

APB (*All Points Bulletin*) is a term used in law enforcement and is a perfect title for this game that is all about the police. The game has two factions, the enforcement agency and the criminals. Gaming websites were calling this game the GTA (*Grand Theft Auto*) of MMOs, with its mix of driving, destruction, and shooting. The game had an estimated $100 million development budget and shortly after its release the company that created APB went into administration (sort of like bankruptcy in the UK). Since then the game has been purchased by another company and is being re-released as *APB Reloaded*.

You can find out more information about *APB* at http://www.apb.com.

Anarchy Online

Anarchy Online is a free-to-play science-fiction-based MMO. The game is played 30,000 years in the future where computers are a fact of life and humans have advanced themselves by attaching microprocessors to their bodies. You play the game on a planet called Rubi-Ka where the Omni-Tek Corporation fights with the Clans. The game has some interesting concepts; for example you can own your own apartment where you can store items from your inventory (although this is only if you don't lose the key to your apartment, otherwise you lose all items stored within it). You also have the opportunity to build your own city, after you have purchased the land to build it on.

Anarchy also uses the micro payments system, which in this case is called premium content. You can purchase extra clothing items or vehicles, such as a jet bike or hover board to help you get around quicker.

You can find out more information about *Anarchy Online* at http://www. anarchy-online.com/.

Champions Online

Ever wanted to be a super hero? *Champions Online* gives you the chance to create a highly customizable character, both in looks and in range of available super powers. Based on the pen and paper role-playing game from the 1980s, now you can create the ultimate super hero. The game allows solo play or the ability to join others to form your very own super team!

You can find out more about the game at http://champions-online.com.

City of Heroes

This is the original super heroes game, with the one ability that everyone wants, the ability to fly! You are tasked with protecting Paragon city from dastardly criminals, villains, and terrifying monsters. The character creation screen in particular has garnered high praise. Some MMOs have limited character sets and so the players end up looking similar, whereas *City of Heroes* has many combinations to give an endless number of crazy, colorful, and interesting costumes.

You can find out more about *City of Heroes* at http://www.cityofheroes.com.

City of Villains

City of Villains is a standalone box product purchase and an expansion to the *City of Heroes* game. It added new content and allowed you to play as a villain in the game. Owning both products meant you can have multiple good and evil characters within the same game.

You can find out more about *City of Villains* at http://www.cityofheroes.com.

Dark Age of Camelot

In *Dark Age of Camelot,* players can join one of the three groups, the Britons, the Celts, or the Norse. The story is set in a world where King Arthur has just died in the kingdom of Albion. *Dark Age of Camelot* is very much a player vs. player game. Player vs. player is where the different groups can attack each other within the game, and can partake in several tasks such as territorial conquest and protecting various relics while trying to capture the enemy's relics. If you are interested in a medieval-based game that uses Arthurian-,Celtic-, and Norse-based mythology, you should check out this game.

You can find out more about *Dark Age of Camelot* at http://www.darkageofcamelot.com/.

DC Universe Online

City of Heroes and *City of Villains* both had a clear run of the super hero games for a while, but with *Champions Online* and now *DC Universe,* they will soon be having some competition. *DC Universe Online* is an MMO that features the DC comic book heroes, such as Batman and Superman. You cannot play these characters, but you can be asked to fight alongside these heroes. *DC Universe* is one of the new breed of MMOs that are multiplatform, the game is currently available for PC and PlayStation 3. This will become more common as game companies try to bring together users from different platforms.

You can find out more information about *DC Universe Online* at http://dcuo. station.sony.com/.

Dungeons and Dragons

In the 1970s a new type of game was created, involving a fantasy setting, storytelling, and the rolling of dice. The game was *Dungeons and Dragons*, a role-playing game that involved a group of people who were the players and one person who was in charge of the story and events called the Dungeon Master. The Dungeon Master would set out a basic scene and the players would decide what they wanted to do with their characters.

The success of the game and its detailed rulebooks were perfect for computer game conversion. The rules were already written about how characters should act with each other based on alignment (good, lawful, evil, and so on), the weapons they could use, and the armor they could wear. *Dungeons and Dragons* has a rich and varied gaming history and this makes the game very interesting to play.

The *Dungeons and Dragons* role-playing game has also been made into an excellent cartoon TV series (from the 1980s) and a not-so-good movie.

If you are in North America, you can find more information at http://www.ddo. com.

If you are in Europe, you can find information at http://www.ddo-europe.com.

Eve Online

Eve Online is a space-based game set 21,000 years in the future. There are a total of five races within Eve, four of which are playable. The game's major playing points are the political alliances that different players and groups of players can bring to the game and its economy-based system. The game uses the economic and political aspects to draw players into the game by creating and breaking alliances. If you have ever played a board game called *Risk*, you will know that alliances are fragile and usually don't last very long. Other MMOs have guilds, which are groups of people who will play together, while *Eve* has corporations.

These corporations can conduct business by mining or manufacturing items and then by selling them to other players. Corporations can also declare war on other corporations, leading to all-out war across the star system.

Eve has regularly hit the gaming news for the way that players have conducted themselves within the game (within the rules), where different corporations have infiltrated other competing corporations and set out to sabotage them.

The political and sabotage aspects of *Eve* make for a very compelling reason to play the game, but it is said that the game can be hard going for the beginner and in some cases too much number crunching when it comes to the economy and working out how to make a profit from various mining and manufacturing activities.

You can find out more about *Eve* from http://www.eveonline.com.

EverQuest

EverQuest is a fantasy-based MMO and was one of first of a new breed of MMO games that featured 3D worlds and characters; the game was released in 1999. At its height it was said to have had over 400,000 subscribers.

I already discussed *EverQuest* earlier in this chapter; for more information about the game, visit http://eqplayers.station.sony.com/.

EverQuest II

As technology improves sometimes game companies find it easier to release a new version of a game rather than update the older version. This is not always the case, and some games like *WOW* and *Ultima* have had in-game engine updates to keep them current. With *EverQuest II*, Sony created a new game engine and based the story 500 years after previous events. The game was released in November 2004 and is a monthly subscription-based game.

SOE (Sony Online Entertainment) announced and subsequently released a free-to-play version of EQ2.

You can find out more information about the game at http://everquest2.station.sony.com.

FarmVille

With the growth in social networking sites such as Facebook, the way companies have tried to reach their audience has changed. This has also meant a change in the way games are presented to the users. Facebook has become a focal point for people to exchange information with friends and acquaintances. Users can post information about their current location, indicate their status, and upload images. Users can also allow games that they play to upload information about how well they are progressing. *FarmVille* is one such game that has been rumored to have millions of users playing it. The game is all about owning a farm, plowing fields, planting seeds, and watching your farm grow. The game is free to play on entry, but like many games, it has a coins system that allows you to pay cash for in-game items and money, which can then be spent on improving your farm quicker than if you were playing in free-to-play mode.

FarmVille is not a traditional MMO with many users running around the same space, but you can add your Facebook friends as farm neighbors and view what they are doing within the farm. Even though *FarmVille* (and *Mafia Wars* mentioned later) is not the type of MMO you'll be making in this book, it's worth a mention and a look.

You can find out more about *FarmVille* at www.farmville.com.

Final Fantasy XI

Released in 2002 first on the PlayStation 2 platform and then on Windows, *Final Fantasy XI* is an MMO based on the extremely popular *Final Fantasy* games. The game has also been released on the Xbox 360, and is therefore the first MMO to be cross-platform. The game has a user base of around 500,000 and is particularly popular in Japan, from where it originates.

You can find out more information about *Final Fantasy XI* from http://www.playonline.com/ff11us/index.shtml.

Free Realms

Free Realms is one of a number of MMOs being released by Sony that will work on both the PlayStation 3 platform and the PC. *Free Realms* is aimed at the younger age market and will be trying to capture some of the users currently using *RuneScape*. It has a very cartoony feel to it, and allows the players to pick from a wide selection of careers, including blacksmith, chef, ninja, postman, and more. The game contains lots of mini-games as well as a card battle/ trading system.

The website for *Free Realms* is http://www.freerealms.com/.

Guild Wars

Guild Wars is a cooperative player vs. player MMO, set in a fantasy world called Tyria. When it was released in 2005 it became an instant hit as it was one of the only MMOs to be free of monthly subscriptions (since then others have followed). Since the release of the first product, a number of expansion packs have been released and according to the developers over 6 million boxed products have so far been sold.

You can find out more information about Guild Wars at http://www. guildwars.com.

A new version of *Guild Wars* is currently in development (and looking very nice too). You can find more information about *Guild Wars 2* at http://www.guildwars2.com

Home (PlayStation)

PlayStation Home is a social networking MMO that provides users a way of meeting other PlayStation users as well as playing games such as chess, Red Bull Air race, and arcades. Home also hosts a growing number of game areas relating to games that have been released on the PlayStation 3.

Star Wars the Old Republic

Star Wars has already had one very successful MMO associated with it in *Star Wars Galaxies*. *Star Wars the Old Republic* is a new MMO in development from Lucas Arts and Bioware. With this MMO the developers are hoping to introduce a more story-driven element to playing an MMO. The game takes place 3,500 years before the rise and fall of Darth Vader.

This is considered one of the AAA big hitters with regards to MMOs. With the size, scale, and scope of the project, it certainly has a chance of emulating WOW's success.

Visit http://www.swtor.com for more information.

Lego Universe

Lego games have become extremely popular in the last few years, since TT games released a number of movie-based tie-ins, starting with *Lego Star Wars* and *Lego Indiana Jones.* Trying to cash in on the popularity of Lego, Net Devil (Gazillion Entertainment), the creators of the *Lego Universe,* have set about making an MMO game that will allow children to create their own in-game Lego items, complete the normal MMO quests, and socialize with other Lego users. The game is aimed at the younger market.

You can find out more about *Lego Universe* at http://universe.lego.com/.

Lord of the Rings

Lord of the Rings is a set of books written by J.R.R. Tolkien, set in a fantasyland called Middle Earth, featuring races of orcs, elves, humans, and hobbits. The story follows a ring of power called the One Ring, which must be destroyed in Mount Doom before the Dark Lord Sauron can retrieve it and turn the lands of Middle Earth into a wasteland and enslave its people.

The books were followed by an animated cartoon, which unfortunately was never finished, though it was released. In 2001 the first of the three movies was released to both critical and commercial success. The rest of the trilogy followed in 2002 and 2003, and is considered by many to be one of the best book to film adaptions. There have been a number of very successful RTS games, and with the success of the movies and the amount of story content available from the books, this was a perfect title to make into an MMO. The game was released in 2007, and has had numerous in-game expansions (called books) and one boxed expansion pack called *Mines of Moria.*

You can find out more information about *Lord of the Rings* at the EU website of http://www.lotro-europe.com and the US website http://www.lotro.com. *LOTRO* is also available in Japan, Korea, and Russia.

Mafia Wars

Mafia Wars is a Facebook game where you start a career in crime as the boss of a mafia group. The game is pretty simple; you can get involved in crimes, use experience points, and buy properties. You can call on the help of other players. It's not an MMO in the traditional sense, but it's where a part of the market of massively online games is moving.

Visit http://www.zynga.com for more information.

Pirates of the Burning Sea

Pirate-based games have always been popular since the very early home computers. The ability to mix land-based and sea-based concepts is an interesting notion that was successfully implemented in a single player game by Sid Meier called *Pirates*.

Pirates of the Burning Sea is an MMO very much in the style of *Pirates*. The game is set in the year 1720. You can play the part of a navy officer, privateer, trader, cutthroat, or buccaneer. You can own your own ship(s), attack other nationalities' ports, or move around on land. You can also customize your character with colorful clothes and add items such as wooden peg legs.

You can find out more information about *Pirates of the Burning Sea* at http:// www.burningsea.com.

Ragnarok Online

Ragnarok Online is a Korean MMO released in 2001, and is now available in many other countries. The game is set in a magical world based on Nordic mythology and graphically it has a typical Asian cartoon feel to it, very much in the style of Manga/Pokemon.

You can find out more information about *Ragnarok Online* and can select your particular country's website from http://www.ragnarokonline.com.

RuneScape

RuneScape is a free-to-play MMO, and is very popular with the teenage market. The main reason for its success is the ability to play the MMO from within a browser. You can also upgrade the account to allow for additional benefits such as more quests, mini-games, new areas to travel to, and the ability to play the game in full screen.

Additional *RuneScape* information can be found at the website http://www.runescape.com.

Second Life

Second Life was covered earlier in this chapter. *Second Life* is not really a game but a social and business experiment that gives the users the opportunity to buy and sell land as well as build, create events, and advertise a particular item or company.

You can find more information about *Second Life* at http://secondlife.com.

Star Trek Online

One of the most anticipated MMOs in development (even more so with the rebooted *Star Trek* movie success) is *Star Trek Online*. The game is being developed by Cryptic Studios, who were responsible for the *City of Heroes* and *City of Villains* MMOs. The Star Trek universe is a rich tapestry of different cultures, races, ships, and worlds. Having a large number of TV series made means there is a wide variety of content they can use within the game. Anyone who remembers the original Star Trek series will certainly be looking forward to Tribbles within the game.

The game allows the players to command a ship and partake in ship-to-ship combat, as well as compete in the normal land-based MMO quests. You can take on the role as an engineer, tactical officer, doctor, and a selection of other roles. The game's universe is set 30 years after the film *Star Trek Nemesis*.

You can find out more information about *Star Trek Online* at http://www.startrekonline.com.

Star Wars Galaxies

Star Wars Galaxies is an MMO based on the Star Wars universe. Released in 2003, it is now over 5 years old. As with many MMOs the game has had many new features added over the life of the product, such as space travel/battles, player housing, creature mounts, and vehicles. You also have the chance of becoming a Jedi (good or evil), manufacturing items, and raiding the republic and empire bases which lead to player-versus-player battles.

You can find out more about *Star Wars Galaxies* at http://starwarsgalaxies.station.sony.com.

Stronghold Kingdoms

Stronghold Kingdoms is a castle-building strategy simulation game (the Castle MMO). The game involves building up your castle and its forces and defeating the enemy. The creators of this game decided that it would be very interesting if you could create your medieval towns and castles, but with many other players doing the very same. This leads to a massive online game with a large number of players fighting to be the ultimate medieval lord.

You can find out more information about *Stronghold Kingdoms* at http://www.strongholdkingdoms.com.

Ultima Online

Ultima Online was discussed previously in this chapter. The game is still going strong after 10 years. It isn't in true 3D, but in isometric 3D, and doesn't have the best graphics compared to the current crop of MMOs, but what it lacks in graphics it makes up for the amount of content and the amount of things that players can do.

You can find out more about *Ultima Online* at http://www.uoherald.com.

Warhammer Online

Warhammer Online was released in 2008 and is an MMO based on the popular Games Workshop fantasy role-playing and board war game *Warhammer*. This game is based on a medieval fantasy setting and not to be confused with Games Workshop's other major game called *Warhammer 40K*.

There are a number of races that you can play in the game, including dwarfs, empire, high elves, chaos, dark elves, and green skins. Recent patches have also added additional characters types such as the orc Choppa and the dwarf slayer.

Warhammer allows the forces of good and evil to fight and lay siege to each other's cities. There are also public quests that anyone in the area can join in and play, which can make for interesting side quests.

Warhammer has also introduced free play, where you can now play the game for free until you reach a particular level.

As of this writing there were around 300,000 active subscriptions on the *Warhammer* game. You can find out more information about the *Warhammer* game at http://www.warhammeronline.com.

WOW: World of Warcraft

World of Warcraft (or *WOW*, as it is also known) is the current king of the hill when it comes to MMOs. The Warcraft mythology was already a successful real-time strategy game brand before the MMO was released. The game was released at the end of 2004; and it quickly established itself as the MMO to play. *World of Warcraft* has a fantasy and medieval theme, featuring a large variety of creatures and enemies, such as pirates, robbers, spiders, bears, wolves, and sheep, to name a few. The game uses a very bright and colorful land, with some very interesting and different areas for the players to traverse, such as mountains, forests, and deserts.

The game currently has over 10 million subscribers, which far exceeds any other MMO to date. *World of Warcraft* has also had a number of very successful expansion packs released since the game's original launch, allowing users to increase the level of characters and travel to new areas within the game.

If you haven't already played the game, I would definitely recommend that you take a look, before you begin making your own MMO. This game has the largest and most committed user base, which means that it is doing things right in terms of game design and content.

To find out more information about *World of Warcraft*, visit the website http://www.worldofwarcraft.com.

TAKE ADVANTAGE OF ANY MMO TRIALS

There is a growing number of MMOs now appearing, and while some current MMOs may be closed down, it does seem that in the future there will be even more growth within the MMO sector. In the early days of MMOs there was less of a need to provide trial software for the game, but now with the increased competition, many of the MMOs listed in this chapter have some form of free trial period available to use. In some cases the trial period may only be 10 to 30 days, but it should give you a good idea of what the different MMOs look like, and how it feels to play them.

It is essential for any MMO creator to take a look at other MMOs and see what they have done right and which areas don't work as well. This will provide you with a useful stepping stone in deciding what type of MMO you want to create as well as give you an idea of what content, areas, and creatures to include in your game.

Note

The MMO market is one of growth and constant change. At the time of writing some of the MMOs mentioned in this book may have been closed down, whereas others will have appeared or gone from a subscription method to free to play. There is fierce competition in the MMO market. It's important to realize that an MMO that does not add new content and updates is unlikely to stay popular for very long.

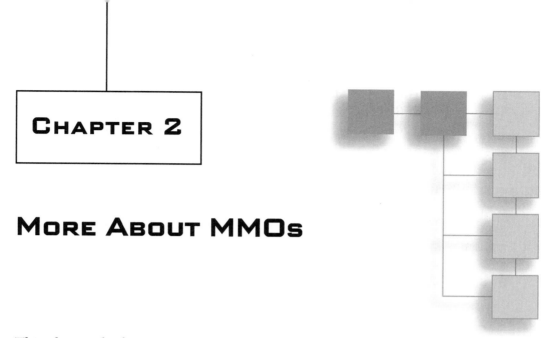

CHAPTER 2

MORE ABOUT MMOS

This chapter looks at MMOs in more detail, including their availability, pricing, and game-play elements. This chapter gives you an overview of the concepts and details of MMOs that you should be considering placing in your own MMO game.

A few of the options contained within this chapter may not apply to your MMO—for example charging a fee or multiple servers—but are included for completeness and for those users who might be considering such options.

DIFFERENT STYLES AND TYPES OF MMOS

There are many different styles and types of MMOs, some of which were mentioned in Chapter 1. For completeness, they are all covered here.

- **Fantasy:** The most popular setting for an MMO is in a fantasy world. This is mainly because it gives the game creation much more artistic license than most other game types. This is also true for games that are not MMOs, as the creators can create their own fantasy story, characters, and creatures.

- **Historical**: Historically-based games are very rare in MMOs, mainly because it is difficult to set an evolving game in a true historical setting. This doesn't mean that a historical MMO is impossible or shouldn't be attempted as there is a lot of material for the game designer/maker to reference. The type of historical event or timeframe you are referencing determines how close you have to stay to the original material or in fact how careful you have to be making a game on it. Recent history has more pitfalls than benefits for the MMO game creator. If you are using ancient history, such as Romans or medieval times, you don't have to make it an exact fit. You can use buildings, clothing, names, and events to fill up your MMO world.

- **Mythology**: Many MMOs use mythology for a background history or story. When making an MMO it is very important to have a background story to give your game some depth, and it ensures that your players can appreciate why they are doing certain quests. The most popular mythology currently used in games is Norse mythology.

- **Modern Day**: There are very few modern-day MMOs, mainly because it is difficult to create a complex story in a modern-day setting. Some MMOs have achieved it using a sprinkling of science fiction or using a particular gaming concept. There are two memorable games using a modern day settings; the first uses police and criminals (*APB*), whereas the other uses spies (*The Agency*).

- **Science Fiction**: Science fiction is a popular area for MMOs, and is probably the second most popular genre in MMOs games. Science fiction-based games can include ideas such as amazing inventions, robots, space, or futuristic concepts.

- **Horror**: Horror is certainly an area that is very much ignored on the whole in MMOs. This is a shame as there is so much potential for this subject matter to make a really interesting MMO. Some games do have creatures or NPCs based on some fictional horror characters, such as zombies and ghosts.

You can see some images from an MMO example made in Realm Crafter in Figures 2.1 and 2.2.

Figure 2.1
A small set of buildings with a castle standing ominously in the background.

Figure 2.2
A small selection of buildings in a town.

GAME PAYMENT METHODS

Chapter 1 mentioned a little bit about payment methods. There are a few different payment methods you can consider for your own games, and it really depends on the overall quality and size of the market that you are aiming for. For example, a commercial MMO may have anything from 10 to 200 people working on it at any one time and so will need to find ways of creating a steady income from the game when it's released, whereas an MMO made by an individual for a few friends will most likely be free. This is not a hard and fast rule and there are many examples of small development teams selling their games on various market places.

Some of the payment methods available to you are as follows:

- **Free-to-play:** Considering the large number of MMOs becoming available as well as the long shelf life of MMOs in general, in some cases lasting more than 10 years, it's difficult for new MMOs to keep a strong user base. Charging a monthly subscription for some of these MMO games is becoming increasingly difficult. This has led to a greater number of free-to-play MMOs. In a crowded marketplace, it is easier to attract people to a game if it is free at entry (there is no payment to go online and play it). There may be other ways for a company/creator to obtain some form of financial payback, including in-game advertising and micro transactions.

- **Monthly subscription:** Charging a monthly fee is typically something that only the larger and more commercial MMOs can do in this increasingly busy market. You will not find non-commercial or independent MMOs with a monthly charge in most cases, because the cost of making a commercial engine that can justify a charge is in the tens of millions. Unless you are working on a costly commercial engine with popular or well known intellectual property, it is best to investigate other methods of payment. The normal price for a monthly commercial MMO is $12–16 per month. The cost of these monthly subscriptions combined with the amount of playing time means that many players subscribe to only one or two MMOs. It is possible that many MMO players wouldn't pay for two full priced monthly subscriptions but would pay for a full priced MMO and a smaller scale MMO with a smaller monthly subscription. A number of MMOs are now appearing with lower subscription fees, to entice users who may decide that they won't miss a couple of dollars a month. Many users are also looking for games that don't require as much time and effort as a full-priced MMO, where they can just log in for an hour every so often and have some fun without worrying about spending lots of money each month on a game they are not playing much.

- **Micro transactions:** Some games have subscriptions *and* micro transactions, but a growing number of MMOs are being released free to play with the ability to earn revenue from the micro transaction method. Micro transactions give the game player the ability to pay a small amount of money for a particular in-game item or advantage. An example of this is in the PlayStation Home community system, where you can pay for furniture, clothing, and even buildings for your in-game avatar. Other games sell items such as more inventory or bank space to store more in-game items or other beneficial items, including spell scrolls and potions. The games can be played without purchasing the items, but are enhanced when players do buy them.

- **Donations**: If you are making an MMO for fun or to show off your game design skills, it is likely that you will not charge any fees for the MMO. You are probably making a game in your spare time; you might want to have some help in paying for any server equipment or other small-scale costs. If you are working on a game that you are not going to charge people for, a good way of helping finance your game is through donations. You can add a simple link on your website asking for donations to help pay for the development of the game. The amount of money you make from such donations won't be much, but might help pay something toward your ongoing costs.

SERVERS AND CLIENTS

To create an MMO, you will need two types of technology. The first is a client PC. This could be a PC running Windows Vista or Windows 7, for example. This is where the MMO software is installed and contains things such as graphics that the players will see and the GUI (Graphic User Interface) that the players will load up to connect to the MMO. The client PC is the machine that the players will use to play the game.

The second thing that is required is a server, located somewhere on the Internet. The server will be running a server operating system such as Linux or Windows Server. The server holds all the information about the game, such as the quest information, player data such as current gold or XP (experience points). The server will also store the player's location within the world. The reason for having a server is two-fold; first, the server needs to be the central logging on point for all clients, and second, the server will be security enabled. If the MMO data was contained on the client PC, it would be easy for the player to find out where the information of XP and gold was stored and amend it. This would allow for wholesale cheating. To store information and data, the server also requires a database; this could be MySQL or some other common database application.

Note

Experience points (XP) are values that players can accrue for completing tasks within a game. These experience points can normally be traded in for skill points, which players can use to upgrade their characters.

For the clients to connect to the server, they need the server's location. Every computer device that accesses the Internet must have an IP address. An IP address contains information about the machine's location by country, the service provider providing the address, and a number assigned to that particular computer.

An IP address consists of a set of four numbers separated by a dot; an example of an IP address could be 127.0.0.1.

Note

The 127.0.0.1 address is called a *loopback* address, as this is assigned automatically to your PC's network card. It is used for testing that your network card is working correctly. If you go to a command prompt and type **ping 127.0.0.1**, you will get a reply.

This IP address is not the same as the one given to your PC by your Internet provider.

Note

As the number of devices that can connect to the Internet has exploded in recent years, the number of available unique numbers is being exhausted. A new numbering system called IPv6 is beginning to be used to replace IPv4. IPv6 and IPv4 are available in Vista and Windows 7, although in most cases the rollout has been slow. On June 8 2011, the Internet Society, together with several other large organizations, will hold a World IPv6 Day, a global 24-hour test of IPv6.

The IP address also contains a unique number given to that machine. It is common for users' PCs to have a dynamically assigned IP address; this means that the machine's IP number does not stay the same. This is fine for general PC use, as you do not need the IP address to stay the same. This is not the case for servers as any MMO client needs to know where the machine is so that the client can connect to it. If the IP address keeps changing the PC will not be able to find the server. This is the same issue when you decide to visit your favorite website in a web browser. Say, for example you type **www.makeamazing.com** into a browser. The browser looks up the name on a special server called a DNS server and translates this domain name to an IP address, at which point it knows how to connect to the server.

So having a static IP address for your MMO server is essential if you want anyone to find it. If you are going to test your MMO at home and have a few friends connect to it over the Internet, you could provide them with the current IP address that your ISP has provided. If you have a server online provided by an ISP then this will be a static IP address.

If you want to set up a server at home with a static IP address, you should contact your ISP (Internet Service Provider) to get a static address.

Note

An ISP is an Internet Service Provider; these are the people that provide you with Internet access.

Note

Not all MMOs will install software to the client PC. In games such as *RuneScape*, the game is played within a web browser (although the user has the option of downloading a client).

THE CHARACTER CREATION SCREEN

In every MMO, the players need a character that they can control and send out into the dangerous world that you have created. Players need an interface that they can use to create their characters; this part of the MMO is called the Character Creation screen. Here the players select a particular type of character—perhaps Orc, Human or Elf—and then select the types of clothes, the look and color of the hair, and even perhaps the eye color and nose shape.

Character creation is considered a very important part of setting an early quality stake in the ground. The Character Creation screen sets the tone for the rest of the game, and a Character Creation screen with few or no options will not fill the player with the initial confidence of what is to follow. Neither do you want a Character Creation screen with so many options that the interface is too busy or confusing. This does not mean you have to sacrifice the number of options that a player can have to customize their characters. Games such as *City of Heroes* have thousands of combinations, but in a very easy-to-use interface. The player can easily spend lots of time just in the Character Creation area of an MMO, making their characters.

It is common for MMOs to allow the players to create multiple characters within a game, but most limit the number to around 6-10 characters. Normally they provide enough character slots to allow players to try all of the different types of characters available in the game.

Note

Some games, especially free-to-play games, will give you an initial number of character slots, and you need to pay a small amount of money (a micro transaction) to add other characters.

GUILDS AND GROUPS

Many MMOs have a lot of complexity and depth, and as you progress through the game, the quests become more complicated and increase in scale. Some quests are extremely difficult to complete without the aid of other people. This could mean joining a group to achieve a quest with people you have just met, or getting help from friends who you have played with before.

One type of group that has become a primary way of keeping in contact with people who you regularly play with is a guild. A *guild* is a user-created group, usually with a user specified name. Some players take guilds very seriously and have a set of rules that players must abide by. Players often come and go in guilds on a regular basis, often joining just to get help completing a certain aspect of a game, whereas others will have many friends and acquaintances whom they regularly play with over a number of years.

Most MMOs have a special screen in their game to create or join a guild. Most of the time you will find out about a guild from another player, who invites you to it if you perform well in a group quest.

Experience and Levels

Your players should accumulate experience points (XP for short) completing quests and killing creatures. XP is usually the basic indicator used to *level up* players. When players level up, they normally acquire new skills, potions, or spells. In some MMOs, the leveling up allows new items every two to four levels gained, so a player would receive new skills at level 2, 4, 6, and so on. Most MMOs have a level cap; this is the maximum level that a player can reach, for example level 50. Once the player has reached this level, they won't be able to gain any further skills or experience points.

MMOs generally release new content or expansion packs that increase the number of levels that a player can achieve.

Note

Using micro transactions, you could charge users to open further levels.

Non-Player Characters (NPCs)

NPCs are the lifeblood of any MMO; these are the computer-controlled characters that you will meet in the course of the game. NPCs are the key characters in the game that will provide the players with quests and little conversational set pieces to move the story forward. In some MMOs, you might have to provide protection for the NPC; perhaps escort them to a particular location or provide them with items before they will interact with you. NPCs can also be used as hired help to complete a particular quest. NPCs are used to help the players discover new areas or new skills by telling the players what to do.

Quests

A quest or mission is one of the ways a player can achieve experience within an MMO, and it can also set a particular task for them to accomplish. Quests are usually given to players by NPCs, but could also be given as part of an ongoing story or a particular event.

Quests can also be used to give the players more information about the world that they are playing within, including learning about other characters, events or its inhabitants.

Quests normally have introductory text and then the relevant player actions; these might be collecting a number of particular items, meeting a character, or killing a number of animals of a particular kind. When creating your own MMO, you have to be very careful that your quests do not end up with the players merely collecting X number of items or killing a lot of creatures. These types of quests can quickly bore MMO players. These types of quests have been given the name of *grinding,* as the players have to complete repetitive tasks over and over again. To reduce the chance of grinding it is important to ensure that your quests are varied, but also that they link to the main story. This way, players can buy into the reason why they are taking on the quests, which makes for a more enjoyable game experience.

To avoid the grinding trap, consider quests that involve more character and story-based progression, such as:

- Rescuing a maiden from a tower.
- Building a clock from a selection of parts to keep a particular character happy.
- Patrolling outside an area to protect the town.
- Escorting an NPC to a particular place.

Maps and Places to Go

An MMO is usually set in a massive world, as you may remember that MMO stands for Massively Multiplayer Online game. This is to give the players many different places to visit and give the game designer the room to create an interesting story across these areas. MMOs host many hundreds or even thousands of players on the same servers at the same time. Having all of these people next to each other on-screen would be very busy and confusing for your players. This would also be a nightmare for the game as the amount of communication between the client and server would be very high and would cause the game to stutter. The characters on-screen might not move immediately when the players press the keys on the keyboard. This delay is called *server lag* and is very detrimental to a game player's opinion of an MMO or any online game.

Because there are many places a player can visit, it is important that the game have a map that the player can refer to. Usually there are two levels of maps—the first is a continent or world map. The second map is a local area map; this shows the location of NPCs and areas of interest. You can see an example of a map that is provided in Realm Crafter in Figure 2.3.

There is one final map that a user might have while playing an MMO game, and that is a mini-map. A mini-map is a small map that is usually situated on the bottom-left or right of the screen and shows close players, NPCs, and objectives.

Death

As Benjamin Franklin once wrote, in this world nothing can be said to be certain, except for death and taxes. In MMOs, death is almost a certainty within the game, and there are a number of ways to handle what happens next.

When the players die in some MMOs, they become ghosts and are placed in a nearby graveyard. They then have to get back to the body of their character to revive them. This is particularly risky if the creature who killed them is still nearby, as it's possible that the player could be killed a second time by the same creature when collecting their possessions. Once the player has been revived, they may have some form of penalty, such as damaged armor or a timed affliction that will reduce the players' stats for a short period of time.

Figure 2.3
This Realm Crafter map could be used as an area map.

Some games allow other players to loot dead players' possessions from their dead bodies. In any game where this is the case, such players take a more defensive line until they can get to a safe place to store any important items safely.

In *City of Heroes,* death incurs a penalty to the experience points the dead player has and the character is then placed in the hospital. This was fine to begin with, but if the player was attempting to complete a difficult area of the game, she could incur a very large negative XP tally, which could make it difficult to level up in the game.

Other ways you can "punish" players when they die is to reduce a number of skill points every time they suffer a death. As with negative XP, there should be a limit to how many points players can lose; otherwise, players might decide to stop playing if it becomes too difficult.

Personally I prefer not to punish my players too much for fear of discouraging players from playing altogether.

INVENTORY

Inventory is where players store their wares that they have purchased, created, or taken off the body of a creature. At its very basic level, an inventory represents a set of bags or rucksack where players store their goods.

The bag system is usually put to good effect by having a limited number of slots or a restricted size. As players increase in levels, they are able to get larger bags and carry more items.

BANKS

A bank has the same use as it does in the real world; it is a place to store valuables. In some MMOs, banks are used only to store money, whereas other games allow you to store any items you find, such as spells, potions, scrolls, and weapons.

MMOs allow players to find many different items on their travels, and carrying all of these items is not an option. Therefore, storing them for future use is important. There is still the issue of limited storage space within a bank; some games restrict storage space, such as *World of Warcraft*, whereas games such as *Ultima Online* have a more unrestricted storage policy.

In games that restrict the number of slots that you can have, you are able to pay the bank to upgrade the amount of slots. As you unlock further slots, the cost becomes more expensive. This is another way to implement micro transactions into your game.

A bank is an important aspect of any MMO and should be available in a number of places so that players do not have to travel halfway around the world to deposit their goods. Banks can be in the players' starting locations or in the main friendly cities and towns.

AUCTION HOUSE AND SHOPS

Many MMOs have sophisticated financial engines running seamlessly in the background. Game worlds run very much like the real world and have an economy that includes the buying and selling of goods, price increases, and price deductions.

An auction house is a way for players to sell items that they no longer want or items of high value. Auction houses are also good places to buy goods that you need to create other items.

Shops can also provide the players with goods such as food, bags, and potions. The laws of supply and demand can even be woven into your game. In *Ultima Online*, when you sell multiples of the same items to the shopkeeper, the price of the item decreases. The same was also true when players purchase many or all of a particular item—the price for those items would increase.

TRANSPORTATION

MMO worlds can be of epic proportions, which if traversed on foot would take the game player many hours to walk across. This would be unacceptable to all but the most hardcore game player, so MMOs have special ways for the player to traverse the game world.

Initially in most MMOs the player moves around the world on foot. Then as the player levels up and begins to make money, other transportation options become available, such as a horse, vehicle, or maybe even a secret portal.

The ability to use a faster method of transport rather than foot is just one level of travel. MMO worlds are still too big to cross with a horse, so other methods are also available. Here are a few examples:

- **Trains/trams:** In *World of Warcraft*, players can travel between two cities using an underground train; this is one form of simple travel that connects to areas of interest.

- **Flying creatures/vehicles:** The ability to connect various areas quickly and easily using flight paths is a positive step so that your players do not have to travel long distances to locations they have already visited. Different flight paths connect to different areas, so players have to find specific flight areas to be able to travel quickly to these new locations. *World of Warcraft* is one such game that contains flying creatures.

- **Boats and ships:** If your MMO is set on multiple landmasses or even planets, you might want to consider a way of connecting these places using boats or spaceships. Most MMOs have some access to vehicles. *Star Wars Galaxies* takes it a step further with land vehicles that can take you across the world and space vehicles that can connect you to planets in a solar system.

In many MMOs, once players have visited a travel point, they have then unlocked it for future use. For example, in *World of Warcraft,* once players have visited a number of locations, they can then fly between them easily.

PETS

To help players in combat situations, many MMOs allow certain character types to have companions. This companion is usually an animal of some kind; for example a tiger, dog, or mythical creature.

There are also MMOs that contain animals that cannot be involved in combat, but are there for the players to collect. Games such as *Free Realms* and *World of Warcraft* allow players to collect animals such as dogs, cats, and birds. In some games, you have to feed your pets to keep them happy, and if the animals are not kept happy they could leave you. This is particularly the case if they are wild animals that you have tamed.

Gamers can become attached to games and in particular to items they collect. For example, many gamers are animal lovers and have affection for in-game creatures. Players can become attached to the items they own in the game world and will therefore play the game over a longer period or even feel that they cannot leave the game and move on to another MMO. Features such as these are very important if you want to retain your user base.

PLACES TO LIVE

Different MMOs have different ways of making the whole gaming experience more realistic or more fun. *Ultima Online* allows players to rest at "hotels" and recover, but it also extends this by allowing players to own their own buildings.

There are a number of benefits to owning a building; first, you can safely store lots of equipment and items you have collected. You can also create a shop where you can purchase an NPC as a shopkeeper and sell goods. In *Ultima Online*, you can build these houses and stores only in particular locations, so very quickly the most popular routes are taken very quickly. The great thing about *Ultima Online* is that there are a large number of building types to select from—players can choose a small hovel, a farm, or even a castle-sized building (with a castle-sized price tag, of course). If players fail to pay the rent on the building, the building will slowly fall into disrepair and finally will disappear, and players lose any goods that they may have stored within the rooms.

If you are able to implement a house-based system within your MMO, it is definitely worthwhile. Allowing the players to have a base of operations which they can relate to, decorate, and purchase items for can make a big difference in keeping your players interested in your MMO. The more your players invest in your game, the more likely it will be that they will continue to play it.

PVP

PVP stands for player versus player. This is a very important aspect of many MMOs and refers to when a player can attack another player. This is a very simple concept but is one of the key selling points of any MMO. In many MMOs, you will find that there are factions or races that are story-wise against each other. In *World of Warcraft*, for example, there are certain servers that are for direct PVP action, so any person from another enemy faction can be attacked. On other *WOW* servers, this PVP action (where a player can attack another player) has to be initiated, at which point a player will be flagged as an enemy of a particular faction for a set amount of time. In *World of Warcraft*, *Warhammer* online, and many other MMOs there are certain areas on the map where PVP action is automatically initiated so any player in that area is at risk from attack by other players.

PVE

PVE is player versus environment and this is effectively what all MMOs do. The player has to fight against creatures or environmental effects, such as water, fire, or ice.

REALMS

The term *realm* can mean a number of different things in MMOs. First, it can mean a single server that contains the world. As MMOs can have hundreds, thousands, or millions of players, it is sometimes impossible to fit them all onto a single server. Each of these servers contains a version of the MMO running independently of the others. In order for players to find their friends, they get a list of realms to choose from when logging in.

Another term is RVR, realm versus realm, where the realm indicates a set group of players, generally those within the same race of characters who fight globally against another race for the spoils of war. This is different than general player versus player, as it normally requires large groups of players from the same race to attack a particular target or area. So while PVP can sometimes include small groups of players battling each other, RVR normally signifies large-scale all-out wars. *Warhammer* online uses both the PVP and RVR game-play mechanics within the game. RVR requires that a particular set of players attack another faction's home city. On success of this attack, the team might gain a number of advantages such as cheaper equipment, more experience points, and so on.

INSTANCES

Because many MMO worlds are large and have many users, there is a risk that too many players are in one area at a set time, which can have an impact on the server's performance. A way of helping reduce this performance hit is to split your users into smaller groups to prevent too many being in one place at one time. This is very important when fighting with a large number of NPCs and a lot of graphical effects are taking place. In most MMOs, there are certain quests that are separated from the main game and are being played only by particular group of players. There may be many groups playing the same quest, but they will not interact with each other and will not see each other within that area of the game. These groups of play are called *instances*.

SUMMARY

This chapter discussed some of the concepts and features that are available in most MMOs. This will be useful as you start to learn about Realm Crafter and implement your own in-game features. Making a good MMO is not an easy or straightforward task, but having knowledge of other MMOs and preparing your ideas will certainly make the process a lot easier. The next chapter looks at how to do some basic game design for your MMOs. This includes how to write your background story, creating and linking quests, and creating a long-term goal for your MMO. I will use three example templates to provide you with the types of information you should consider collecting before starting on your MMO—*Zombie Invasion*, which is a modern day zombie MMO, *Mercury Project*, an alien invasion MMO, and *New Colony*, a space-based MMO.

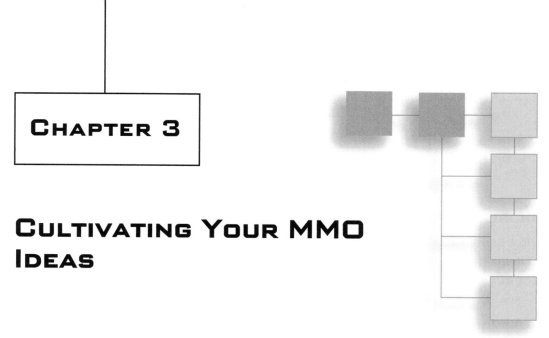

CHAPTER 3

CULTIVATING YOUR MMO IDEAS

This chapter explores how you can come up with ideas for your MMO games. Covered here is how to generate a list of different game ideas, how to pick the best one to start development, how to create a back-story, characters, quests, and overall game play mechanics.

Note

Some of the ideas listed in this chapter can be done through options in the Realm Crafter software, whereas others may have to be done using Realm Crafter's own scripting language. Many of these ideas are found in commercial MMOs.

GETTING AN IDEA

Before you begin making any games, you need to have a good idea about what you want to make. It doesn't matter if you are making a game for fun, a semi-professional, or a full commercial game, all game design and development begin with the initial game idea.

So, how do you begin to get a good game idea? Here are some ways to get started:

- **Brainstorming:** This is the process of just randomly thinking of ideas.

- **Playing some games:** Why not play some already-made games; these can be a great starting point for game ideas.

- **Researching:** There are a multitude of books, magazines, and game/video websites in which you can find large amounts of relevant information.

Brainstorming

You can brainstorm on your own, with your family members, or with other people working on the game with you. If possible you should be in the same room/location; if not, video conferencing is the next best thing; and if that is not available then use voice chat.

Brainstorming is the process of thinking out loud about your game ideas. You should not be thinking in detail at this time, but just getting an idea of the type of game you might want to make. Write down every idea but don't evaluate them at this point. This means if someone suggests an idea that you think is not very good, you should still write it down. Do not criticize or judge the idea at this point. When making a game, it is easy to dismiss initial ideas as being poor, but they may actually end up being good with some changes. If you dismiss any ideas at this point you may be ruling out a future good idea. You may also upset a fellow teammate if you say every idea he or she has is rubbish. This person might no longer get involved in suggesting ideas. This part of the process is about generating ideas, not preventing them.

Here are some ideas on how to create a brainstorming session:

- **People:** Try to get everyone in the same room. If you can't do this, ensure everyone has video conferencing or at least voice chat. If you are using voice chat, consider how people are going to present their ideas, as people are more likely to talk over each other in this setting.

- **Taking notes:** Think how you are going to record everyone's ideas, this could be recorded or hand-written on post-it notes or notepads. Ensure that the method allows for quick collation of the data, as there will likely be a lot of notes and ideas flowing at once.

- **Start:** Give a brief idea of the aim of the brainstorm. This should be the overall idea of what you are trying to achieve. For example, we are going to make an MMO or we are making an FPS (First Person Shooter). Try not to give too many details, as you want people to give random ideas, rather than be selective based on what you have presented to them. For example, if you say, "we want to make an MMO, maybe in medieval times," the brainstorm session will likely follow the path that you have suggested. If you don't have any idea at this time of what game you will make, don't make any particular suggestion at the start.

- **End:** Ensure you have an end time for your brainstorming session. If you are doing this on your own, you can select short or long brainstorming sessions, whatever best suits you. If people have travelled a long way, you may want to have a number of sessions in a day, broken up by coffee/lunch breaks.

- **Post brainstorming:** Ensure that the initial brainstorming session notes are given to everyone who attended the meeting at a later stage. It is impolite to get people to take the time to give input, and then not provide them with a set of meeting notes within a few days of the meeting.

Note

You can brainstorm at different times throughout the development of the game. If you have already decided to make a particular type of game, for example, you might need to brainstorm about the introduction. In this case, it should be the particular subject that you are brainstorming about. An example of this could be that you have decided to create an MMO about robots that have taken over a planet, and you can take the role of a human or a robot. You need at this point to brainstorm about the goal or purpose of the robots on the planet.

Playing Games

While brainstorming, it is recommended you play some games. Playing other games is a good way of coming up with new ideas and concepts. You could be playing a particular game, for example a game about jousting. By playing this game you suddenly get a game concept for a game that involves horse battles. The game idea might not even be in the same genre, but sometimes a small idea can quickly grow into a full game.

In this book you are learning about making your own MMO, so you might be able to get ideas from the following:

- **Playing other MMOs:** This is definitely a good place to start. You are making an MMO game, so it is a good idea to find out what makes a good MMO. I have played many MMOs over the years and some of my favorites are *Ultima Online, World of Warcraft,* and *City of Heroes.*

- **Playing certain game genres:** Even though you are making an MMO, there are many other games that might be useful in playing. For example if you are making an MMO about a world that has been ravaged by nuclear war, playing *Fallout* would be useful. Or, if you are making a game about medieval times, you could look at the *Ultima* series of isometric single player games.

While playing these games, make sure you have a notepad and pen handy to jot down any good ideas that you come across, or things that you like (or don't like!).

Researching Ideas

Playing potentially competing games is a good way of getting ideas, but it's not the only place to get great ideas for your MMO games. Some other ways to research ideas are as follows:

- **Books:** There are many sources of great information available at your local library. These books could be historical, fictional (stories), or technical books, such as army uniforms, gun types, maps (city and topography), architecture, and vehicle guides. Games companies usually base their games on real-life places or equipment. For example, the world in GTA (*Grand Theft Auto*) is based on real places (with the names changed for obvious reasons). These types of books are essential if you are trying to come up with ideas or at least create a believable world.

- **Magazines:** Magazines can provide useful insight into a particular subject area. Although they contain less detail than books, they can still be a good place for inspiration. If you were thinking about making a medieval-based MMO, magazines such as *Wargames* and *White Dwarf* (with its

Warhammer game) would certainly be a good place to start. If you are looking at a game with many vehicles in it, there are a large number of car magazines, such as *Top Gear,* that you can consult.

- **Movies**: Movies and TV shows can provide lots of inspiration for your games. They don't have the depth or accuracy of historical or factual books, but do contain character interactions, which are very important in bringing a sense of realism to games. Even if you are making a game that contains zombies or aliens from another planet, the game has to be believable or the players won't be engaged with the story/game. There are many games asking for players' time, so if your game is not engaging enough they will decide to move on to a different one. This is a bigger problem with MMOs because the investment in making such games is quite large, so it's important to keep the number of subscribers as high as possible.

Note

You can use games, books, and films for inspiration, but be careful not to duplicate others' ideas. Using general game ideas such as an MMO that contains dragons is fine, but if you decide to use images that look and are named the same as an existing game, this could be a problem. You cannot use other people's trademarks or products without permission from the trademark owners. For example, if you are making an MMO that has vehicles in it, you could not legally use a road car that is owned by someone else. Consult a legal representative for the exact details on your rights and responsibilities.

Cultivating Your Idea

Once you have done the initial research you should have a better idea of the type of game you want to create. You should create a list of the best ideas that you have so that you can see them all in one place. Don't make the list too big, as this will make finding the right MMO idea a lot harder.

Before you create your list, you should think about some key aspects of making an MMO. Doing so will make your list more streamlined and more accurate:

- **Technology:** How big is the game going to be? Are you making it for just a few friends or are you hoping to make it for a large number of people? What hardware will you use, a home computer and a broadband connection or a server?

- **Team:** The number of people on your team and their skills will determine what type of MMO you can create and might also define the scope/size of the project. Knowing the skills on your team will also help you identify any shortcomings. Do you have enough writers, designers, and graphic artists, and do you need a programmer?

- **Obtaining and creating assets:** An MMO needs assets, which are the graphics and sounds that appear in your game. The type of game you create might be limited based on the assets you can buy, make, or use. If you are using free assets off the Internet, there may only be enough assets of a particular time frame (for example, modern) and this may have a direct effect on the type of game you can make. If you have a 3D artist you will have more room to be more selective in your MMO choice.

- **Difficulty and time:** These two items are directly related; the more difficult and complex an MMO, the longer it will take to create. Do you or your team have time to create an MMO over the course of two years or are you intending to make a small area first and build it up step by step?

Now that you have a better idea of the resources you need and have access to, you can start to make your list of MMO ideas that fit within your capabilities. I recommend that you keep the list as simple as possible. Create a simple brief that makes it easy to recall the general basis of the game. You can see a simple example of a list in Figure 3.1.

Figure 3.1 shows three possible games to consider; these ideas are separated into the following column headings:

- **Game Name:** The name of the game. This is only a placeholder name, but allows you to quickly remember what each line item refers to.

- **Introduction:** This is a brief introduction to the game. This is not meant as an in-depth discussion of the game in question, but instead is a quick description to remind you of the game idea.

- **Core Factions:** The starting point of what groups/races/character types will be part of the game. I will break this idea down further later in this chapter.

Game Name	Introduction	Core Factions
Zombie Invasion	A chemical spill takes place in a small town in the USA, the first people who arrive at the scene find the injured driver of the vehicle, who then attacks them. This begins the Zombie Invasion.	Humans – Non Government Humans – Government Zombies
Mercury Project	A probe comes back from its mission to Mercury to collect space dust. The probe crashes on re-entry in the desert. As a team races to collect the probe, local residents near the crash site start to disappear.	Humans – Non Government Humans – Government Various Aliens
New Colony	A group of space travelers set up home on a previously unexplored planet, believing it to be uninhabited. Unfortunately, the planet is home to the Robots, a number of robot races who live underground.	Humans – Space travellers Robots – Friendly Robots - Unfriendly

Figure 3.1
A list of potential games.

MAKING A STORY

Now you have an idea for the type of MMO that you want to create. You need to begin to fill in some gaps so that you can develop the game idea in more detail. This in turn will help you design the game in more detail.

This section takes the three game ideas listed in Figure 3.1 and expands them, so that each contains more in-depth information. When you are designing your own games, you should do this on a separate document for each project. You can use these templates, or you can amend them as you see fit.

Note

You should be careful working on multiple projects at the same time, as it can become confusing (you may mix up concepts between games), and also be very distracting. Jumping from one idea to another can slow down your progress on one particular idea. This isn't a problem early on in the development of your games, but as you delve deeper into your game design, it's best to focus on one game only.

When making a game and generating a story, you have to consider questions such as:

- Why is the player in the current location/predicament?
- Who are the player's friends and whom does the player know?
- Where does the player go on a normal day?
- What resources are available in the player's current location?
- What outside influences may have an impact on the player's game and the game world?

Let's now begin to expand on the three simple ideas.

Zombie Invasion

The Zombie Invasion MMO begins in a small US town. Initially, the player is taking a fishing holiday at a nearby log cabin. The player is slowly introduced to the zombie problem via the news on the radio and by helping local townspeople with issues.

- **Project name:** Zombie Invasion.
- **Starting location:** Small town, with a population of around 500 people.
- **Starting location brief:** A small American farming town, with one main street, and a cluster of buildings in and around the main town. There are a number of outlying farms and a small selection of shops, a bar, a pharmacy, a sheriff's office, and the like.
- **Starting location of player:** The player has a log cabin on the edge of the woods, where he takes a regular fishing holiday.
- **Starting resources:** The log cabin has a small selection of food that the player has purchased from town as well as some equipment, such as an axe, fishing gear, and shotgun (with a small number of bullets).

Let's now look further into the factions:

- **Humans – Non-government**: These include townspeople, such as the local DR, teacher, sheriff, and general townspeople such as families and farmers.

- **Humans – Government:** You might have a number of agencies involved in this game, including the National Guard, an unknown health department group, and the FBI. Some might be working with the town while others could be working against it.

- **Zombies – Human-Based:** You might create multiple groups of zombies. First you can have different human-based zombie groups with different characteristics, such as slow and weak, fast and strong, and perhaps even some that explode when killed.

- **Zombies – Animal-Based:** What if animals could become zombies as well? This allows the scope of the enemies to be greatly increased, and their menace might show itself in different situations or locations than with the human zombies.

Note

You could include the sheriff on the government list, but as I want the government to be outside agencies, I have included the sheriff as a non-government (friendly). This is because the local sheriff is working for the local people. During the game, the players will not know precisely whose side the government is on. This allows you to create some interesting quests, and also have a level of intrigue in the ongoing battle with the zombies.

Mercury Project

A probe crashes in the desert. You are the sheriff of a town and have been told to set up roadblocks and prevent any townsfolk from approaching the probe. The space agency is sending a team to collect the samples. The player is introduced to the story when local townspeople start disappearing, and the player has to do simple quests for the space agency and FBI.

- **Project name:** Mercury Project.

- **Starting location:** Small town, with a population of around 1,500 people.

- **Starting location brief:** Small American mining town.

- **Starting location of player:** At a roadblock, just outside of town. The main town is like many small towns; many of the facilities are within short distance of each other. What makes this town interesting in terms of the game is that it also contains a mining facility. This is a great place to have many caves and interesting enemies. A desert also surrounds the town, so the area is very secluded and has a single highway going in and out of the area (to the nearest big city).

- **Starting resources**: Access to small arms, shotguns, and ammunition.

You can now look further into the factions:

- **Humans – Non-government:** These will include townspeople, such as the local DR, teacher, sheriff, and general townspeople such as families and farmers.

- **Humans – Government:** There could be a number of agencies involved in this game, including the National Guard, an unknown space agency group, and the FBI. Some could be working with the town while others could be working against it.

- **Aliens:** These would take the form of simple alien blobs to complex alien creatures and alien humanoids (the brains).

New Colony

The player is a member of an alien race looking for a new home. They find what they believe to be an uninhabited planet that has plentiful food, water, and supplies. It seems like the perfect place to set up home. The player is part of a number of forward groups, setting up communications and basic amenities for the main population to beam down at a later stage. The planet of course is not uninhabited and has a number of Robot races, ready to attack the colony. Early quests would set up the initial storyline of needing to set up communication and gather food. There would be quests such as introducing players to the alien robot races and perhaps losing communication with another forward base.

- **Project name:** New Colony.

- **Starting location:** On board one of the space carriers currently orbiting the planet.

- **Starting location brief:** The ship Frontier is one of five population carriers; the ship also contains a small security and science detail. The five population ships are escorted by a single battle cruiser. Further ships will follow once bases and resources have been set up.

- **Starting location of player:** The player is part of a science or security detail, currently on the ship awaiting orders to beam down to one of the forward bases. The player is stationed on a ship, and completes a number of quests before travelling down to the initial base.

- **Starting resources:** Access to basic laser weapons, rations, and science equipment.

You can now look further into the factions:

- **Humans – various:** Includes various groups of humans, such as political groups, scientists, security officers, farmers, and families

- **Plants:** Some dangerous species of plants that can attack the player

- **Robots:** Various robot groups, such as robot spiders, humanoid soldiers, and so on

- **Creatures:** Various creatures also inhabit the planet, such as boars, space cows, and the like

Note

You may notice that the first two MMO ideas are set in a small town, whereas the third deals with an initial small colony. Starting small like this allows you to create a small area in which you can more easily control events. Many MMOs start in a small area before opening up to a bigger world. This could be a training/learning area where you introduce the story to the players or show them how to play. Many MMOs begin in a small area, allow the players to gain a few levels and upgrade their skills before they move out into the wider and more complex world.

CREATING MAPS AND PLACES TO GO

When you begin to design your MMO, you need an idea of how your initial areas will look, and what areas are available in your world. Even if you are just creating a starter area or a single zone, you will still need to map out these basic areas.

You might separate map creation into three levels:

- **World map:** This is a high-level map of your entire game world. If your world is particularly large or complex, it might need several maps. Think of this as the state/county view.

- **Area map:** A close up map of a particular location. Here you might see areas such as swampland, desert, buildings, and important landmarks.

- **Building/inside map:** You might need to map inside a particularly complex building or cave complex.

N o t e

When you are beginning to create your world maps, you don't need to have an amazingly artistic and well-drawn map. Start off simple using MS Paint or any simple drawing package, and then begin to make it more complex. Any map you make at this stage does not have to reflect an end product. Maps are generally works in progress for much of the design stage.

Some basic examples of starter maps can be seen in Figures 3.2, 3.3, and 3.4.

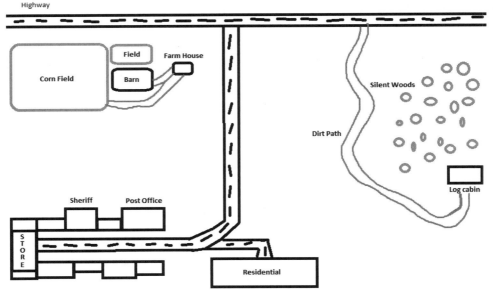

Figure 3.2
Map of the town in Zombie Invasion.

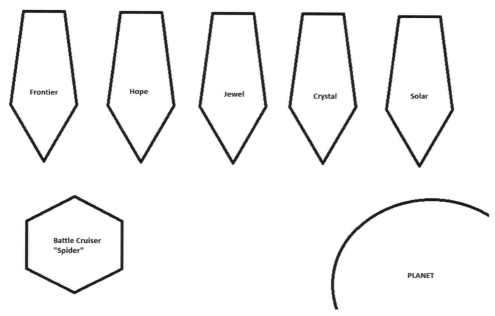

Figure 3.3
Simple high-level map of the New Colony game space.

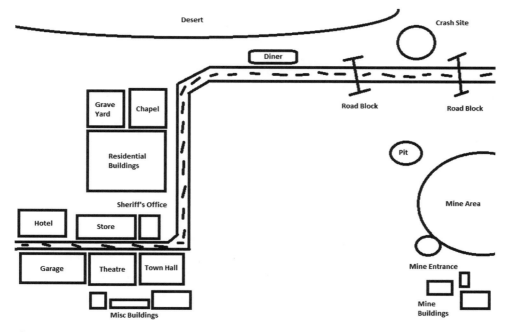

Figure 3.4
Map for Mercury Project.

Map Research

Making the various maps that you will need in your MMO can be quite a task. You can make things easier by using other sources as inspiration. Some ideas:

- **Landscape books**: You can purchase or borrow a landscape book from the library.

- **Topology maps:** Topology maps show different land/sea surfaces on a map, such as mountain and sea heights.

- **Google maps and real places**: Google Maps is an extremely useful tool for creating games based on different landscapes and places. If you are making a game that's based on the real world, for example being located in America or in the United Kingdom today, you can use Google Maps to help you start making your game maps. If you are going to create a game that is slightly older, such as a gangster game in the 1950s, Google Maps may still help as you will be able to find the old parts of a city that haven't actually changed that much from a layout point of view. You may have to look at historical documents to get a better overall picture, though.

- **Aerial maps**: There are many photographic resources (including Google and books mentioned previously) that allow you to get a bird's eye view of a particular landscape. These can form the basis of very useful examples while building your own worlds. Want to know what features you might see in the countryside or in a desert? By consulting real-life pictures you can get an idea of how the land and buildings are structured. If you are making a game that is not based on the earth, such as the New Colony example, you can still use real life to get some inspiration and ideas. You may have to make some changes to represent your world if it is wildly different than the world you live in.

- **Historical maps**: If you are making an MMO game based on a particular time frame, such as a medieval-based game (even if it's not based on a true historical time—perhaps you are making a knight game with modern technology), historical maps can be filled with useful information.

Note

Please note that you cannot use exact copies of any real world map, as these are generally copyrighted by the companies that created them. You can use the general layout as inspiration for your own maps. So for example you should not use any copied images or material in the world map screen, but draw your own.

Note

In many commercial games, they will use maps as an inspiration and create their own worlds as the basis of a map. For example, San Andreas and Liberty City from *Rockstar* are based on real places. Other games use countries as inspiration, either by using a real country in the game or creating a new country.

Visualizing Your NPCs

Now that you have looked at a basic story structure and have been thinking about what the world might look like, you need to start thinking about the people in your game. NPCs (Non-Player Characters) are characters that the player has no control over and are controlled by the computer. There are two types of NPCs that are used within an MMO:

- **Interactive NPCs:** These are characters that the player can interact with, talk to, and receive quests from.

- **Non-interactive NPCs:** These are characters that you cannot interact with, and include characters that populate a world, such as friendly people populating the area or enemy characters that attack you on sight.

This section of the book looks primarily at interactive NPCs. Now that you have three game ideas and some basic maps, you need to begin building some of the characters within the game that the players will interact with. The initial areas in your game world should be relatively small. This provides a good starter area for the players to get used to the game's controls and its general game play, and at the same time you can introduce them to the story. In some MMOs, the starter area is a game zone that the player doesn't return to after completion. In other MMOs, it is just another area within the game world that the player can go back to.

If the area is a one-time play area, where the player completes some basic tasks and never visits again, you should not have too much character interaction, except perhaps to explain how to play the game and provide some basic story conversations.

You are now going to create a number of basic characters that the player can interact with within the games.

Some initial characters that the player can meet in the Zombie Invasion MMO can be seen in Figure 3.5; characters from the Mercury Project are shown in Figure 3.6; and characters from New Colony are shown in Figure 3.7.

Name	Job Title/Role	Basic Description
Alex Ryan	Sheriff	Popular sheriff has been in the role for over 3 years. The Sheriff is in his early 40's.
Alicia Smart	Deputy Sheriff	The newly promoted deputy sheriff is well liked and trusted individual within the town.
Ruth and Giles Scott	Farm Family	One of a number of local farm families.
Lucas David	Hunter	Local hunter, who the player meets close to the log cabin. Lucas introduces you to the first quest in the game, to find his hound dog that went running off into the forest. The hunter has seen a number of strange sights in the forest.
Dr John Smith	Local Doctor	Local Doctor that has many years of experience. This doctor will ask questions of the player, and provide further feedback on what the unknown health official is asking of the player.
Jones Bain	Town Mayor	The mayor is an aging politician who is extremely strong minded. The mayor will not allow any outside agencies to overrule the rights of the local people.
Health Official	Unknown Health Official	Unknown health official that asks the player to do missions to get an idea of the scale and problem of the zombie invasion, including obtaining samples so that the government can find out more about the attacks.

Figure 3.5
Initial characters in the Zombie Invasion game.

Name	Job Title/Role	Basic Description
Joseph Thomas	Deputy Sheriff	Your deputy, will ask for your help to protect the local civilian population.
Jack Zire	Space Agency Person 1	One of the two space agency personnel that will ask you to perform quests, some quests which may be questionable.
Joshua Creed	Space Agency Person 2	The second of the two space agency personnel. Joshua wants to help you avert disaster which has beset the small town.
Agent	FBI Agent	You do not know the FBI agent's name, and only know him by the name "Agent". You will get various quests to protect the local civilians.
Alice Appleton	Diner Waitress	The closest building to the crash site.
Zac Travis	Garage Mechanic	Mechanic whose son has gone missing. His son was last seen in the vicinity of the crash site.
Karl Vance	Mine Boss/Owner	Karl Vance is the owner of the local mine. He is not a very popular figure as he closed the mines recently (leading to job losses) in order to sell the land.
Jane Harris	Hotel Receptionist	A stressed hotel receptionist who has to deal with lots of people who need putting up in the local hotel as the main route out of town has been closed.

Figure 3.6
Characters in the Mercury Project MMO.

Name	Job Title/Role	Basic Description
Aldan Scott	Security Officer	Provides basic quests in securing any forward bases.
Christian Staff	Science Officer	Provides quests for retrieving data to help improve research.
Liz Beta	Provisions Officer	Supplies on the ship will last only a short while; Liz will ask you to find new provisions on the planet.
Buzz Tobin	Terra-forming Person	Buzz is the terra-forming officer who ensures any planet is safe to live on. Quests will check that the planet is habitable.

Figure 3.7
Characters in the New Colony MMO.

Note

If you are struggling to come up with different character names for the NPCs within your game, you can always use the Internet. There are many websites, such as baby-naming sites, that can be quite useful when thinking up different names. When you try to think of names on your own, it is very easy to end up with all surnames beginning with the same letter or with the first names being too similar. It is also a good idea to not use famous people's names for your characters. Many writers use software or even write their own name-generation system, whereby you can enter lots of first name and surnames and then click on a button to generate a new name.

ADDING WORLD ITEMS

You need your worlds to be populated with items that the player can use, as well as items that make these worlds more believable. Some items that the player can pick up could be combined to make other items or have a resell value (which can make the player some money). The sort of items you should consider in your worlds might fall under the following categories:

- **Weapons:** Most (but not all) MMOs contain fighting, be it with aliens, robots, creatures, or zombies, so you will need to have something to fight the hoards with. In some cases, you can combine weapons or have different ammunition to make them more effective.

- **Armor and clothing:** Wearing items can change the look of a character (and make your world seem less monotonous) while giving the player the opportunity to find unique items from quests. Clothing can also be a useful modifier in terms of providing protection when attacking or defending against other creatures/characters. Some armor will be heavier to wear but provide good protection, whereas other armor will provide less protection but will be lighter and allow the players to run around the world for longer/faster.

- **Food:** Food can be used to good effect in your MMO games. First, it can be used to increase health and other player stats. Recovering particular stats such as health is an approach used in many MMOs, or you could also make it increase a stat to higher than its normal level (to a maximum amount).

- **Manufacturing:** In most MMOs you can combine items to make a new item. This manufacturing can be in the form of creating new weapons or decorative objects. In the game *Ultima Online,* you can chop up some wood, do some wood-working, and buy some additional items to make a clock, which you can put in your own home or sell. Manufacturing can add a lot of depth to your game, but it does require lots of combinations to be effective. You also need to take into account the issues of supply and demand if you decide to have some market/buy/sell system. In *Ultima,* you can make a lot of the same item. However, when selling the same item to an NPC shopkeeper, the more you sell of an item, the lower the price you get, until the point at which the shopkeeper doesn't want any more of it.

- **Household and general items:** Making your world more believable is a big step in ensuring that your game can immerse the player in the game world. The ability to buy random items such as household goods, chairs, tables, and furniture might seem like a pointless exercise, but it can allow the players to express themselves and decorate their game homes anyway they want. The ability to manufacture items as well as buy them can add a lot of depth to an MMO.

All of the mentioned groups can add a lot of value to your MMO, because different items can cost more to the player and are something to aspire to, whereas some items might be unique or rare.

Here are some ideas for the different types of items that you could find in different MMOs (in no particular order).

Weapons:

- Axe
- Short sword
- Long sword
- Two-handed sword
- Rifle

- Pistol
- Shotgun
- Knife
- Crossbow
- Composite bow
- Bow
- Hammer
- Pike
- Mace
- RPG (rocket-propelled grenade)
- Grenade
- Laser gun

Weapon ammunition:

- Bullets
- Pellets
- Arrows
- Bolts
- Stones
- Darts

Armor:

- Chain mail
- Plastic armor
- Steel armor
- Bullet-proof vest
- Leather armor
- Gloves

- Boots
- Helmets

Clothing:

- Hats
- Gloves
- Boots
- Trousers
- Tights
- Skirts
- Kilts
- Gowns
- Capes
- Tops

Accessories:

- Rings
- Necklaces
- Earrings
- Glasses
- Jewelry

Household:

- Chairs
- Fireplace
- Beds
- Bookcases
- Tables
- Picture frames

- TV
- Radio
- Printer
- Computer
- Carpet
- Lighting
- Clock

Food:

- Fruit
- Cakes
- Potatoes
- Bread
- Drinks (water, mead, and so on)
- Pies
- Cooked meat
- Soup

Food Substances:

- Flour
- Grain
- Fruit
- Uncooked meat
- Spices
- Stock
- Sugar
- Vinegar
- Butter

CREATING YOUR BASIC QUEST LISTS

Earlier in this chapter, you learned about NPC characters and how to give them a basic background story/description and detail their job titles. You can see these details in Figures 3.5, 3.6, and 3.7. Now you can start to build up some basic quests. Some basic reasons why someone might do a quest are as follows:

- **Collect:** A common quest in MMOs is to collect a number of a particular item, such as a flower, bug, body part, or other miscellaneous item.

- **Deliver:** Take an item or items to a person or place.

- **Defeat:** The player is sent to defeat a number of enemies, either in an area that the player already knows, or as a way of opening new areas for the player to explore.

- **Investigate:** These types of quests are used to expand on the story, allowing the player to visit new locations.

- **Rescue and help:** This is used as a story mechanic; the player must rescue someone either from a difficult situation or from a particular enemy.

- **Travel:** The player must visit a particular NPC or travel to a particular town. These types of quests are usually meant to get the player to move to a new area once most of the quests are completed in the area that they are currently in.

- **Manufacture:** You will need to manufacture some items. This could also involve the collect quest, where you have to go to a particular area and collect items to be able to build the specified object.

Now that you have a basic set of quest templates, you can begin to think about how you will generate your quests. The best way to do this is to use a program such as Excel to generate a spreadsheet of the quests. You may find that you have a lot of quests, so you can use Excel's tabs (which allows you to separate data on different pages).

Some of the things that you should consider putting in your quest list are as follows:

- **Quest giver:** The name of the person who provides the quest.

- **Quest level:** The level range of the quest so the player can determine whether the quest is within their current level range. This is useful as the player can decide if they want to accept a quest that might be many levels above their current level. Some MMOs have a limit to the number of quests that you can accept.

- **Quest description:** A designer's description of the quest.

- **Quest description display:** The quest text that is displayed to the player.

- **Quest success criteria:** The success/failure criteria of the quest.

- **Chained:** Is this quest linked to other quests? In most MMOs, this feature allows you to string together a number of quests that all relate to the same story/character/area. For example, you could have a single NPC give you five quests that relate to a particular story.

- **XP:** How much XP (experience points) will the player get for completing a quest? The level of the character (compared to the quest level range) will normally define the amount of XP that the player gets. For example, if a player is level 50 and the quest level is level 20, the player will be able to easily complete the quest. The amount of XP the player will get will be 0 or very small. This will also work the other way; when the player is a lower level than the quest level, the player will receive bonus XP. You can make this simpler by having a base amount of XP for completing a quest and then apply a modifier to work out the final amount of XP. You may want to specify the minimum amount of XP for completing a quest regardless of the modifier, for example 100 XP. You can see an example of the modifier table in Figure 3.8.

- **Reward:** In addition to receiving XP for completing a quest, the player may also receive gold (or whatever currency exists in your game) or an item bonus. It is very common to receive both money and the ability to select from a group of items as a bonus for completing the quest.

- **Completion text:** The dialogue of the NPC spoken to the player at the completion of the quest.

Now that you have an idea of the headings that you want to track within your quests, you can start to build a selection of quests, as shown in Figure 3.9.

Quest LVL Difference	XP Modifier
-10	+1000
-9	+800
-8	+750
-7	+650
-6	+625
-5	+600
-4	+590
-3	+575
-2	+300
-1	+250
0	0
+1	-25
+2	-75
+3	-100
+4	-125
+5	-150
+6	-200
+7	-250
+8	-300
+9	-450
10+ (and above)	-500

Figure 3.8
An XP modifier table.

Quest Giver	Quest Level	Quest Description	Quest Description Display	Quest Criteria	Chained	XP	Reward	Completion Text
Lucas David	1	Find Dog - This will end with the player needing to find the dog's remains and then going back to the player.	Thank goodness I've met someone, I was beginning to get very worried. I was out hunting with my dog, but there's something strange going on in the woods. My dog has run off, perhaps you can help me find her, her name is Bess. To be honest I am too scared to go back into the woods, so perhaps I can stay here at the cabin while you go and look for her.	Find dog's collar/remains	Y - 7	400	Shot gun pellets	[Sob] [Sob] My poor Bess, thanks for finding this. There is something evil lurking in the woods. I am too distraught to make it back to town, buy you should go and warn the Sheriff. I found this ripped fabric covered in blood on the floor where I was hunting, I am sure the Sheriff will want to look at it.
Lucas David	1	Find equipment left in the woods	Could you do me another favor? I was too scared to hang around in the woods north of here, so I left all of my hunting gear. I had some pictures of my dog in my bag, and I would really want it back. There are some supplies there also that you are welcome to use, I don't need them anymore.	Find lost supplies		500	Food - cake, sandwiches	I really appreciate getting my pictures of Bess. [Sob] [Sob]
Alicia Smart	1	The deputy Sheriff is in charge at the police station as the Sheriff is dealing with the incident at the vehicle chemical spill	Thanks for bringing this evidence to us. Not sure what we can do about it right now, as we are pretty stretched dealing with the chemical spill on the highway.	Provided with ripped fabric.		250	None	None.
Alicia Smart	1	Deputy Sheriff wants you to go and check out the missing person at the Scott farm.	We are having problems contacting the Sheriff over the radio. Unfortunately I have enough problems of my own as we have had reports of the one of our farmers going missing, Ruth Scott called us about 20 minutes ago, we sent out a deputy, but have heard nothing since. I cannot leave the station for the moment, I know it's alittle much to ask a visitor for help, but you seem like an upstanding person, I wouldn't normally ask, but we would really appreciate it.	Go and meet Ruth Scott, listen to her story and accept her quest.		1000	None	None.
Alicia Smart	2	Take radio and spare battery to Sheriff at road accident location.	Hey look, if you take this radio and spare battery over to the Sheriff, just north east of here on the highway, perhaps we can get communication back up and running.	Take Radio and spare battery to Sheriff		1000		We now have contact with the Sheriff, thanks for helping us out. He has reported that he was attacked by the ambulance crew, what is going on out there?

Figure 3.9
An example of a quest spreadsheet in Zombie Invasion.

As you can imagine, it can get quite complicated as you begin to build the number of quests. It is also possible that you might decide to make changes to your characters, locations, and story as you begin to build up your quests. Quests are a key component to any MMO, so don't think that once you have written them you won't need to change them. You should expect to improve your quests as testing of your game reveals issues.

It is best to start off with detailing the quests for each of your key NPCs within the starter level, and then slowly build them up and create linked quests and quests that take a player to a new area. Start off small and build upon a solid base of quests. Doing so will improve your game considerably and will ensure that any issues that might arise are spotted early on.

Considering Areas versus Difficulty

When you begin to create your maps, you will need to consider the different levels of enemies in that particular area. It is common for the player to be able to defeat a single enemy within the same or next level, while multiple enemies of a higher level become more of a problem. These groups of enemies (called *mobs*) can pose a danger to new players, and so you should try to spread the enemies out in the early levels.

If you are making a starter area, you should put enemies of the same area close to the player, and then slowly build up the levels. Once players are at a reasonable level and you have introduced them to a particular set of game rules, you can then send them on their way to complete harder quests.

You can see an example of how to arrange your first few levels in Figure 3.10.

As you begin to build your other areas you will need to create a mix of enemy levels. Most MMOs have a range of levels within an area, and some will be too difficult for the player to initially defeat. The main reason for this is that the player could level up as she goes through an area, but then there will be no further reasons for the player to return to a particular area. So if you have level 1, 2, 4, and 12 within an area, but it is likely that the player will only reach level 5, that means the player will have to move out to another area before coming back and completing the required quests.

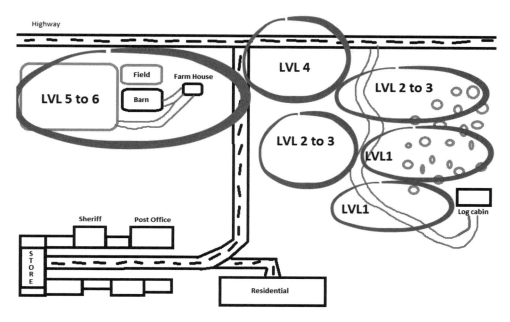

Figure 3.10
A beginner's area with an idea of the enemy levels.

Note

Do not make the level ranges of the enemies too high within the first few areas, because your players will get defeated trying to beat those high-end enemies, and will most likely become frustrated with the game. Slowly introduce the player to difficultly and mob groups. Ensure your players fully understand the concept of levels and difficultly before placing them in dangerous areas.

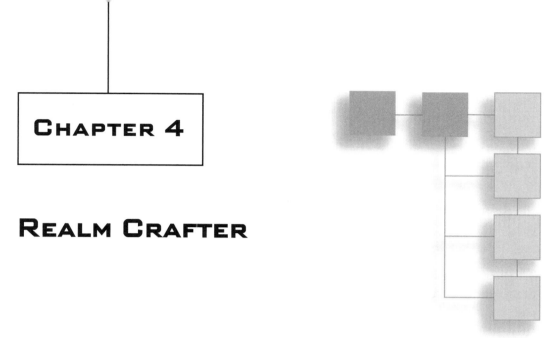

CHAPTER 4

REALM CRAFTER

Realm Crafter is an easy-to-use but powerful MMORPG creator. Realm Crafter takes away many of the headaches of creating your own MMO game, leaving you to concentrate on your concept, ideas, and story.

Creating a commercial MMO can take many millions of dollars and many tens or hundreds of staff. You won't be able to compete with these types of MMOs for budget or resources, but Realm Crafter will make it easier for you to create your very own MMO on a much smaller scale. It will also allow you to slowly add new features as you increase your gaming world when you are ready to do so. Realm Crafter's set of editors and tools will allow you to create your world, characters, and quests quickly. Realm Crafter also allows a level of scripting, so the more experienced game creator can create more complex worlds and events.

Note

At the time of this writing, there isn't a Realm Crafter Professional demo, although the developers state they are currently working on one.

REALM CRAFTER'S SYSTEM REQUIREMENTS

Realm Crafter Professional is a massively multiplayer online role-playing game creator, which is designed to create games that many people can play at the same time, in the same game world. This means that you need to be able to create your game on a machine that is accessible by people over the Internet.

Due to the scale of a game that can be made in Realm Crafter, the technical requirements are a little more complicated than a normal game-creator system.

MMOs require two network technologies, which in MMO terms are classified as the client and the server. The client is the player's machine and the server is the machine that the client's PC connects to in order to access the MMO data.

The server needs to be a Windows-based operating system, running a database to store the MMO information, which can be MySQL. The server also requires a static IP address; this is an Internet number that indentifies the server to PCs around the world. I will go into more detail about this later in this chapter.

You may be concerned about the cost of setting up a server to run your MMO. I will show you ways of keeping the costs as low as possible. The aim of this book is to be able to create an MMO and allow a few friends to play online initially. Once you have your MMO up and running, you can then decide if you want to allow more players to have access to it, and how to keep the costs as low as possible.

The term server means different things to different people. In the context of the MMO, you are going to create a server, which is a machine that will accept connections/logins from other PCs and store the MMO data. This type of server is common in networked computer games where one PC is the server and the other PCs connect to it to play the game.

When you connect to a company's website on the Internet, the pages of the website are stored on a server. A server is a more powerful computer and can allow multiple connections at the same time. Such servers run server operating systems such as Linux and Windows. These types of servers are more expensive than PCs but do allow scalability.

In this book, you learn how to set everything up on a PC so you do not need to worry about buying a server. Realm Crafter will work perfectly on your PC and allow a limited number of users to have access to it. If you later want to increase the number of people connecting to your MMO, you can also purchase a server from one of the many web-hosting companies that can provide this type of service.

Note

A web host is a company that provides access to a website or web space on its servers. Many people use these hosting companies to host their websites and upload files.

Realm Crafter requires the following system specifications:

- **Minimum server:** P2-600 MHz, 128 MB RAM, and Internet connection with a static IP.

- **Minimum client:** P4-1.3 GHz, 512 MB RAM, sound card, GeForce 5500 / Radeon 9800 or higher (128MB video RAM), and Internet or LAN (local area network) connection. Windows 2000/XP/Vista/Windows 7 and DirectX 9.0c or above.

- **Supported file formats:** B3D, 3DS, X, JPG, BMP, PNG, TGA, DDS, WAV, and OGG.

INSTALLING REALM CRAFTER PROFESSIONAL

When you have purchased Realm Crafter from the Realm Crafter site at www.realmcrafter.com, you will receive an email with details on how to download the software. Once you have logged in to the secure site, you will see a list of items that you can download. These items can include:

- Full version of the software.

- Any beta versions of the software.

- Sample projects that provide examples of various levels.

- Additional content such as graphical icons, weapons, and spells.

Once you have confirmed that your PC has met the system requirements, you will be ready to install the Realm Crafter software.

The Windows operating system you're running—Vista or Windows XP—determines the exact process you need to follow to install Realm Crafter successfully. The steps for each operating system are covered in the following sections.

Beginning the Install on Windows XP and Windows 7

To begin installing Realm Crafter on your Windows Vista or Windows 7 machine, follow these steps:

1. Ensure you are logged in as an Administrator.

2. Download the full version of the program from the Realm Crafter website. Double-click on the setup file to start the installation process.

3. You can now follow the "Main Install Process" heading, which will be discussed later in this chapter.

Beginning the Install on Windows Vista

To begin installing Realm Crafter on your Windows Vista machine, follow these steps:

1. If you are running the Vista operating system, ensure you are logged in as an Administrator.

2. First you have to disable User Access Control (UAC) to successfully install Realm Crafter. To do so, you need to click on the start bar and select Control Panel. Select User Accounts and then select Turn User Account Control On or Off. You can see this in Figure 4.1.

3. Unselect the checkbox to turn off UAC, as shown in Figure 4.2. You will now need to reboot your PC.

4. Once your PC has rebooted, right-click on the Realm Crafter Professional executable and select Run as Administrator.

5. You can now follow the "Main Install Process" heading.

Main Install Process

The installation process will begin and extract a number of files to your hard disk. Once this extraction process completes, the Welcome dialog box appears, as shown in Figure 4.3.

Tasks
Create a password reset disk
Manage your network passwords
Configure advanced user profile properties
Change my environment variables
See also
Parental Controls
Make changes to your user account
Change your password
Remove your password
Change your picture
Change your account name
Change your account type
Manage another account
Turn User Account Control on or off
Administrator
Password protected

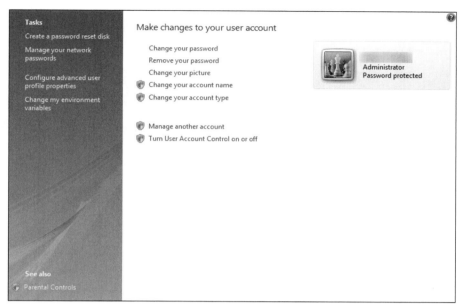

Figure 4.1
The Vista User Account management screen.

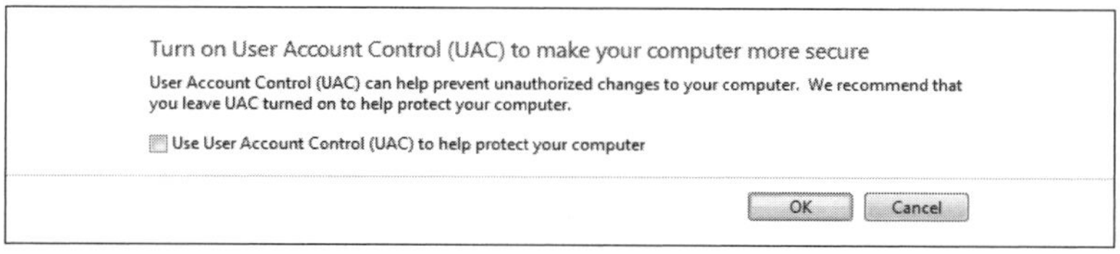

Turn on User Account Control (UAC) to make your computer more secure
User Account Control (UAC) can help prevent unauthorized changes to your computer. We recommend that you leave UAC turned on to help protect your computer.
Use User Account Control (UAC) to help protect your computer
OK
Cancel

Figure 4.2
Turn off the UAC setting.

Read the welcome message and click on the Next button to continue with the installation.

You will now see the License Agreement dialog box, which contains license information about the software, as shown in Figure 4.4. Read the license information, accept the terms of the license agreement, and then click on the Next button to continue with the installation.

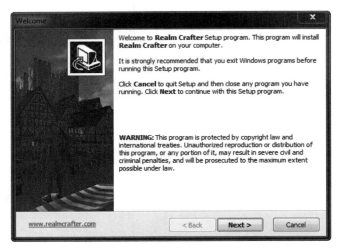

Figure 4.3
The Welcome install dialog box appears.

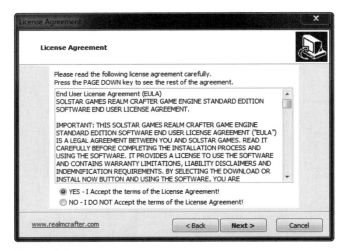

Figure 4.4
The License Agreement dialog box.

Note

You can click on NO - I DO NOT Accept the Terms of the License Agreement, and this will cancel the installation.

You will now be presented with a Readme screen, which contains additional information that is not covered in the License Agreement, as shown in Figure 4.5. Press Next to continue.

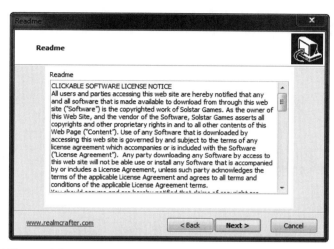

Figure 4.5
The Readme dialog box.

The User Information dialog box will now appear and will take your login username and place it within the Name edit box automatically. Click on the Next button to continue with the install.

You will now be able to choose the default installation directory, as shown in Figure 4.6. The default path places the Realm Crafter files within the Program Files folder. You can change the default path by clicking on the Browse button. Click on the Next button to continue with the installation.

N o t e

> You will notice in Figure 4.6 that the Choose Destination Location dialog box lists how much hard disk space is required for the installation of Realm Crafter. Ensure you have enough space or choose another disk.

You will now see the Set Program Shortcuts dialog box; this allows you to change the text name that appears in the Start/Programs Menu bar. It is customary to keep with the default, so click on the Next button to continue.

Figure 4.6
The Choose Destination Location dialog box.

You will now see the Confirm Setup Settings dialog box, which details the selections you have made through the initial install process, as shown in Figure 4.7. If you are happy with your previous install selections, click on the Next button. Click on Back to change any of the previous settings.

Figure 4.7
The Confirm Setup Settings dialog box.

On clicking the Next button you will be asked to confirm if you want to back up any previously created Realm Crafter projects. If you have never used Realm Crafter before, you don't need to worry about this option and can click on No. If you have files from a previous version, click on the Yes button (the following examples assume you have selected No).

As the program is copying files to your hard disk, you will see the Copying Files dialog box shown in Figure 4.8.

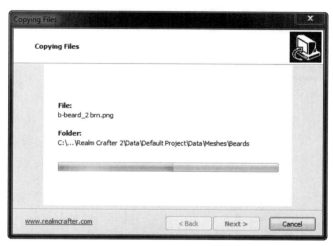

Figure 4.8
The Copying Files dialog box.

Once the file installation is complete, a Setup Complete dialog box will appear. This dialog box advises you that the installation is being checked. Once this has completed you will then be asked to reboot your PC, as shown in Figure 4.9. Select Yes to restart the computer.

LOADING REALM CRAFTER FOR THE FIRST TIME

To run Realm Crafter you will need to run the application as an Administrator. To start Realm Crafter, click on the Start button and then select All Programs > Realm Crafter, as shown in Figure 4.10. Right-click on the Realm Crafter option and select Run as Administrator.

Figure 4.9
The Setup Complete dialog box.

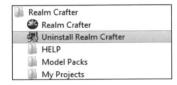

Figure 4.10
Running Realm Crafter from the Start button.

Note

If you don't want to right-click on the Realm Crafter text and select Run as Administrator each time you launch the application, you can also configure it to do this automatically each time. To configure this, right-click on the Realm Crafter text and select the Properties option from the pop-up menu. On the shortcut tab, click on the Advanced button, and then ensure that the check box Run as Administrator is checked. Then click on OK.

The full version of Realm Crafter Pro requires you to confirm your user account details that you were provided when you purchased the software. A dialog box will appear, asking for your username and password that were provided when you purchased the software. You can see the dialog box in Figure 4.11. Once you enter the information and click on the OK button, it will connect to the Realm Crafter system and confirm your login details. You will then receive a message

Figure 4.11
The full Connect to Realm Crafter dialog box that you see the first time you run the application.

box informing you if the process was successful. Click on OK to close the dialog box. You will need to click on the All Programs > Realm Crafter > Realm Crafter menu item again and then select Run as Administrator.

You will now see the Real Crafter Project Manager, which is where you can see any programs that you have already created and quickly get access to them. You can see the Realm Crafter Project Manager in Figure 4.12.

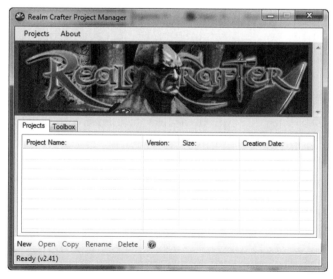

Figure 4.12
The Realm Crafter Project Manager dialog box.

CREATING A NEW PROJECT

To create a new project, click on the New option, listed at the bottom of the Project Manager. You will then be asked if you want to create a new project, as shown in Figure 4.13. Click on Yes to create a new project.

Figure 4.13
The Realm Crafter Create Project dialog box.

Note

You can create a new project by choosing the Projects > New Project menu option at the top of the dialog box or by clicking the New option at the bottom of the Project Manager.

Realm Crafter will begin to create a new project. This process requires a number of files to be created and so it might take a couple of minutes. Once Realm Crafter has created the new project, it will be listed as New Project in the Projects tab, as shown in Figure 4.14. You can rename the project file before you start to do something that more aptly describes your project.

USING THE PROJECT MANAGER TOOLBOX TAB

The Project Manager toolbox tab provides quick access to some key Realm Crafter tools that you will need to use throughout your project.

These include:

- **Game Editor:** This is the standard Realm Crafter editor where you create your MMO games.

- **Test Server (Normal):** From here, you can test your MMO server, configure any login messages, and view any particular zones you have created.

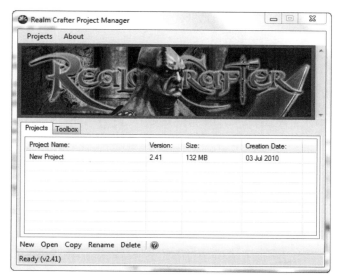

Figure 4.14
The new project added to the Projects tab of the Project Manager.

- **Scripts (Visual Studio):** This allows you to launch Visual Studio and load a pre-built solution that contains all of the key scripts for your game. You must have Visual C# Express to use this option.

- **Test Client:** Check that your end user client is working correctly. This will load your game and allow you to connect to the server. This allows you to test that your client menus and game are working correctly before distributing the client to your end users.

You can see a list of the toolbox items in Figure 4.15.

N o t e

You can get a free version of Visual Studio from Microsoft called Visual Studio Express. You can find out more information and download instructions from the following address: http://www.microsoft.com/express/.

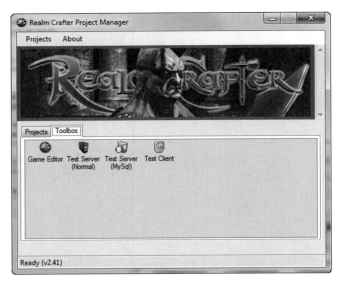

Figure 4.15
The Project Manager toolbox.

Starting Your Project

Once you have created your project using the New option you can access it by double-clicking on it. This will open the editor for this project. You are able to save the project as another file once you are within the project.

You can see an opened project in Figure 4.16.

Note

Every project you create is filled with a basic set of data so that you can test your game straight away. This includes the screen configuration, basic area to walk around in, and a character player.

Realm Crafter Tour

The Realm Crafter interface consists of a number of tabs that provide access to the editor screens.

The default tab that Realm Crafter loads is the Project tab. You can see the Project tab in Figure 4.16. The Project tab isn't the only tab available, of course.

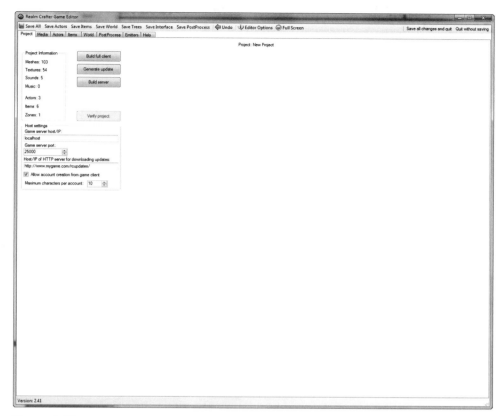

Figure 4.16
The first project open in the Game Editor.

The Realm Crafter program consists of several other tab windows that provide access to common features. You can see all of the available tabs in Figure 4.17.

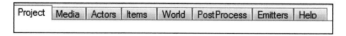

Figure 4.17
The tabs available in the Realm Crafter program.

The tabs are defined as follows:

- **Project:** From the Project tab you are able to build the client and server software for your MMO. This screen also provides project statistics and server connection details.

- **Media:** This is the location for all of your graphics, sounds, and 3D models that you want to access within your MMO.

- **Actors:** It lists all of the games characters that will appear within your MMO world. It also contains information such as general description, gender, associated faction, and appearance. By default there are three actors provided with a starter project; these are human and two variations of a lizard folk.

- **Items:** Anything that can be picked up by the player is an item. This can range from treasure items, weapons, armor, and potions.

- **World:** Within the World tab you create the zones/worlds in which your players will walk around and play the game.

- **Post Process:** This allows you to add special graphics effects to your game. You can add effects such as bloom, brightness, and monochrome.

- **Emitters:** Particle effects are special graphical effects that you can add to your MMOs, such as smoke, fire, and blood splatter. Particle effects are used in all modern computer games. From within the Emitters tab you will be able to amend already created particles or create new ones.

- **Help:** Access the help for Realm Crafter Professional.

Note

Under some of the Realm Crafter editor tabs are additional tabs; I will be covering these other tabs as we discuss each of the editor options.

You may notice in the task bar that there are two Realm Crafter icons, as shown in Figure 4.18. The blue icon represents the Realm Crafter Project Manager dialog box and the red icon represents the Realm Crafter Game Editor. You can close the Realm Crafter Editor by clicking on the X in the top-right corner of the application window. This will bring you back to the Realm Crafter Project Manager.

Figure 4.18
The Realm Crafter icons in the Windows task bar.

Summary

The following chapters progress through the Realm Crafter application tabs and help you begin to add content to your test project. The upcoming chapters will show you the process required to get your game up and running as quickly as possible.

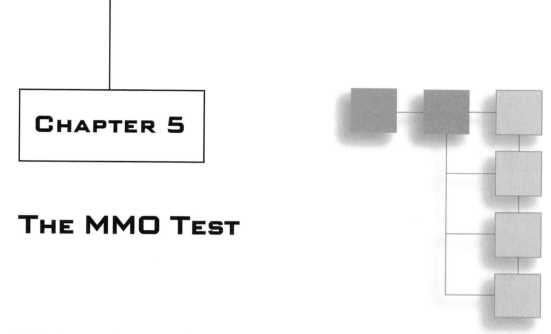

CHAPTER 5

THE MMO TEST

This chapter shows you how to run a simple test to confirm your MMO is working correctly. You may wonder why you would test your MMO before you have actually created anything. A blank default Realm Crafter project contains everything it needs to run a test MMO, including a player and a world. By running the test, you will have a better idea of what you are creating as you go through the different editors.

THE SERVER

As explained in Chapter 4, you need two things to run an MMO successfully. You need a server that will contain the important data such as user passwords and login accounts and you need a client to allow the end users to play the game.

The first thing you need to do is start the server. The server will need to be running any time you want anyone (including yourself) to be able to access the MMO game. Follow these steps to start the server:

1. Ensure that the Realm Crafter Project Manager is running.
2. You must have at least one project file listed in the Projects tab to continue.

3. Click on the Toolbox tab on the Project Manager dialog box.

4. Double-click on the Test Server (Normal) option.

This will bring up the Realm Crafter Professional Testing Server dialog box, as shown in Figure 5.1.

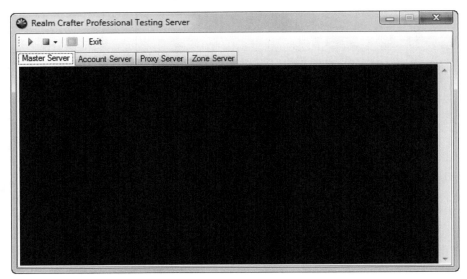

Figure 5.1
The Realm Crafter Professional Testing Server dialog box.

Realm Crafter Professional is aimed at giving MMO creators the ability to scale their MMO over a number of servers. If you are going to make an MMO for a few friends, you can do this on a single server. However, when you start to consider the number of users you could have using an MMO, the biggest problem most companies have is insufficient scalability. A lack of scalability causes users to suffer poor performance or to be unable to access a server because it is too busy. Many new MMOs suffer this problem when they are first launched because buying too many servers can be costly, and it's difficult to predict the number of concurrent users who will access at one particular time. The original Realm Crafter had only a single server, and so if you were looking at trying to make a professional MMO, you would be limited by the amount of users who could access a single server. The way Realm Crafter Professional solves this is by creating a number of servers; you can improve performance by adding servers.

Before you start learning more about the various servers, it is important to understand the term *cluster*. A cluster is a common server word (very much like the term *farm*) that means that multiple servers belong to the same group.

In Figure 5.1, you can see four possible tabs:

- **Master Server:** This server manages all of the game servers; it is the game world administrator. The server is the central data repository. Any changes made to this server will propagate down to any other servers. There can be only one Master Server in a cluster.

- **Account Server:** This server deals with authenticating (checking) that a user has the rights to log into the game. It will also present the users with the ability to select a character. In Realm Crafter Professional there is no graphical account front end for managing users, but you can edit a script called AccountDatabase.cs, which allows you to create more complex web-based front ends to user account logins and payment processing systems. Many MMOs require that users have web accounts in order to manage payments and upgrades to their accounts.

- **Proxy Server:** A *proxy* is a forwarding service; it will receive a connection and then forward it to the right address. In Realm Crafter Professional's case it is the only part of the server that is visible to the player, and will direct the player to the Account Server.

- **Zone Server:** An MMO game is made up of many zones. A zone server allows you to split up areas of your game into zones and as such have a server represent a particular zone. This ensures that you can provide maximum performance for the heaviest traffic areas. These are usually main city areas where people congregate.

N o t e

Concurrent and total users are two important words in MMO games. When a company sells an MMO, the number of copies it sells is the total number of possible users. Concurrent is the total number of actual users accessing the MMO at any one time. When figuring out concurrent numbers, you need to take into consideration time zones (different users will log in at any one time) and initial free trial time (more users will be logged on during the free 30-day trial period).

Testing Server Toolbar

Across the top of the Testing Server application is a selection of buttons. These allow a basic level of management of your servers.

Figure 5.2
The Testing Server buttons.

The buttons can be seen in Figure 5.2 and consist of the following (from left to right):

- **Start:** Start the servers. This is required for the users to connect to the game.
- **Stop:** Stop the servers; this can be a soft or hard stop. A hard stop will close all connections straight away, whereas a soft stop will close all services correctly before shutting down. Unless there is a serious problem with your servers, you should use soft stop.
- **Web Browser:** Allows you to view traffic data in a web browser.
- **Exit:** Exit the Testing Server. If you are running the server and click on Exit, it will advise you that exiting the server will result in stopping the service.

Note

The Testing Server application is also available in the tool tray, located in the bottom-right corner of your Windows operating system (next to the date and time). You can access the Start, Stop, Web Browser, and Exit options by right-clicking on the Realm Crafter Server icon.

Starting the Server

In this section, you'll learn how to get your server up and running, which will allow users to connect to the default MMO that is created as part of every project. Follow these steps to get your server up and running:

1. Ensure that you have started the Realm Crafter Project Manager.

2. Ensure that there is at least one New Project; if there isn't, choose Projects > New to create one.

3. Click on the Toolbox tab.

4. Double-click on the Test Server (Normal) button. This will bring up the dialog box mentioned in Figure 5.1.

5. Click on the Start button represented by a small green triangle. By clicking on this button you will start up all four servers (by default these are set to your PC IP address).

6. Four boxes will appear and then disappear, and then some text will appear in the Master Server console, as shown in Figure 5.3. This shows you if the server started correctly. If you see the text "Server Started," then it has been successful.

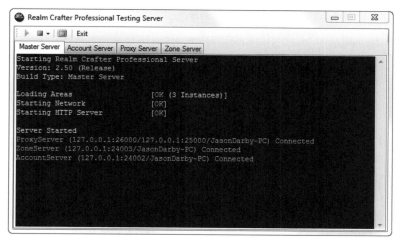

Figure 5.3
The Server Started messages.

Note

By default, the services will start up on IP address 127.0.0.1. This is called the loopback IP address and is used locally. If this process fails, there may be a problem with your network card or drivers.

If you try to start the client without starting the server, you will get the error message shown in Figure 5.4.

Figure 5.4
The client error message when trying to start a game when the server is disabled.

The Client

Now that the server is running, you can learn how to run the client and take a look at some of its features. The client is the software that is installed on the users' PCs that will allow them to play the game. This section uses the default MMO in order to show you what to expect when you begin creating your own games. Follow these steps to access the test client:

1. Ensure that the Realm Crafter Project Manager is loaded.

2. Ensure that there is at least one project.

3. Click on the Toolbox tab.

4. Double-click on Test Client.

A window will now appear and after a few seconds will display a login menu, which can be seen in Figure 5.5.

Using the login screen shown in Figure 5.5, the player can generate a new account or log in to an existing one.

Note
You can prevent players from creating accounts through the client software within the Realm Crafter Editor.

Client Settings

Once you have clicked on the Settings button found in the bottom-right corner of the New Project application window, a dialog box will appear with a number of tabs.

Figure 5.5
The MMO login menu.

These tabs can be broken down into the following:

- **Graphics:** Allows you to configure/change your graphic options, such as resolution, full-screen or window view, and so on. This is very useful for those people running more/less powerful graphics cards as they improve the performance or look of the game depending on their card. You can see the graphics options in Figure 5.6.

- **Controls:** Allows you to view and change the mouse and keyboard controls for the game. You can see a selection of commands in Figure 5.7. You can change an option by clicking on it with the left mouse button. The text will change to red to show that you can change it. You then click on a key or mouse button to change the option.

- **Other:** Allows you to change the volume of the game, as shown in Figure 5.8.

Figure 5.6
The Graphics Options dialog box.

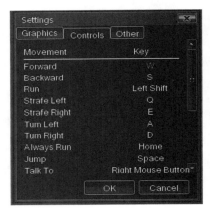

Figure 5.7
The Controls Options dialog box.

Figure 5.8
The Other options dialog box.

STARTING THE GAME

Now that you have explored all of the menu options, this section will take you through the process of running the game to show you what happens. Ensure you have the menu system displayed and that the server is running.

You will now be presented with a login dialog box. This will contain the login details of the Administrator. You also have the option of creating a new user.

1. Enter a username, a password, and a valid email address; you can see an example of this in Figure 5.9.

Figure 5.9
The login box with some user details entered.

2. Click on the Create Account button. A message will appear advising you that a new account has been created, as shown in Figure 5.10.

Figure 5.10
The New account created dialog box.

3. Click on OK to close the dialog box.

4. Click on the Login button.

5. You will now be taken to a Character screen, which currently contains no player characters associated with this account, as shown in Figure 5.11. Here you can view any existing characters as well as create or delete characters that will play in the world.

Figure 5.11
The character screen.

6. Click on the New Character button to create a new character.

7. You will now see a Character Creation screen where you will select the type of character you want to play and assign any stats, as shown in Figure 5.12.

8. On the left side is a Character dialog box, which allows you to select from a drop-down box. There you can choose from the different types of characters that are available. In this example there is a single entry of Human. Most of the options here haven't been configured. Click on the Face right arrow to scroll through some different options.

9. On the right side of Figure 5.12 is an Attributes dialog box. This is where the stats for the player are displayed. In this example, the player has five points that they can apply to various player attributes, such as health, mana, and strength.

Figure 5.12
The Character Creation screen.

10. At the bottom is a place to add a character's name. In this example, I have typed the name Jasned.

11. Click on the Create Character button to create the character.

12. You will now be taken back to the blank character screen.

13. Click on the name of your new character, which in this example is Jasned. You can also use the left and right arrows at the bottom of the screen to rotate around your created character.

14. Once you are happy with your selection, you can click on the Start Game button to enter the game world.

15. Your character will be dropped into the game world. You may also find that a number of dialog boxes have been displayed. Close them and you will then see your character onscreen as shown in Figure 5.13. You can move around by using the keys described in Figure 5.7.

Figure 5.13
The character placed in the game world.

Touring the Game Interface

This section takes a quick look at the components that make up your game, as you will be making changes and configuring them later. The settings shown in this section are as follows:

- **Compass:** Shows the direction that you are looking/moving in. You can see the compass in Figure 5.14.

Figure 5.14
The compass showing the direction that you are moving in.

- **Action Bar:** Allows the players to use quick keys to initiate certain actions quickly; this could be to drink a potion or use a weapon such as a wand or sword. You can see the action bar in Figure 5.15. The action bar also contains a number of predefined quick keys that I will cover shortly.

Figure 5.15
The action bar with a set of quick buttons ready for the players to place objects that they want to use.

■ **Chat Window:** Displays anything that you say to other users in the game, but also any global chat that players will type into their windows. You can see some example chats in Figure 5.16. To access the chat, press the Enter key, type in your message, and then press the Enter key again to send your message.

Figure 5.16
The chat window with an in-game chat example.

Predefined Quick Buttons

On the action bar is a set of eight predefined quick buttons. You can see a close-up of these buttons in Figure 5.17.

Figure 5.17
The eight pre-defined quick buttons.

These buttons are as follows:

- **Chat:** The speech bubble icon represents a chat action key. This will allow you to bring up the chat box where you can type your message. Type your message into the window and press Enter to continue.

- **Map:** This brings up the game map. The default image is just a random set of images and is something that you will need to replace later when making your MMO.

- **Inventory:** This will contain items that you have collected from other NPCs or have purchased. It will also give you an indication of how much money you have. Items can be stackable, which means you can have multiple items in one square as long as they are of the same type. You can see an example of the inventory for the default player in Figure 5.18.

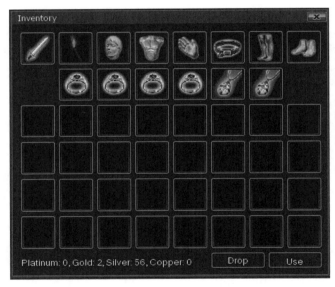

Figure 5.18
The Inventory screen.

- **Abilities:** Lists all the abilities that your character has.

- **Character:** Details the character stats that your player has, including any reputation, money, level and experience as well as particular attributes. You can see an example of the character stats in Figure 5.19.

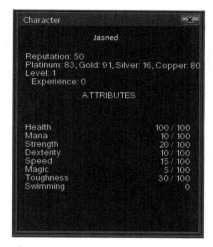

Figure 5.19
The Character's stats screen.

- **Quests:** Lists all available quests. The default is blank.
- **Party:** Details the members of your party.
- **Help:** Provides a default set of text that you can configure to provide in-game help. The text file is located in the \data\game data\help.txt file.

Now that you have been introduced to the main components of the MMO game interface, it is time to exit the game. You can do this by pressing the Esc (Escape) key. Upon pressing the Escape key, you will see a dialog box appear, as shown in Figure 5.20.

Figure 5.20
The Menu dialog box.

Using the Menu dialog box, you can access the settings, log out, exit the game, or resume the game and continue to play.

BROWSER STATS

Once you have an MMO game up and running with users playing your game, you will need to keep track of how your server(s) are performing, and what kind of performance your users might be getting from your game.

Realm Crafter Professional provides some basic information about how your game is being used in the form of a web-based interface.

To access the browser stats, you need to be running the Testing Server. Once the dialog box is open and the server services are running, you can then select the browser button.

To access the stats you will need to enter your login and password to the Admin account for this particular MMO. The default settings are "Admin" for user and "password" for the password. When the password dialog box appears, as shown in Figure 5.21, you enter the login and password details.

Figure 5.21
The login. and password dialog box.

Note

The screenshot in Figure 5.21 is from Internet Explorer; you may find that other browsers display the content differently.

The web browser administrator is separated into a number of options:

- **Global:** Displays global stats about your cluster, including the number of servers, the number of players, and how long the server has been running. The number of servers in the cluster does not equal individual servers, but services. A useful option here is to see the load on the servers. A low load means your servers are handling the account and user requests; if you are getting a heavy load (displayed as red text) for a period of time, you should consider moving a service to another server to lighten the load and give players a better play experience. See Figure 5.22.

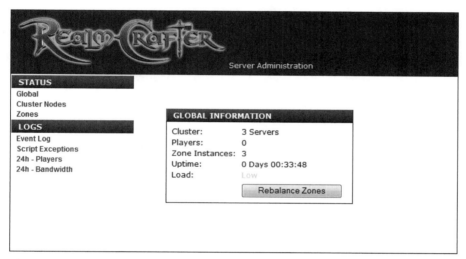

Figure 5.22
The Global Status page.

- **Cluster Nodes:** All the servers that are involved in the cluster, including account, world, and proxy servers. It displays the properties and IPs of the servers, as well as the number of clients and bandwidth usage. See Figure 5.23.

- **Zones:** Information about the zone instances in your cluster. In the default game project this includes the default zone and the main menu areas (character screens). See Figure 5.24.

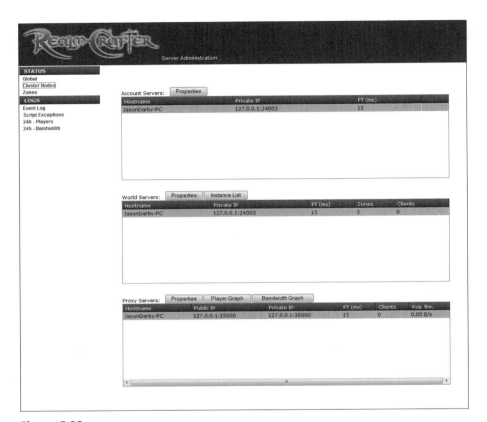

Figure 5.23
The Cluster Nodes page.

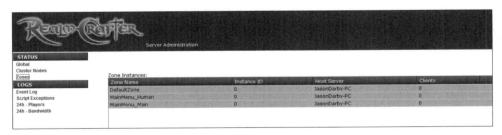

Figure 5.24
The Zones page.

■ **Event Log:** Displays important logging information about the servers. This will also display any error messages such as a server not starting. See Figure 5.25.

Figure 5.25
The Event Log page.

- **Script Exceptions:** Because an MMO will run many scripts, from playing a spell effect to transferring a player to a particular zone, it is important to track when scripts do not run correctly. This screen will display any errors in the scripts that are being run in the game. See Figure 5.26.

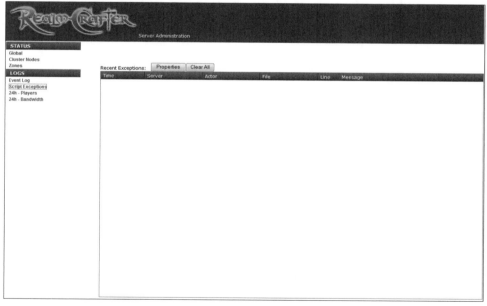

Figure 5.26
The Script Exceptions page.

■ **24h–Players:** Displays a player count over the last 24 hours. This is very useful for determining if there is a regular spike in the number of players playing the game at any particular time. This is helpful in seeing when most of your users are logging in to play the game. See Figure 5.27.

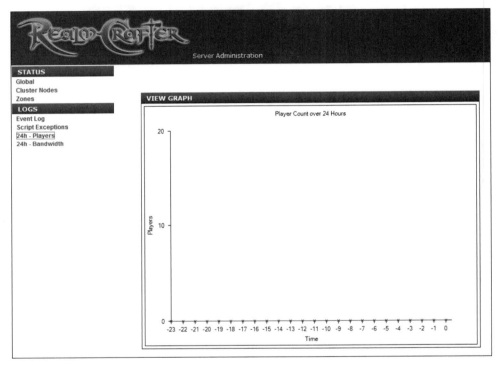

Figure 5.27
The 24-hour player's page.

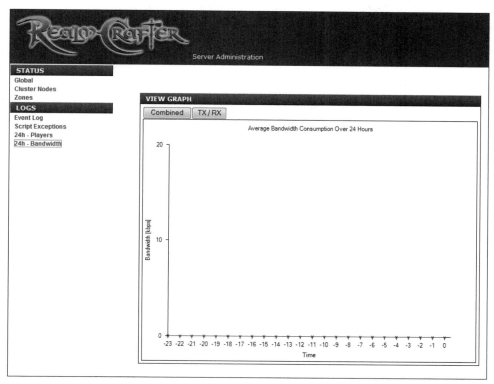

Figure 5.28
The 24-hour bandwidth page.

- **24h–Bandwidth:** This gives a 24-hour view about when the most band-width for your game is being used. Typically, the more players online, the more bandwidth your game uses. This screen shows you the exact amounts being used. See Figure 5.28.

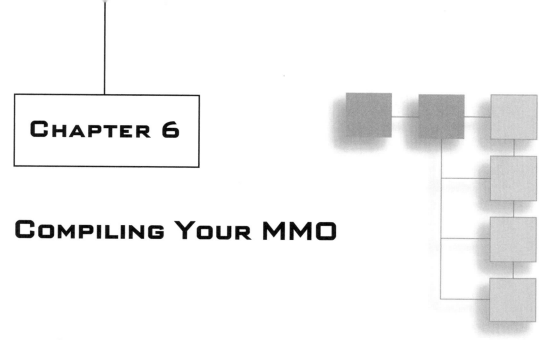

CHAPTER 6

COMPILING YOUR MMO

Compiling your MMO in order to generate an executable that you can give to users is something that you typically do after you have made your MMO. Even so, I am covering this subject at this time because it is part of the first tab called Project, and as you make your MMO you should be generating builds so that it can be tested. Testing your MMO as you build various areas is very important and a great way of saving a lot of bug fixing at the end of your project.

BUILDING A FULL CLIENT

Ensure Realm Crafter is open and you have double-clicked on a project to open the Realm Crafter Game Editor. The Project tab will be open by default, as shown in Figure 6.1.

The Project tab can be split into the following sections and options:

- **Project Information area:** Provides basic information about your game, including the number of textures, sounds, and zones.

- **Host Settings area:** By checking or unchecking the Allow Account Creation from Game Client, you can allow or prevent users from creating user accounts from within the client application. If you uncheck this box, you must have an alternative method of allowing users to create

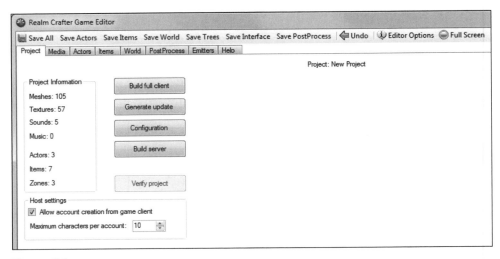

Figure 6.1
The Project tab.

accounts, such as from a website. You can also define how many characters a user can have per account. A good starting number is about five or six characters. Some free-to-play MMOs have a limited number of characters and the player can upgrade to more characters for a small fee.

- **Build Full Client button:** This option will build a full client that you can then distribute. As your game gets bigger, the full client will continue to grow in size. The original *WOW* came on five CD-ROMS, but would be on many more CD-ROMs if released now with all of the new content Blizzard added to the original game.

- **Generate Update button:** This will generate a patch update since the last full build. This is smaller than a full-client build and allows you to distribute a smaller file to your users.

- **Configuration button:** Allows you to configure aspects of the master server, the password, and other servers within your cluster.

- **Build Server button:** Builds the server software that is required to run on the server.

- **Verify Project button:** Use this button to verify that the project has been built correctly.

Once you are ready to build a full client, click on the Build Full Client button. You will receive the build message shown in Figure 6.2.

Figure 6.2
Full Client Build warning message.

If your game is particularly large, it may take many minutes to compile all of the files. This example uses the default project, so the compilation will take only a minute or two.

1. Click on the OK button.

2. You will see at the bottom of the Realm Crafter Game Editor a small bar that turns green as it completes the compile.

3. Once the compile is complete, you will get a Build Client dialog box, as shown in Figure 6.3.

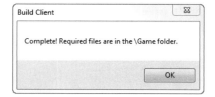

Figure 6.3
Build Client complete dialog box.

4. Click on OK to close the dialog box.

Now that you have built the client, the files will be located in the following directory (based on default installation path and your project being called New Project):

C:\Program Files\Solstar Games\Realm Crafter 2\Projects\New Project\Game

BUILDING AN UPDATE

By generating an update to your game instead of a full build every time, you can provide your current users with a smaller set of files, which means fewer files that need to be downloaded. This is better for those who are on a restrictive download policy with their ISP and saves your current users a lot of time. To generate an update, follow these steps:

1. From the Realm Crafter Game Editor window, click on the Generate Update button.

2. If you haven't built a full client, you will get a message as shown in Figure 6.4.

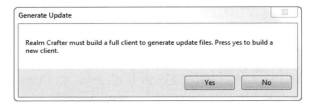

Figure 6.4
The Generate Update message.

3. Click on Yes to build the full client. Depending on how big your game is, this process can take a while. With the default project, it should take no longer than a minute or two.

4. Upon build completion, you'll see the message box shown in Figure 6.5.

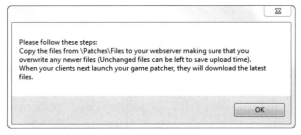

Figure 6.5
The build update process dialog box.

5. To allow users to use the latest files you will need to copy the files from your Patches\Files folder to your web server where you are storing your client updates.

CONFIGURING YOUR SERVERS

All of your server configuration can be done through the Configuration button on the Project tab of the Realm Crafter Game Editor window. By clicking on the Configuration button, you can change the details for the master, proxy, zone, and account servers.

1. Click on the Configuration button in the Realm Crafter Game Editor window.

2. A configuration dialog box will appear, as shown in Figure 6.6.

3. Once you have finished changing the details, click on Save or Cancel to exit the dialog box.

In Figure 6.6 you can see all of the server details, starting with the Master Server:

■ **Address:** This is the public IP (Internet Protocol) address for your Master Server. If you have installed Realm Crafter Professional on your computer, this will be your current IP address assigned to your computer by your ISP (Internet Service Provider).

■ **Port:** Computers have a variety of Internet ports that various applications can use to communicate from your computer to the outside world. Using protocols such as HTTP, FTP, and communicating with MSN requires a range of port numbers. The default port for the Master Server is 25001.

■ **Master Proxy:** This lists the selected Master Proxy for the Master Server, which in the case of Figure 6.6 is MyMachine.

■ **Web Username:** The username for logging into the web admin page.

■ **Web Password:** The password for logging into the web admin page.

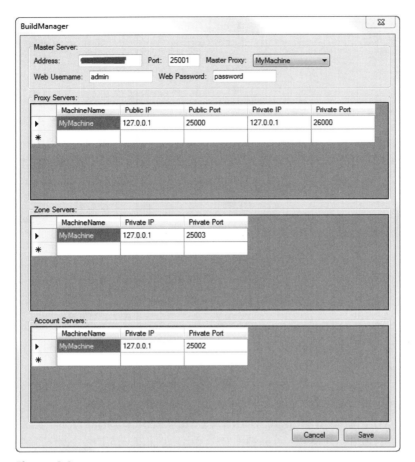

Figure 6.6
The Configuration dialog box contains the server details.

By default, the Proxy Server is the machine where you have installed Realm Crafter Professional. This also has a public and private IP and port. The benefit of this is that you can have two network cards in the Proxy Server and allow one network card to be public facing while the other is internal. This ensures that your Proxy Server can communicate across the public and private networks safely.

The Zone Server is the machine where you installed Realm Crafter Professional by default. This is only private facing and has a private IP and port.

And finally, the Account Server also uses the default settings and has a private IP and port.

Note

You will notice that all of the IP address fields listed in Figure 6.6 (except for the Master Server for which I have deliberately deleted the IP address so that it's not detailed in the book) contain the loopback IP address of 127.0.0.1. This is a special IP address given to all network cards. If this IP address does not work, there may be a problem with your network card or drivers.

BUILDING THE SERVER

The Build Server option in the Game Editor window allows you to create an executable which can run on a server and which takes one of the four key roles in the Realm Crafter Professional cluster—Master, Zone, Proxy, or Administration Server.

1. Click on the Build Server button from the Game Editor window.

2. Once the build is complete, a dialog box will appear, as shown in Figure 6.7. This message box advises you about where the files have been placed—in this case, in the \Server folder.

Figure 6.7
The Build Server dialog box.

3. Click on the OK button to close the dialog box.

If you navigate to the following area, you will see a set of folders, as shown in Figure 6.8:

C:\Program Files\Solstar Games\Realm Crafter 2\Projects\New Project\Server

MasterServer	23/12/2010 16:53	File folder
MyMachine	23/12/2010 16:53	File folder
MyMachine.0	23/12/2010 16:53	File folder
MyMachine.1	23/12/2010 16:53	File folder

Figure 6.8
The server roles folders, which contain executables.

The folders in Figure 6.8 are the different server roles. If you want to run a particular service on a particular machine, double-click on that particular folder and then run the associated executable. So for example, you would double-click on MasterServer and then double-click on MasterServer.exe to run the Master Server. That particular server service will then run, as shown in Figure 6.9.

Figure 6.9
The Master Server service is running.

Note

At the time of this writing, these server services work best on Windows-based machines. They can be configured to work on Linux servers, but you need to make further adjustments. Please consult the Realm Crafter Professional Wiki at the following link to find out more information (you must have a username/password registered with realmcrafter.com to access this article):

http://realmcrafter.com/rcpwiki/index.php?title=Documentation:Server:BuildingACluster#Linux_Servers

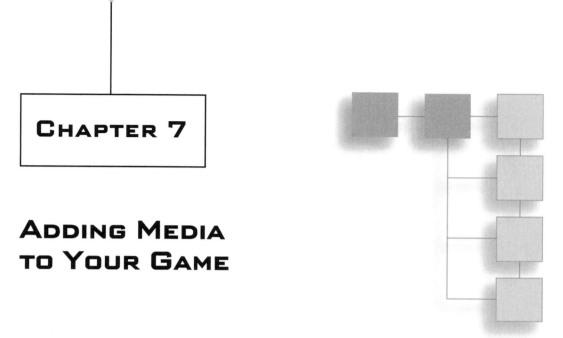

CHAPTER 7

ADDING MEDIA TO YOUR GAME

This chapter explores the types of media you can use in your games, and the options available from the Media tab. The options in the Media tab allow you to prepare your 3D content, sound, and music for your game. In this chapter, you'll add some content to the demo example files.

To access the Media tab, you need to have created a Realm Crafter project. Open the Realm Crafter Project Manager and double-click on the project you created (unless you have renamed it, it was called New Project in previous chapters). Then click on the Media tab.

You can see the default set up of the Media tab in Figure 7.1.

TYPES OF MEDIA

There are a number of types of media available in Realm Crafter, as follows:

- **Meshes:** Think of any 3D-based object in a computer game or MMO, such as a character, table, car, sword, house, or one of hundreds, perhaps thousands, of 3D objects within a game world. If you remove the skin of that object, you will be left with a mesh. A mesh is a number of polygons connected together to form the shape of an object.

- **Textures:** As you can imagine, a 3D object with just a mesh would look pretty boring in a computer game. To give an object a lifelike appearance

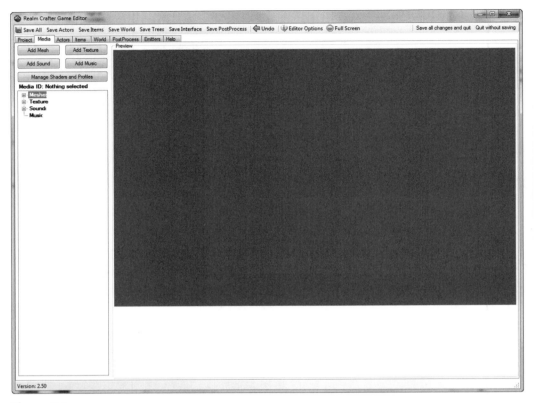

Figure 7.1
The Media tab of the Game Editor.

you need to add a texture to it. A texture is an image that is placed on top of the mesh and gives the object its color and texture. If you think of a human being with a suit of armor on, the texture would need to include all the different colors being represented, such as skin tone, armor color, and cloth. A texture created by a 3D program is displayed as a flat image; this image is then wrapped around the 3D object. Figures 7.2 and 7.3 show a face of a 3D character and as suit of armor, respectively, as flat textures.

▪ **Sound:** In MMOs, sounds include sound effects, such as walking, hitting, drinking, and weather noises. These are the sounds that your game needs to appear more realistic.

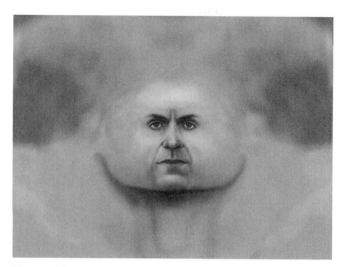

Figure 7.2
A face texture.

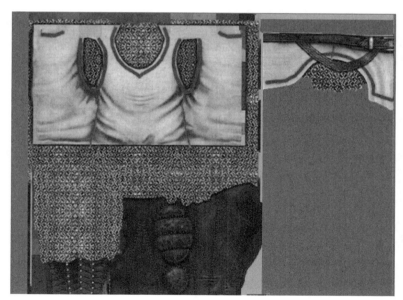

Figure 7.3
A suit of armor texture.

Think of a game with no sound effects; it would be like watching an old black-and-white silent movie with no sound. A game without sound would be a lot less immersive, and this is why game companies put a lot of value on the sound in games.

■ **Music:** Adding music to your games can also add to its overall quality of your MMO. Music can be used to great effect, such as when you have entered a particular zone or friendly capital city, or perhaps when the player enters a dangerous area. You should be careful not to mix music with actions that a player might make, as it may become difficult to hear the actions taking place. For example, you shouldn't play music when a player is fighting with an enemy.

Note

A *polygon* is a shape created using a set of straight, non-intersecting lines. These lines will end up with a closed shape and no lines will cross over any others. A triangle is an example of a polygon. All lines are connected, and none crosses over any others. By connecting a number of polygons together, you can create a 3D shape. The more polygons within a 3D object, the smoother and higher quality the 3D object will be, and the larger in size.

The media formats that are supported by Realm Crafter are as follows.

Meshes:

■ **B3d:** Blitz 3D format. Blitz is a game-creation package that has its own 3D format. The original Realm Crafter (standard) was made using Blitz, and many of the original models were created in this format.

■ **Eb3d:** This is an encrypted B3d format. This ensures that the 3D models cannot be used in another application without the use of an encryption key.

■ **3ds:** Autodesk 3ds Max is a high-end 3D creation product that is used extensively in the games and movie industries. You can find out more about the 3ds format at www.autodesk.com.

■ **X:** The X format is a model format from Microsoft. It was created for DirectX 9 and should not really be used as a model format in your own games.

Textures:

- **BMP:** The Bitmap file format is a common graphics format used in print, web, and game creation. It is supported in most free and paid graphics packages and you will have no problems finding a package that will support it (for example, Windows Paint).

- **JPG:** The JPG format (also called JPEG) became extremely popular for use on web pages on the Internet. The format is very good at reducing the file size of an image by reducing the quality of the graphics image. Some images can look extremely low quality when using JPG at its highest settings, so there is a trade-off between image quality and size. The JPG format is widely supported by art packages.

- **PNG:** PNG is a lossless data compression format; this means the format can reduce the overall file size of the file while keeping the quality high. The file is compressed and once opened needs to be uncompressed. This can lead to large memory usage in games with lots of images. As with BMP and JPG, this format is widely supported.

- **DDS:** The DDS (Direct Draw Surface) format was created by Microsoft, initially for use in DirectX applications (starting from DirectX 7). You can find out more about DDS format at the following web link: http://msdn.microsoft.com/en-us/library/bb943990(v=VS.85).aspx.

- **TGA:** The TGA format is not widely used and you may find issues with packages not supporting this format.

Sound:

- **Wav:** WAV is a popular sound format that has been in use for many years. The only general downside of using WAV is that its sound files can be quite large. The WAV format is supported by many applications, such as Windows Sound Recorder, and music players such as iTunes and Windows media player.

- **OGG:** As WAV files can be quite large, other formats have become more popular in use, and one such format is MP3. One potential issue when using MP3 within games is that there may be a potential charge for using this format. OGG is a good alternative as it is license-free and it is more efficient (smaller in size) than WAV.

Music:

- **OGG:** Good format to use, as mentioned previously, but may need specialist sound applications to save in this format.

- **MID:** MIDI is a format that has been used in games for a very long time. You can connect a MIDI compatible music device to your computer and connect it to a supporting software application, and then create your own music effects.

- **WAV:** WAV is a good format for music, but can be on the large size. You can use third-party applications such as Adobe SoundBooth to convert WAV files into lower quality files to reduce the file size.

- **MOD:** MOD is another format that has been around for a very long time. I would generally recommend using WAV or OGG formats when possible.

- **S3M:** This is a format based on MOD. Unless you have S3M formatted files, it is recommended that you use WAV, OGG, or MIDI.

- **XM:** Another old format that you shouldn't use unless you have files formatted in this way.

- **IT:** Another old format that you shouldn't use unless you have files formatted in this way.

TOUR OF THE MEDIA TAB

The Media tab allows you to upload your content, ready to use within the game. Within the Media tab are a number of options as shown in Figure 7.1. These are as follows:

- **Add Mesh button:** Allows you to add a number of new meshes to your project.

- **Add Texture button:** Allows you to add a number of new textures.

- **Add Sound button:** Allows you to add sound to your project.

- **Add Music button:** Allows you to add music to your project.

- **Manage Shaders and Profiles button:** You can manage any graphics shaders and their respective profiles. This will allow you to apply graphical effects to your media.

- **Media Tree:** Displays all of the meshes, textures, sounds, and music within your project in a tree-like structure. You can expand any tab by clicking on the + sign and collapse it using the – sign.

- **Preview screen:** The Preview screen by default displays a blue background, but when you add 3D content, it will display the content. It will also display a Play button for music and sound so you can listen to it.

Note
___

Every item added to the project is given an ID; every item is unique and has its own ID number. This means that even if you add two items that are exactly the same, Realm Crafter treats them as different objects.

___

To give you a better understanding of how you view and interact with the various options, the next sections look at some of the media in more detail.

Viewing a Mesh

Follow these steps to look at a typical mesh in the Media tab:

1. Click on the + sign next to the Meshes text on the Media Tree. This will expand the Meshes item and display any items or folders under it.

2. Expand the Actors group.

3. Expand the Lizardman group.

4. You will see two items within this folder; the first is an animated lizardman and the second is an animated lizardman with armor mesh.

5. Click on either of the items to display the mesh of the object in the preview window, as shown in Figure 7.4.

Some media types also have a set of extra options associated with them; in the case of meshes, you will see a set of additional options shown in Figure 7.5.

Figure 7.4
The mesh of the lizardman.

Figure 7.5
Additional configuration options for a mesh object.

Some of these additional options allow you to change features of the mesh, such as object scale and the level of detail.

Note

Level of detail (or LOD as it is commonly called) is an extremely useful technique for improving the available memory of a game by reducing the quality of the texture of objects that are far away. If your character is standing next to an object, you would want to display a high level of detail for that object. This would ensure that objects close up look as good as they possibly can. When an object is far away, the human eye cannot see all the detail in a highly graphical texture, so there is no point in wasting precious memory and resources showing details that can't be viewed anyway. Within Realm Crafter you can pick from a high, medium, or low level of detail based on the distance from the player's viewpoint.

Viewing a Texture

Textures can be applied to meshes, used for the skybox or terrain, or used for graphical effects, such as particles.

1. Expand the Texture group from the Media Tree.

2. Select any of the objects within the groups in the Textures folder.

Recall that Figures 7.2 and 7.3 showed examples of two textures.

Note

A *skybox* is a graphic texture that is applied (wrapped) around the world to create the sky. You can create your own skybox or edit a current one for use in your project.

Note

Terrain textures are the graphic images that you use for the ground within your MMO. So you might have a grass, sandy, or dirt-based terrain image, for example.

Note

A *particle* is a graphic effect that you can place within your MMO. Particle effects are used extensively in modern-games to display effects such as smoke, explosions, blood splatter, and fire (and many more).

Viewing Sounds

The sounds group contains all of the current sounds within the default project.

Click on the Sounds group in the Media Tree to expand it.

In the Sounds tree, you will see three items currently applied—footsteps, water, and forest. Click WAV files, called Carefulstep2 and dampstep. These are two different walking sound effects. Select one of these items and then click on the Play button that has appeared at the bottom of the Preview window, as shown in Figure 7.6. You will hear the sound effect play.

Figure 7.6
The Play Sound properties dialog box.

IMPORTING CONTENT

You can import additional content or your own into Realm Crafter, so that you can change the look, feel, sound, and theme of the MMO. This section of the chapter shows you how to import content into Realm Crafter.

Note

This section does not show you how to create your own content, as there are many different products available to create your own sounds and 3D objects.

When you have purchased Realm Crafter Professional, you will also have access to a large amount of other content that you can use within the product. You can download content such as player characters, game props, item icons, spell icons, and weapons. You will need to log into the Realm Crafter site to download the extra content.

Once you have the various EXE installation files, double-click one of the EXE files to begin the installation. Doing so will install the content into various folders in the following location:

%System Drive%\Program Files\Solstar Games\Included Content.

You may also find content in the following location:

%System Drive%\Program Files\Solstar Games\Model Packs.

Importing 3D Content

Importing 3D content requires a little more work than adding sounds or music. This is because every project you create has its own folder structure, which requires you to place any content you are using into that folder.

When you create a project, it is added to the following location:

%System Drive%\Program Files\Solstar Games\Realm Crafter 2\Projects.

The first project you created in this book was called New Project and a folder was also created for that project within the Projects folder. Your content was then stored further within these folders:

- New Project\Data\Textures
- New Project\Data\Meshes

Follow these steps to get your content into Realm Crafter:

1. If you are using your own content, create two folders—one called Meshes and the other called Textures. Place the relevant content within each of these folders. For example, if you have a zombie character, you would create a Zombie folder within the Meshes folder, and within that Zombie folder will be the zombie mesh.

2. If you are importing content from one of the downloaded model packs, it will already be in the relevant folder structure. In this example, you will be importing a Bear model into the game (the model comes from the downloadable content from the Realm Crafter site).

3. Copy the Bear Mesh (model) folder, which is in a location similar to:
   %System Drive%:\Program Files\Solstar Games\Model Packs\Animals\bear
   This needs to go in the Meshes location for the particular project you are working on. So for this example, the mesh folder is in the following location:
   %System Drive%:\Program Files\Solstar Games\Realm Crafter 2\ Projects\New Project\Data\Meshes\Actors
   And its full path is:
   %System Drive%:\Program Files\Solstar Games\Realm Crafter 2\ Projects\New Project\Data\Meshes\Actors\Bear

4. Copy the body.bmp and head.bmp files from the following folder:
   %System Drive%:\Program Files\Solstar Games\Realm Crafter 2\ Projects\New Project\Data\Meshes\Actors

Place these two files into the Bear folder. You can see an example of the Bear folder in Figure 7.7.

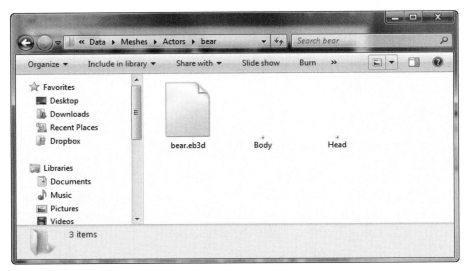

Figure 7.7
The Bear folder for the mesh example.

5. Now you need to copy the textures for the Bear into the relevant Textures folder. Copy the file Bear2 from the following folder:

   %System Drive%:\Program Files\Solstar Games\Model Packs\Animals\Textures

6. Navigate to the following location:

   %System Drive%:\Program Files\Solstar Games\Realm Crafter 2\Projects\New Project\Data\Textures\Actors
   Create a folder in here called Bear; this will contain the texture file. You will see this folder in Figure 7.8. Paste the Bear2 file into this folder.

7. Load Realm Crafter.

8. Double-click on the project where you copied your mesh and texture files. In this example, it was called New Project.

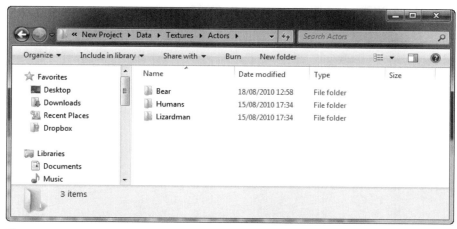

Figure 7.8
The Bear folder holds the bear texture.

9. Click on the Media tab.

10. Click on the Add Mesh button.

11. Navigate to your project folder. In this example, that would be: %System Drive%:\Program Files\Solstar Games\Realm Crafter 2\Projects \New Project\Data\Meshes\Actors\bear.

12. Select eb3d, or if you are importing your own content, the supported file format and then click on Open.

13. You will now be asked if you want to import the object as an animated object, as shown in Figure 7.9. Choose Yes.

Figure 7.9
The Add Meshes dialog box.

14. You will now be asked if you want to encrypt the object, as shown in Figure 7.10. Choose Yes. This will protect the object so that it can only be used in Realm Crafter.

Figure 7.10
Import a mesh as an encrypted object dialog box.

15. If you expand the Meshes and then the Actors folder on the Media Tree, you will see the bear object (or navigate to the file location that you imported). Since it was placed into its own folder, it will also have a folder in the Media Tree. Expand that folder and click on the mesh object to display the object in the preview window. An example is shown in Figure 7.11.

16. Now you need to import the texture, so click on the Add Texture button, which in this example is located in the following directory: %System Drive%:\Program Files\Solstar Games\Realm Crafter 2\Projects \New Project\Data\Textures\Actors\Bear

17. Select the texture and click on the Open button.

    You now have to select the relevant graphic effect to apply to the image, such as alpha channel, mask, and so on, as shown in Figure 7.12.

18. Navigate to your texture and click on it. You can now see the texture displayed in the Preview window, as shown in Figure 7.13.

Note

The settings you select within the texture settings will depend on how you created the 3D meshes and textures. Consult your 3D tools documentation for more information.

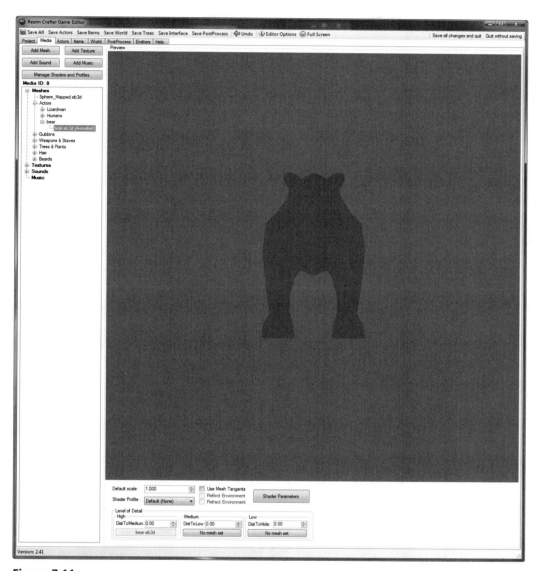

Figure 7.11
The mesh previewed within Realm Crafter.

Figure 7.12
The Texture Settings dialog box.

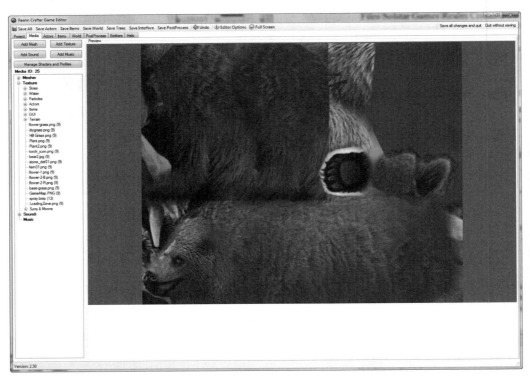

Figure 7.13
The imported texture.

SUMMARY

You now know how to import your 3D content and its relevant textures into Realm Crafter Professional. Chapter 8 shows you how to pull in this content so that it is associated with a particular actor, set up its animations, and allow the object to be a player character.

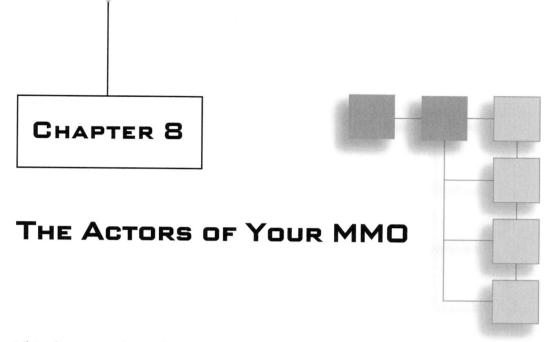

CHAPTER 8

THE ACTORS OF YOUR MMO

This chapter explores the Actors tab in Realm Crafter. If you consider a movie, it contains actors, some who are the stars of the film, and others who are bit part players that you notice in the background or who have only a few lines of dialogue. An actor in Realm Crafter is exactly the same; any character within your MMO is an actor, from the player's character that they control, to a group of enemy characters who the players will fight, to a bit part non-player character who stands in a shop selling goods.

To begin this section of the book, you need to have a project already created and the Realm Crafter Game Editor loaded and on the Actors tab.

TOURING THE ACTORS TAB

Let's now take a look at all of the various options within the Actors tab. Within the Actors tab are five main sub-tabs, as shown in Figure 8.1.

These five main sub-tabs are as follows:

- **Actors**: This is where you create your actors for your MMO game as well as set up if the actor is a player character or a mount, and other options such as how much XP the player would get for killing.

Figure 8.1
The additional tabs in the Actors tab.

- **Factions**: The Factions tab allows you to set up the rivalries between various groups. Is one group friendly with another, or are they at all-out war?

- **Animations**: Allows you to set up the different animations that an actor will have, such as walking, running, and attacking.

- **Abilities**: These are abilities that the player can initiate at any point, such as heal self, heal other, or poison. If you have played other MMOs, you could call them spells or buffs.

- **General Settings**: Allows you to configure a number of general settings, such as combat delay times and currency amounts.

N o t e

A *mount* is an actor within an MMO that the player can ride around the game world. In a game like *Ultima Online* or *World of Warcraft,* a mount could also be a horse, an ostrich, or perhaps even a dragon. You could be making a game in a Sci-Fi setting and so the mount could easily be a robot or a vehicle.

Actors Sub-Tab

The Actors sub-tab is the first of the five sub-tabs available. You can see the initial screen in Figure 8.2, the application window is separated into three sections.

- **Actors Tree Pane**: Here you will see all currently available actors within your game. Having already played a test of the MMO, you will recall that you can select a human or lizard creature.

- **Setup**: This section includes a description of the actor and some basic settings. This description is not used in-game and is for the game developer's benefit only. The following options are available in the Setup section.

Figure 8.2
The Actors tab.

- **Race**: You can set up multiple races to associate your actors with, for example Human and Lizard.
- **Class**: You can create multiple classes of a particular race. For example, if you were making a fantasy game, for your human race you could have the following classes: Wizard, Thief, Soldier, and Worker.
- **Genders**: You can create gender-specific actors and you can also make them non-gender-specific. This is useful if you are creating an

actor who doesn't need to be associated with a gender, for example an animal or alien. You can select from the following options, male and female, male only, female only, and no gender.

- **Home Faction**: Defines the actor's faction. In the case of the book's default project, there are two factions, humans and traders.
- **Description**: Type a description for the actor.

■ **Properties**: The properties area consists of four additional tabs—Behaviour, Appearance, Attributes, and Preview.
- **Behaviour**: Main configuration options for the actor.
- **Appearance**: Change the appearance of an actor.
- **Attributes**: Change, add, or delete an attribute.
- **Preview:** A small preview window of the actor.

Note

Above the Setup field are three buttons—New Actor, Duplicate Actor, and Delete Actor. These buttons allow you to create a new actor, copy an already created actor, or delete an actor from the left actors tree pane.

Note

If you were creating an MMO from scratch you would remove the current actors and replace them with your own. These are the default actors that allow you to test the MMO client straight away without needing to do any initial work.

Note

Attributes are values that are assigned to an actor that contain things such as human characteristics and skills. Examples of attributes include health, mana, and swimming.

The following sections discuss the Properties tab's options in more detail.

Modifying Actor Behavior

The Behaviour tab contains configurable items associated with the selected actor; Figure 8.3 shows the available options.

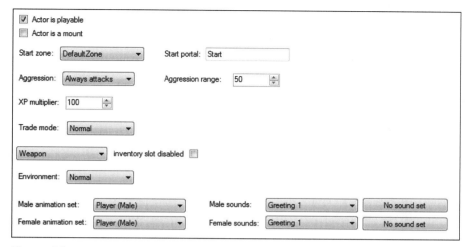

Figure 8.3
The behavior settings for the current, selected actor.

The options that are available are as follows:

- **Actor is playable**: This will allow you to select this actor as a playable character.

- **Actor is a mount**: Configure the actor as a mount, which is a character that your player will be able to ride, such as a horse or vehicle.

- **Start zone**: The starting zone for this character. This is very important for a player character, as this will decide where they will start the game.

- **Start portal**: You can create multiple start portals; this allows you to specify a starting location for a character, which could be different for another character.

- **Aggression**: When you walk around the MMO world certain factions will react to you. The aggression drop-down box allows you to configure this particular actor's aggression. This can be set to Passive, Defensive, Always Attacks, and Non Combatant. You could, for example, have a wolf that is set to defensive, so it wouldn't attack you, but if you attack the animal it will defend itself.

- **Aggression range**: If you set an actor to be aggressive to the player, you can set the range at which the actor will take notice of the player and attack. The lower the number the closer the player will need to be to the actor for it to initiate its attack.

- **XP multiplier**: How much XP (experience points) the player gets for killing this particular actor. This is a modifier based on the player's current level.

- **Trade mode**: Determines whether the actor is a trader, cannot trade, or is a trade pack animal (an animal that carries trade items).

- **Weapon**: The actor's default weapon.

- **Inventory slot disabled**: Determines whether the actor's inventory slot is available; if this is disabled you cannot give the actor any items.

- **Environment**: The environment that the player exists in. The options are normal (ground), swimming only, flying only, and walking only.

- **Animation sets**: Which animation set is associated with this actor.

- **Sounds**: The initial sound that is associated with this actor.

Note

An MMO consists of multiple areas, called *zones*.

Modifying Appearance

The Appearance tab allows you to configure the 3D mesh with specific details. This is particularly useful when you have a group of actors but want each one to look slightly different. In this case, you could use the base actor, duplicate it, and then make changes to the appearance. You can see the appearance options in Figure 8.4.

The options in Figure 8.4 are placed in three groups—Male, Female, and General. The male section allows you to configure items such as hair, face, body, and beard, whereas the female options allow hair, face, and body changes. You can also configure multiple versions by selecting variations such as first male hair, third male face, and so on.

The general settings allow you to configure options such as hair color and various *gubbins*, as well as the blood texture to use when the player gets hit.

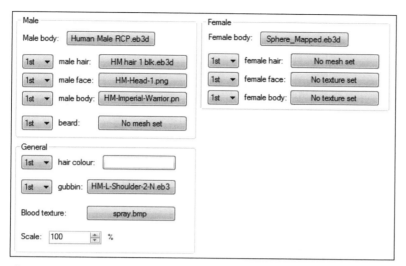

Figure 8.4
The Appearance tab options.

N o t e

Gubbins are small 3D objects that can change the appearance of another 3D object. So in the case of a medieval warrior, the gubbins could be extended shoulder pads, spikes on arm armor, add-ons to a helmet, and so on.

Attributes

Attributes are values that can increase or decrease and can have a dramatic effect on the player's character. There is a set of default attributes and resistances that are applied to each character. The great benefit of this system is that you can give different actor groups different starting values. You can see these values in Figure 8.5.

Some examples of this could be:

- **Shark**: High swimming attribute.
- **Elephant**: High strength and high toughness.
- **Poison Ant**: High poison resistance and high speed.
- **Fire Zombie**: High fire resistance but perhaps wouldn't be too tough (rotting flesh may not be tough).

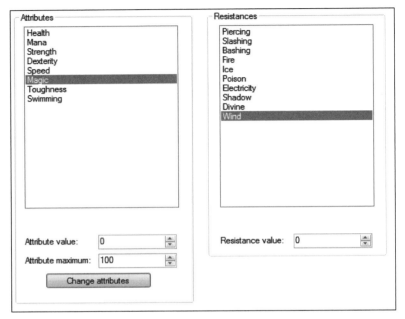

Figure 8.5
The attributes and resistances options.

▪ **Tree Monster:** Has bark, which gives it a high toughness attribute but low resistance to fire.

You can create your own attributes by clicking on the Change Attributes button. You can see the Change Attributes dialog box in Figure 8.6.

The following options are available:

▪ **Add attribute**: Adds a new attribute.

▪ **Remove attribute**: Removes the selected attribute.

▪ **Rename attribute**: Changes the name of the currently selected attribute.

▪ **Attribute is a skill**: Changes an attribute to a skill. A skill is something that you can learn as you play the MMO.

▪ **Hide attribute from players**: Hides this value from other players.

▪ **Fixed attributes**: The fixed attributes are the default set of attributes that are required for the game.

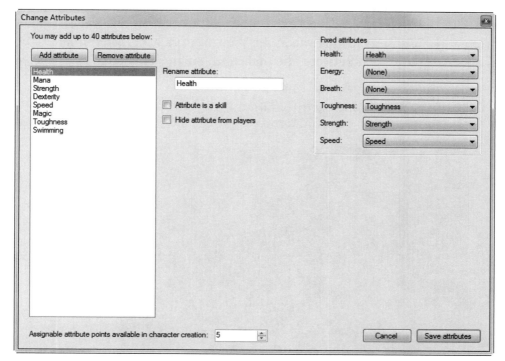

Figure 8.6
The Change Attributes dialog box.

- **Assignable attribute points**: You can set the total number of points a player can assign to their attributes when in the Character Creation screen.

- **Cancel**: Cancels any changes.

- **Save attributes**: Saves any changes you have made and closes the dialog box.

Note

You can add up to 40 attributes.

Previewing Your Actor

The preview screen gives you a small window where you can preview the actor you have amended. You can hold down your left mouse button and move the mouse to spin the actor around, so you can see all views. You can reset the view to its original position by clicking the Reset View button. The male/female radio buttons allow you to switch between the male and female versions of the selected actor.

You can see the preview window in Figure 8.7.

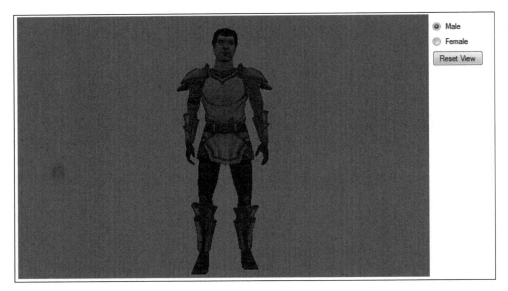

Figure 8.7
The actor preview window.

Before moving to the other tabs within the Actors tab, it's time to create an actor.

CREATING AN ACTOR

In this section, you'll create an animation for a 3D mesh and texture that have been imported. In this example you'll create a bear actor. You can use any other already imported media if you want.

1. You will need to be in the Actors > Actors tab.

2. Click on the New Actor button; this will create a new actor called New Actor [None].

3. Next you must choose a race for your actor. If you are following along with the chapter example, type **Great Bear** (you may use whatever you want to classify your imported media).

4. Leave the class blank and type a description to describe the actor.

5. As the Bear is not a playable character or a mount, leave both those options unchecked.

6. Change the aggression to Always Attacks, so when the players are close enough, the bear will run towards them and attack.

7. Change the animation sets to Bear.

8. Click on the Save Actors button to save the newly created actor. You can see an example of the new character's settings in Figure 8.8.

Figure 8.8
The newly created actor.

Congratulations, you have created a new actor.

Now that you have created the actor, you need to configure its appearance. Doing so will allow it to pick up the correct mesh and texture associated with this actor name. Follow these steps:

1. Click on the Appearance tab.

2. Click on the Male Body button, which is currently set to Sphere_ Mapped.eb3d. This will allow you to choose a mesh, as shown in Figure 8.9.

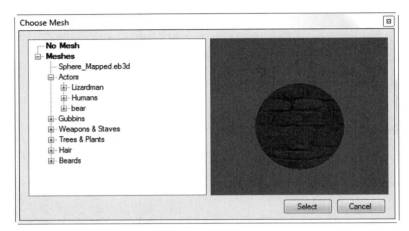

Figure 8.9
The choose mesh dialog box.

3. Expand the Actors tree item and then expand the Bear group.

4. Click on the bear.eb3d (Animated) item. You will now see a preview of the mesh such as the one shown in Figure 8.10.

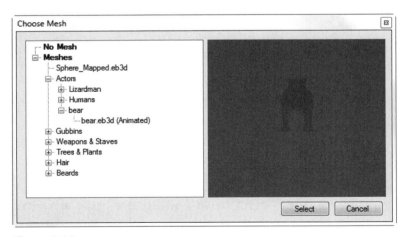

Figure 8.10
The selected mesh.

5. Next you need to apply a texture to the object. In this case, you need to apply the texture to the body. Click on the male body button, which will display a matrix of textures that are currently set to None. Select the 0,0 slot (the upper-left corner). The Choose Texture dialog box then appears. Expand the Actors > Bear groups and then select the bear2.jpg item. You will then see the texture appear in the Choose Texture preview window, as shown in Figure 8.11.

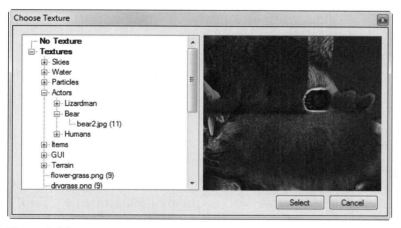

Figure 8.11
The Choose Texture dialog box.

Leave the attributes for this actor at the defaults. Next, you can check the preview to see if the bear is working correctly.

1. Click on the Preview tab.

2. If you have correctly followed the steps, you will see an animated bear in the preview window (or another model if you selected a different model to import/display). You can see the bear preview in Figure 8.12.

CREATING FACTIONS FOR YOUR ACTORS

In any MMO game there are groups of characters that will be friends, enemies, or neutral to other groups. You can create a high level of group interaction by using the Factions tab, which is next to the Actors tab.

Figure 8.12
The bear preview.

Some examples could be:

- If you were making a Zombie game, you could create a Humans group, and also create multiple zombie groups that would be enemies to the Human group. Perhaps you have an MMO where you play a Zombie, and there are certain groups that are not friendly to you, such as Humans or other zombie types.

- If you were creating a medieval game, you could have a number of European groups being friends with each other while others would be enemies.

- On a more local scale, you could create a game in which there are the distinct groups of humans, such as traders, raiders, and thieves, all with varying degrees of friendliness.

The ratings range from –100 to 100; –100 is unfriendly and 100 is friendly. To create a new faction, click on the New Faction button. To delete a faction, select a faction and click on the Delete Faction button. You can also rename a faction if you decide to change its name at a later time.

You can see the Factions tab information in Figure 8.13.

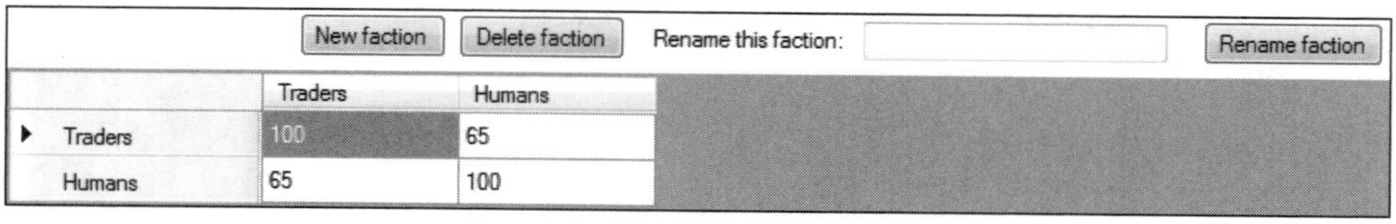

Figure 8.13
The Factions tab.

ADDING ANIMATIONS TO YOUR ACTORS

The Animations tab allows you to create animations for any actors that you have created/imported. An *animation* is a set of defined moves that an actor (and its associated body parts) can make within the game such as riding a horse, fighting, dancing, waving, and dying. To find the Animations tab, you should ensure the Actors tab is selected and then choose the Animations sub-tab.

You can see the basic screen setup for the Animations tab in Figure 8.14.

The Animations tab is split into a number of sections:

- **Actors list**: This is a list of predefined actors within the MMO software. Some are available from the downloaded objects.

- **Buttons**: Create a new animation, copy (duplicate) an animation, or delete an animation set from these options.

- **Animation set**: A list of animations within each actor. For some actors you may have only a small number of animations; for example, in the case of a fish you may just want a swimming animation, whereas in a player you may want many more.

- **Add animation button**: Adds an animation set to the selected actor.

- **Remove animation**: Removes an animation set from an actor.

- **Rename animation**: Renames the animation set name.

- **Animation start frame/end**: An actor can contain many animation frames that do many different movements; you can specify the frame number that applies to this animation set.

- **Animation speed**: Changes the percentage speed of the animation.

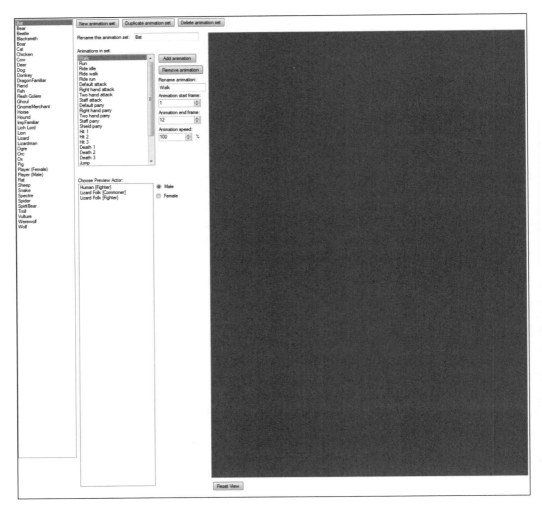

Figure 8.14
The Animations tab.

- **Choose preview actor**: Select a currently created actor to display in the preview window.

- **Male/Female**: Radio boxes that allow you to select male or female versions of an actor (if they are available).

- **Preview window**: Displays a preview of the animation.

Before you can create your animations, you will need to add the object as an actor. You may remember in Chapter 7 that you imported a 3D mesh and texture of a bear (although you may have imported some other 3D object). In the next section, you'll use that bear again.

Creating Animations

The Animations tab allows you to map a particular name to an animation. This animation set can then be called in-game using a script. All animation frames are created within the 3D Mesh. For example, there might be 10 frames of a character running and five frames swimming, but when Realm Crafter imports these meshes, it doesn't know what each of these animation frames is associated with. In the Animations tab, you can create an animation set called "running" that will map to those frames that are associated with running.

Before you create an animation you must have already done the following:

1. Imported your media.
2. Created your actor.

Note

When you imported your 3D model, you were given the option to import a mesh that was animated. It is very important that if your model is animated, you select this option; otherwise, you will not be able to animate the 3D object.

In this section of the chapter, you'll take a look at how an actor you have imported is configured in the Animations tab.

1. Under Choose Preview Actor, you will see an actor that you have imported. In the previous examples, this was a bear actor (you may have imported an alternative model). Click on the name in the Choose Preview Actor list to select it.
2. Click on the animation list on the left and select Bear.
3. You can select the different animation sets such as walk, run, and see the bear in the preview window update.
4. To add your own animation, click on the Add Animation button.

5. Type the name of the animation into the Rename Animation edit box.

6. Enter the animation start frame; this is the first animation frame that relates to the name of the animation.

7. Enter the last frame of this animation.

8. Enter the speed of the animation.

9. Once you have created an animation set, you will need to ensure that you save it. You can do this by clicking on the Save All button.

Note

It is important to remember that not all animation sets will work for every character. These are default names that have been predefined.

Note

Any new animations that are not part of the default set are controlled by scripts within your game. For example, you might create an animation of the player's character playing an instrument, and you may then initiate that animation when the player types/plays music in the chat window.

GIVING YOUR ACTOR SOME ABILITIES

Abilities are basically spells or buffs that you can use on yourself or others to help or hinder progress. If you have ever played an MMO before, you probably have come across spells/buffs. This is where you can apply a positive or negative effect on your player or on another player/enemy. Some examples of these abilities are:

- Heal self
- Heal others
- Poison enemy
- Hide self
- Increase speed
- Increase armor
- Increase damage

In most MMOs, these buffs are given fancier names such as Elemental Damage. You can see the default screen for the abilities in Figure 8.15.

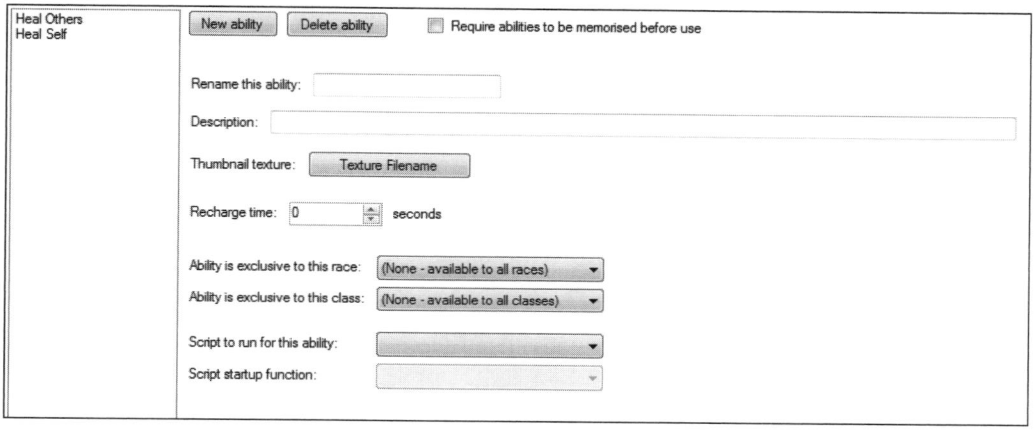

Figure 8.15
The Abilities screen.

The abilities screen has the following setup:

- **Abilities tree**: Lists all of the available abilities.
- **New Ability button**: Creates a new ability.
- **Delete Ability button**: Deletes the currently selected ability.
- **Require abilities to be memorised check box:** Requires the players to memorize the spell before using. This will allow you to set up a limited number of slots for which abilities can be used at any one time.
- **Rename this ability**: Renames the current selected ability.
- **Description**: Holds a description of the ability.
- **Thumbnail texture**: A small image used to represent the ability.
- **Recharge time**: Shows how long the players have to wait before they can reuse the ability.
- **Ability is exclusive to this race**: Indicates whether this ability is restricted to a particular race.

- **Ability is exclusive to this class**: Indicates whether this ability is restricted to a particular class.

- **Script to run for this ability**: When the ability is used run a particular script. An example of this is that you could have an ability to create a campfire. You could have a script that generates a fire when the player has selected this ability in the game.

- **Script start-up function**: You may have a number of functions (script tasks) contained within a script. This allows you to specify the particular main script that contains your script function. So you might have a script called myabilities. Within this script you might have five functions, all of which cast different spells.

TOURING THE GENERAL SETTINGS TAB

The General Settings tab displays a number of general game settings that affect the Actor/player character within the game. You can see this screen in Figure 8.16.

Figure 8.16
The General Settings tab.

The General Settings tab is split into a number of sections:

- **Combat**: Details about combat times, faction ratings, and damage display.
- **Visual**: Player/actor visual items for nametags and chat.
- **Loot Bag**: The loot bag is a bag that the player can get access to when they have defeated an enemy.
- **Currency**: The currency (money) that is used within the game world.
- **Radar/Mini Map**: Used to configure the mini-map that shows nearby items in the world.
- **Other**: Starting values for reputation and player money.

The following sections discuss these areas of the General Settings tab in more depth.

Combat Section

This section defines the combat options used within the MMO:

- **Combat Delay time**: When an actor attacks, there is a timed delay before he is able to attack again; this is the delay time. The time frame is entered in milliseconds, so 1,000 means a delay of one second. To increase the number of attacks, you decrease this value.
- **Combat Formula**: This allows you to select from four possible combat methods, which use different calculations to work out the combat success:
  - **Normal Formula**: The default setting.
  - **No Bonus/Penalty from Strength**: Do not use strength in any calculations.
  - **High Damage, High Defence**: Will test damage against defense in calculations.
  - **Use Attack Script**: Use a special attack script that you can modify to configure your own combat formulas.
- **Damage Display**: Specify how you want to display any damage sustained.

- **None:** No damage displayed.
- **Floating Number:** Display damage as a number.
- **Message in Chat Area:** Display the amount of damage in the chat window.

Note

The Use Attack Script option uses the Attack.rsl script file.

Visual Section

The Visual section defines how certain visual aspects of the game are managed, such as:

- **Show Nametags:** Defines whether it will display the name of the user's characters.
  - **Always:** Always show the nametags.
  - **Never:** Never show the nametags.
  - **Only on selected actor:** Show nametags only on the actor that is currently selected.
- **Valid View Modes:** In many games you have different possible views, such as first-party or third-party view. You can enable or disable the views here.
  - **First Person Only:** Only display first person view.
  - **Third Person Only:** Only display third person view.
  - **Both:** Display both first and third person views.
- **Disable Actor -> Actor collisions:** This will allow actors to walk through other actors, by switching off their collisions.
- **Use chat bubbles:** Creates a chat bubble that contains the chat text above the actor who is speaking.
  - **Never:** No chat bubble is shown.
  - **As well as text:** Show a chat bubble as well as text.
  - **Exclusively:** Show only the chat bubble, and no text in the chat window.
- **Chat bubble text colour:** Change the chat bubble text color.

Note

First-person view is when you are looking from the eyes of the actor. This is a very common view used in many modern first person shooter games, such as *Modern Warfare* and *Medal of Honor*. Third-person view is when the camera/view is behind the actor, such as with *Assassin's Creed.*

Note

Game objects usually have a collision box around them. This means when one 3D model walks/collides into another, the objects can push against each other. It is common to turn this off in MMOs as it ensures that other players do not block entrances of buildings or locations. Leaving this option on could lead to players abusing the system and stopping other users from getting to various locations.

Loot Bag Section

When you kill another character in the game, such as an enemy, they may have a loot bag on their possession. A *loot bag* is the graphical representation of an item that has been dropped by the defeated enemy that the player can pick up. The Loot Bag Mesh option allows you to select a mesh to represent the loot bag item.

Currency Section

All worlds need currency, but the type of currency is totally up to the designer. If you are creating a futuristic game, you could come up with weird and wonderful names for your currency, whereas if you are basing it on a real-world example, you might create a realistic currency.

- **Tier 1**: Base currency that you want to use; the default is copper.

- **Tier 2**: Second tier currency as well as the amount of currency that it takes from tier 1 to make tier 2. So it might take 100 cents (tier 1) to make one dollar in tier 2. The default in this example is set to Silver.

- **Tier 3**: Tier 3 currency amount, which in this case is Gold.

- **Tier 4**: Tier 4 currency amount, which in this case is Platinum.

Radar/Mini-Map Section

The Radar/Mini-Map section allows you to configure a mini-map of the player's local surroundings.

- **Discover map in**: At the time of this writing, this option and its functionality were not yet available.

- **Show actors on radar**: Allows you to specify which types of actors to display on the mini-map. It is common to show friendly, NPC, and Enemy actors on the mini-map to allow players to locate them easily.

Note

By clicking on the checkboxes for any of the actors, you can select a mesh that will represent that actor on the mini-map. So you could select a small red square to represent an enemy actor.

Other Section

You have already learned about the player's reputation and currency in this chapter, but the Other section allows you to specify starting values for these values.

- **Initial player reputation**: Sets the starting value for the reputation of the player. The default value is 50.

- **Initial player money**: You can also set the starting value for the player character; this is using the base tier and has a starting value of 50.

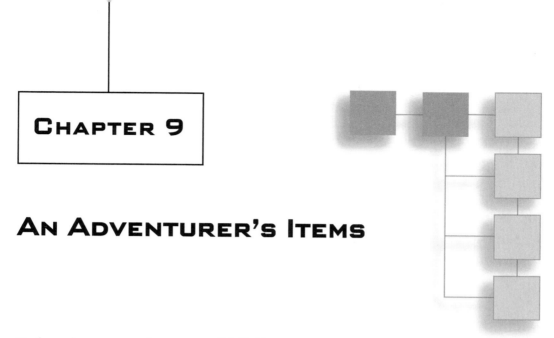

CHAPTER 9

AN ADVENTURER'S ITEMS

It doesn't matter what type of MMO game you create, you will always need items for your players to collect. You read about items briefly in Chapter 3; recall that items are objects that your player can carry, use, cast, attack with (weapons), or manufacture. These items are very important to your world, mainly because the players will need some items to use as they go about the world. They also provide collectables that the players will work hard to gain.

TOURING THE ITEMS TAB

You can access the items information from the Items tab. You can see the Items tab with some default information already displayed in Figure 9.1.

In Figure 9.1, you can see that the Items tab is split into a number of groups. These groups are:

- **Item list**: A list of all the currently created items.

- **Buttons**: A selection of buttons to create a new item, to copy an item, to delete an item, and to remap gubbins. There are also two checkmark box items, which will be discussed shortly.

- **General properties**: A selection of common properties for each particular item; these include the value of the item, how heavy it is, and if it can be stacked.

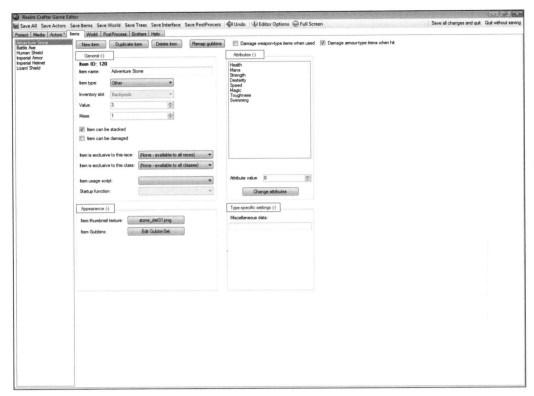

Figure 9.1
The Items tab.

- **Appearance**: Change the item thumbnail's appearance and change the gubbin set that the item is associated with.

- **Attributes**: If an item can make changes to a player's attributes, you specify any particular item values in this section of the program.

- **Type-specific settings**: Any settings specifically for an item. This entry is based on the item type.

The next sections discuss each of these areas of the Items tab in more detail.

Item List

The Item list contains all of the objects that exist within your game. The list can get quite large and so can be difficult to manage if you are not careful. All objects are added to the list in alphabetical order, as shown in Figure 9.2.

In the default project, the items that appear are all fantasy-based and may not be exactly what you want for your own games. Use these test items to look at the different settings that each of the objects have and how the items might affect the player's attributes.

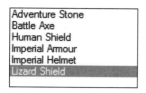

Figure 9.2
The default project list of items.

Buttons on the Items Tab

There are four buttons and two checkboxes that you can use within the Items tab. These can be seen in Figure 9.3.

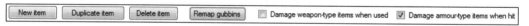

Figure 9.3
Buttons and checkboxes that allow for adding, deleting, and configuring of items.

The buttons are as follows:

- **New Item**: Generate a new item.

- **Duplicate item**: Copy a particular item and generate a new item from it. This is useful when you have a range of similar weapons that you want to create, such as swords, that might have a similar set of options.

- **Delete Item**: Remove an item permanently from the list.

- **Remap Gubbins**: This allows you to map an item to a different part of an actor's body, such as shoulder, arm, or shin.

The checkboxes are as follows:

- **Damage weapon-type items when used**: As with most items in the real world, the more you use something, the more wear and tear it gets.

So when you use a weapon, it will slowly become damaged. Enable this checkbox to allow any weapons that are used to accrue damage.

■ **Damage armor-type items when hit**: If your armor continues to soak up hits from a weapon, over time it will become dented, scratched, and damaged. Select this checkbox to ensure that armor gets damaged over time when hit.

General Properties

The general properties area of the Items tab contains all of the key properties of an item, as shown in Figure 9.4.

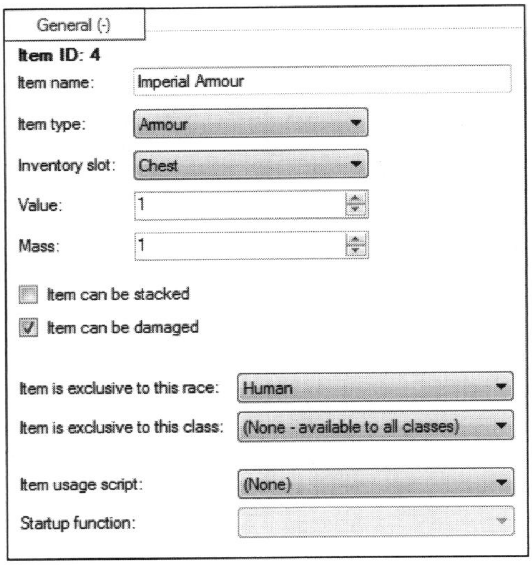

Figure 9.4
General properties of Imperial Armour.

The following options are available:

■ **Item name:** The name of the item.

■ **Item type:** The type of item. This can be a weapon, armor, ring, potion, food, image, or other.

■ **Inventory slot:** The inventory slot where the item can be placed. For example, if you have a legs inventory slot, most likely you will be able to place trousers, kilt, or leggings in that slot.

- **Value:** The value (cost) of the item.

- **Mass:** How heavy the item is.

- **Item can be stacked:** Some items can be stacked on top of each other and take less space within a player's inventory. Think of an inventory slot as a small cube area within a bag. Smaller items are more likely to be stackable, such as bolts for a weapon or food items such as berries.

- **Item can be damaged:** Check this box if you want the item to show damage.

- **Item is exclusive to this race:** Is this item used only by a selected race? This allows you to limit the object to a particular race. This is useful if you have an item that has been used by a race for centuries and is part of their culture.

- **Item is exclusive to this class:** You might have multiple classes within a race, such as healer, warrior, and mage. If so, you might want to limit items between classes. For example, a healer might not be able to use the heavy weapon of a warrior.

- **Item usage script:** Is there a script associated with a particular item? You could create a glow effect if the player is wearing a particular ring, for example.

- **Startup function:** If the item usage script has been selected, when will the script be run? By default, this is during the main function.

Appearance

The Appearance section of the Items tab defines the look of the item you are creating/editing within the game. Here you can specify the thumbnail image that will be used in the game's inventory system. The Items tab displays a collection of 3D objects, such as a shield. This shield must also have a thumbnail representation for when it has been placed in the player's backpack/inventory. You can also edit the gubbin set. The gubbin set is a set of predefined templates that you can configure for an item's position, for example in the left or right hand, or on the back of the character.

You can see a close up of the Appearance area in Figure 9.5. A close up of the item thumbnail texture is shown in Figure 9.6, and a gubbin set is shown in Figure 9.7.

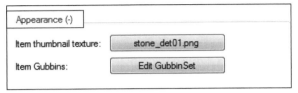

Figure 9.5
Close up of the Appearance section of the Items tab.

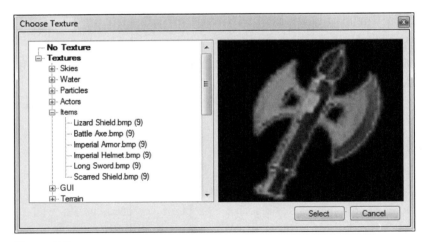

Figure 9.6
Thumbnail texture for the battle axe.

Attributes

Attributes are the key traits that make up your character, such as its health or strength. In many MMOs it is possible to modify these values when placing a particular ring on a finger or when using a certain type of sword.

Changing a character's attributes when the player applies certain objects to his character can really help make the items that the character collects interesting for the player. Every time that player kills an enemy, he will be wondering what loot he can take and will be comparing the stats of the object to see if it has

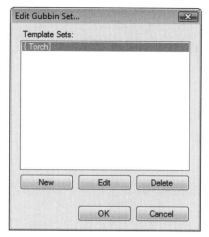

Figure 9.7
The Edit Gubbin Set dialog box.

better attributes than the items he currently has. This is a technique that was used very successfully in games such as *Diablo* and *Borderlands* (not MMOs).

You can also edit these attributes by clicking on the Change Attributes button. This button is covered in detail in Chapter 8.

Type-Specific Settings

Certain item types have additional properties that can be applied only to them. In Figure 9.8, you can see an example of type-specific settings for the weapon type.

Figure 9.8
Type-specific settings for the weapon type.

CREATING AN ITEM

In this section, you'll learn how to add an item. For this example, you are going to create an item called Lords Armour, which will be enchanted and give the wearer additional strength and increased health attributes.

1. From the Items tab, click on the New Item button.

2. Type the name **Lords Armour** in the Item Name box.

3. Change the item type to Armour.

4. Leave the inventory slot as Chest, as this is a chest plate.

5. Change the value to 15.

6. Change the mass to 3.

7. Check the Item Can Be Damaged checkbox.

8. You are going to make this item exclusive to humans only, so select the Item Is Exclusive to This Race drop-down box, and then select Human.

9. Let's limit this to the fighter class, so click on the Item Is Exclusive to This Class drop-down box and select Fighter.

10. Since you don't have a specific thumbnail texture made for this item, let's use one of the stock images. Click on the Item Thumbnail Texture checkbox and, under items, select Imperial Armor.

11. Click on the Strength attribute, and then enter an attribute value of 2.

12. Click on the Health attribute and then enter an attribute value of 3.

13. Press the Save Items button to save any changes that you have made.

Congratulations, you have created your very first item!

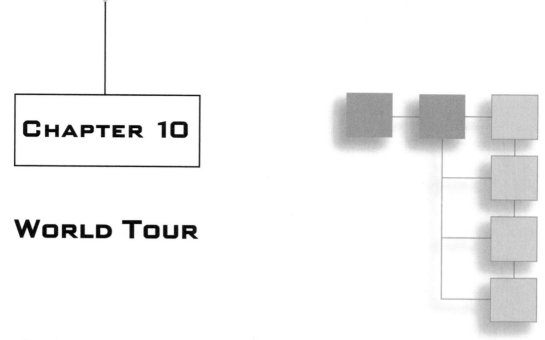

CHAPTER 10

WORLD TOUR

This chapter takes you on a tour of the main options in the World Editor tab, which is where you will spend a lot of time making your game worlds and placing your characters and world objects, such as trees and buildings.

TOURING THE WORLD EDITOR

Accessing the World Editor is simple, just follow these steps:

1. Ensure you have the Realm Crafter Project Manager loaded and then double-click on a project (preferably a default new project that you haven't made any changes to).

2. Once the game data has loaded into the Realm Crafter Game Editor, click on the World tab.

3. You will now see the World tab and a blank area loaded, as shown in Figure 10.1.

4. You will also see a large number of buttons, as shown in Figure 10.2.

The World screen shown in Figure 10.1 can be split into a number of areas, as follows:

- **Buttons**: These are quick buttons that you can use to access the main options for the World tab.

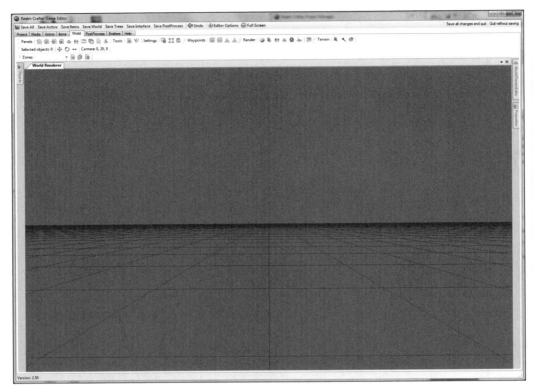

Figure 10.1
The blank world in the World tab.

- **Panels**: Additional property boxes that can appear from the left and right side of the World Editor.

- **World Renderer and World Tabs**: By default there is a single tab called World Renderer, which shows you a blank scene in which to create your game area. By default, the World Renderer tab displays a blank blue area ready to contain your scene. Additional tabs can appear when accessing various options.

The buttons shown in Figure 10.2 are separated into the following groups:

- **Panels**: Property boxes that can appear from the side of the World window to provide additional information. They can also provide a way for the game creators to select data, such as objects.

Figure 10.2
The World tab buttons.

- **Tools**: Tools to help refresh (update) any scripts or edit lighting within the game world.

- **Settings**: Access the setup options for zones and year settings.

- **Waypoints**: Create a set of waypoints, which are points within the game world where a character or NPC can move to.

- **Render**: Describes how the world (or 3D objects) is displayed within the game. Different rendering options display objects in different ways and can use more or less memory. The Render options can provide a quick and easy way to move objects within the world (as objects that use more memory will take longer to render and move).

- **Terrain**: The ground that the player walks upon. This section allows you to configure the terrain options, such as applying terrain automatically or designing a new terrain.

- **Selected objects**: Options related to moving and rotating a selected object.

- **Zones**: A single area in your game world. You normally have multiple zones in an MMO. Here you can view, create, or delete zones.

LOADING THE DEFAULT WORLD

With every project that is created, there is a default world. You can load this default world and use it as the basis of your first zone. You can then use it to add items and get to learn the editor.

In the Zones area there is a drop-down box where you can select any of the zones that you have already created. You will notice there are currently three zones, as shown in Figure 10.3.

These three zones are:

- **DefaultZone**: This is the default world that the player enters and walks around in.

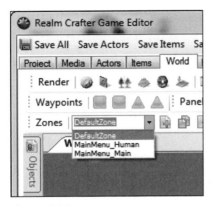

Figure 10.3
The three default zones.

- **MainMenu_Human**: This is the world that is in the background when the player selects the Human character.

- **MainMenu_Main**: This is the world that is displayed in the background when the player has entered the Character Select menu screen.

On selecting the DefaultZone, the default world will load as shown in Figure 10.4.

Moving Around the Default World

A zone can be quite large and so it's very important that you know how to move around the world. The following information will help you move quickly around any world that you have created.

- **Look**: To look around the world, hold down the spacebar and then move the mouse in the direction that you want to look. To stop looking, release the spacebar.

- **Zoom in/Move forward**: Hold down the spacebar and then press the left mouse button to move forward within the world.

- **Zoom out/Move backward**: Hold down the spacebar and then press the right mouse button to move backward within the world.

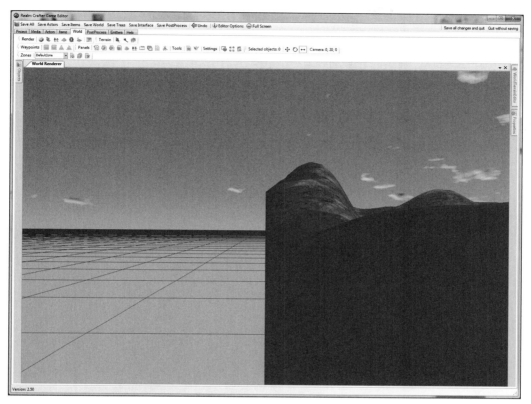

Figure 10.4
The default world loaded.

TOURING THE WORLD EDITOR'S BUTTONS

This section takes you through each of the button sections found on the World Editor so that you have an idea of what they do. Those buttons that are particularly important you will read about in more depth throughout the book.

Panels

Panels are property windows that can appear from the left or right side of the application window. These panels can contain varying degrees of information. Some just display data, whereas others allow you to edit information contained within them.

You can see some panel tabs on the default project such as Objects on the left side or World Terrain Editor and Properties on the right side of the World Renderer window. If you move your mouse over one of the panels, it will expand and show you the contents of that panel, as shown in Figure 10.5.

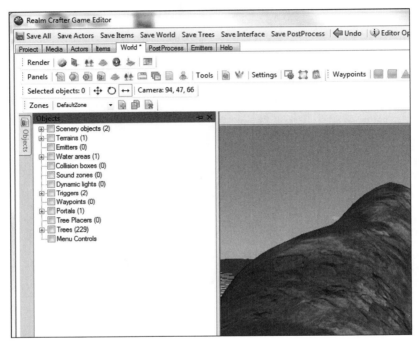

Figure 10.5
The Objects panel, expanded.

When you move your mouse away from the window, the panel will automatically hide itself. This sometimes can be frustrating if you are viewing/clicking on an item in the world and want to see the properties update in the panel, but the panel then disappears. You can solve this by clicking on the pin icon on the right side of the panel window, as shown in Figure 10.6. Clicking this pin will leave the window in place. When you are ready to hide the window, you just click on

Figure 10.6
The hide/unhide panel pin.

Figure 10.7
A close-up of the Panel icons in the toolbar.

the pin again. The X icon will close the panel. If you click this, you can reopen the panel by clicking on the relevant panel icon in the toolbar.

You can see a close-up of the Panel's toolbar icons in Figure 10.7. An explanation of what each icon does from left to right is as follows:

- **Create Panel**: This icon allows you to create a number of predefined objects and place them within the world, such as in-game objects, trees, and collision boxes. You will look at the Create Panel in more detail in Chapter 13.

- **Render Panel**: This will turn on or off the World Renderer window; the default option is on.

- **Properties Panel**: When you edit specific information, the Properties panel will display this information within its window. By default, this panel is blank.

- **Objects Panel**: The Objects panel lists all of the different objects that are currently contained within your game. You can see the Objects panel in Figure 10.5.

- **Terrain Editor**: The Terrain Editor allows you to make modifications to the terrain within your game.

- **Tree Editor**: The Tree Editor will bring up a new tab that allows you to create your own trees, including branches and leaves. This allows you to create different shaped trees using a basic set of 3D objects, allowing you to create a mix of objects from the same base set of components.

- **Interface Hierarchy**: This displays in-game components that will be used within the MMO in a tree-based interface. These in-game components contain items such as interface design and locations. The Interface Hierarchy requires the Interface Editor to also be selected for any data to appear.

- **Interface Editor**: The Interface Editor displays any interfaces that are selected in the Interface Hierarchy. Within this editor you will see any dialog boxes and game dialog boxes such as inventory, chat windows, and their in-game screen position once selected in the Interface Hierarchy list.

- **Script Editor**: Here you can edit existing scripts or create your own. Scripts are an important component to any MMO and you will need to learn how to create scripts to give your MMO the features it requires to make it interesting. (You learn more about scripting in Realm Crafter in Chapters 14 and 15.)

- **Toggle Gubbin Tools**: The Gubbin Editor is used to precisely position objects from the game world onto an actor. For example, the torch that you see in the default game was placed using the Gubbin Editor. Other items include armor, hats, hair, and weapons.

Note

You may see different panels on the left and right sides of the World Render window; if this is the case don't worry, because it is very easy to switch panels on and off using the Panels buttons.

Tools Icons

The tools section of the toolbar contains only two icons, as shown in Figure 10.8. They are defined as follows:

Figure 10.8
The Tools toolbar icons.

- **Refresh Scripts**: When you're writing scripts that have an impact on the world, it is important to refresh them, and this will reload them into the Editor.

- **Edit Light Functions**: You can create a set of light functions that are very useful for providing lighting effects. The editor has a default effect that generates a flickering effect (similar to a light with a problem, flickering on and off). You can see the options available in the Edit Light Function dialog box shown in Figure 10.9.

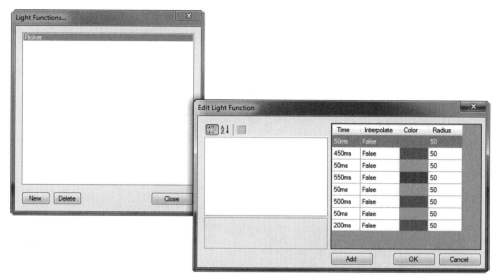

Figure 10.9
The Edit Light Function dialog box.

In Figure 10.9, I have selected the Edit Light Functions button and then double-clicked on the Flicker option to open the Edit Light Functions dialog box. From there, you can see a number of settings to change the light.

Settings Icons

The settings toolbar include settings regarding how the zones are set up and how they are affected by time, date, and seasons. The two icons can be seen in Figure 10.10.

Figure 10.10
The Settings options.

The options are defined as follows, and discussed in more detail in the following sections:

- **Zone Setup**: Setup options relating to this particular zone such as its location, fog color, and viewing distance.

■ **Year Setup**: Create your own year and seasons. You can use an earth-
based setting (with minor changes to represent the location of where
your game is based) or set up something unique to your own game
planet.

Zone Setup Dialog Box

You can see the Zone Setup dialog box in Figure 10.11. The settings for this
dialog box are as follows:

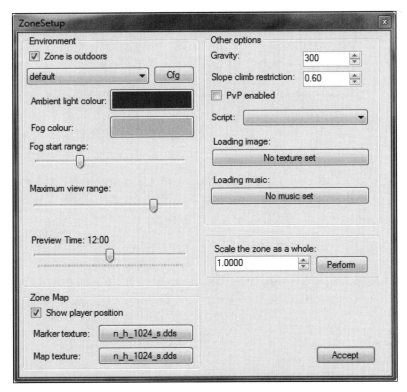

Figure 10.11
Zone Setup dialog box.

■ **Zone is outdoors**: Determines whether the zone is indoors or outdoors.
In the original Realm Crafter product, this flag was used to prevent the sky
appearing indoors, but most of that functionality has been transferred

to the SDK (Software Development Kit). You can still access this information through scripts if required and make particular changes depending on what is selected for the zone.

- **Drop-down box (and Cfg)**: The drop-down box specifies the default environment in which the zone is set up. By default, this is the normal day/night cycle that you see when playing the game. Using the SDK, you can create further environments such as a polar world with an aurora, or a space base with the planets around.

- **Ambient light colour**: Determines what color you want the lighting to be.

- **Fog colour**: The color assigned to fog. Fog is very useful for covering the world in the distance, so the player cannot see what is far away and has to travel closer to an area to find out.

- **Fog start range slider**: By moving this slider, you can change how far in the distance the fog will start to appear.

- **Maximum view range slider**: This changes the viewing distance that the player can see. The longer the view, the more processing power the client will need to display the game zone.

- **Preview time (+time)**: Once you have configured your day/night cycle, you can use the preview time to make the sun rise and set. By moving the slider from left to right you can simulate sunrise/sunset process. In the default game you can also see the moon rising and setting. Scrolling through the time is quite an interesting and nice effect.

- **Show player position**: Show the player position on the zone map (the map can be accessed while in the game).

- **Marker texture**: This is the image that you want to represent the player in-game, it could be a simple arrow, a circle, or something fancier like a small shield image or character icon.

- **Map texture**: The texture image that you want to use for the zone map.

- **Gravity**: Gravity defines how quick the player will rise and fall when pressing the spacebar while playing the game. In most cases the default option should suffice, but if you are making an MMO in space you may want to change these settings to give it a more realistic feeling based on the setting.

- **Slope climb restriction**: You can restrict a character from walking up a particular slope height.

- **PvP enabled**: This area will allow (or disallow) Player versus Player battles. In many games, there will be certain zones where players can fight each other. It is important to note that PvP is not usually included in player starter zones.

- **Script**: If you want to run a script when the player enters a zone, you can specify it here.

- **Loading image**: You can display a loading image when this zone is loading. This is a nice feature to give the player something interesting to look at while they wait for the zone to load. It could be a particular scene that the player will be visiting, such as a vista or landmark, or it could be of common characters.

- **Loading music**: While the zone loads you can play loading music. This music will have been already loaded into the Media tab, and can then be selected via the No Music Set button.

- **Scale the zone as a whole**: This option is no longer used and may be removed in a later version of the software.

Note

Player starter zones are the first locations that a player will appear in at the start of any MMO. These areas are usually quite small and enclosed from the rest of the game world, allowing the player to quickly and easily get used to the basics of the MMO. They might include fighting, casting spells, buying items, and going on basic quests.

Year Setup Dialog Box

Using this option you can specify the length of a year in your world and determine the types of seasons available. This allows you to mimic earth settings, where you may want to change the length and time of the seasons depending on your location. Or you can set up a different year length and seasons to mimic your new planet. You can see the Year Setup dialog box in Figure 10.12.

Figure 10.12
The Year Setup dialog box.

The options within the Year Setup dialog box are as follows:

- **Year length**: How long is the year; the default is to 365.

- **Month:** This drop-down box allows you to configure up to 20 months within your year. The settings for length/time are changeable for each month.

- **Name**: The name associated with the particular month number; in this case month 1 is January.

- **Length**: The number of days in a month.

- **Time compression**: A game world's time is not usually the same as the real world, so an hour in the game does not equal an hour in playtime. The reason that they are different is generally because players would rarely see game world interactions such as the sun rising or setting if they never play at the times when that would occur. Game worlds are usually sped up so that the player spends a few hours playing the game, and this equates to a day or two in the game world. The default setting is 240; this means that the game world is running 240 times faster than it would in real life. If you do want to set it to real time, change the value to 1.

- **Season**: You can specify up to 12 seasons.
- **Name**: The name of the season that you are configuring. In the case of Figure 10.12, it is winter.
- **Length**: The number of days that the currently selected season will last.
- **Current year**: The current year that the game is set.
- **Current day**: Out of the specified number of days in the year length, specify the current day.
- **Season dawn hour**: When will dawn take place in the current season.
- **Season dusk hour**: When will dusk take place in the current season.

Note

You do not need to call your seasons the same as those used in English; this is particularly useful when creating a game based on a totally new world. You could call them Phases, Solstice, or any other combination that you find suitable.

Note

When you are creating a new year setup that is not the same as the default earth setting, you should consider writing it on paper first so that you can work out precisely what you want before you input it into Realm Crafter.

Waypoints Icons

Waypoints are used in everyday situations. When you are traveling from location A to location B, and then decide you want to get some gasoline, that gas station is a waypoint. Actually, all three locations are considered waypoints. In a computer game, an AI character might have a patrol route, and each point is part of the path of where the character will walk.

Once you have added a waypoint object (which is discussed in more detail in Chapter 13), you can connect or delete links to it using the buttons in the toolbar, which are:

- **Waypoint Link A**: Specify that a waypoint object is Waypoint Link A.
- **Waypoint Remove A**: Remove a waypoint linked to A.
- **Waypoint Link B**: Specify that a waypoint object is Waypoint Link B.
- **Waypoint Remove B**: Remove a waypoint linked to B.

You can see the Waypoints icons close-up in Figure 10.13.

Figure 10.13
The creation and removal of waypoint links using the icons in the toolbar.

Note

Only NPCs (non-player characters) can follow a waypoint. The waypoint system is fairly rudimentary, but should provide some use for basic movements of NPC characters.

Render Icons

Rendering is the process of taking a computer game object such as a tree, castle, ground, or world and displaying its textures. When you are designing a large level in any type of game and you have a large number of objects, moving around the game world can be very slow if all objects are displaying their best quality textures. When a level designer is creating a game and placing objects within the world, she may turn down certain aspects of the textures so that they use less memory and players can then move around the world quicker.

The Render icons are shown in Figure 10.14 and are defined here, from left to right:

Figure 10.14
The Render buttons close-up.

- **Toggle Scenery**: This allows you to turn off the scenery within your game world. Scenery consists of items such as water and game objects like treasure chests. These are items that dress up your world.

- **Toggle Grass**: Grass isn't the floor of your game world but objects that resemble grass strands; these would be in the form of grass blades and grass based bushes.

- **Toggle Trees**: Used to switch on or off the trees within your game.

- **Toggle Terrain**: The terrain is the physical floor that your character walks upon. It can be quite confusing when you turn this option off unless you are working at a higher level such as the top of a building.

- **Toggle Editor Objects**: Any editor objects that have been added such as portals and triggers will be removed.

- **Toggle Terrain Collision Radius**: This will display the effective area of the collision area on the terrain. On switching this on, the terrain will turn green.

- **Reload Shaders**: Any rendering effects that you have applied to the world will be reloaded.

In Figures 10.15 and 10.16, you can see the different effects of toggling some of these options.

Terrain Icons

You can see a close-up of the Terrain group in Figure 10.17; the terrain group consists of the following three options:

- **Auto Texture Terrain**: This will automatically texture the terrain. This is a quick way of applying various textures easily to your terrain, which then gives you more time to fine-tune the terrain.

- **Import Terrain**: Includes three methods for creating a terrain map quickly. You will look at this in more detail in Chapter 12.

- **Grass Types Editor**: The grass type's editor, shown in Figure 10.18, allows you to edit various grass types, including the determining of their coverage and scale. This is very useful for generating a varied landscape.

Figure 10.15
The default world with some trees and a terrain object.

Selected Objects Icons

You can see a close-up of the Selected Objects icons in Figure 10.19. The group consists of the following options:

- **Selected Objects**: Displays the number of selected objects. When you click on an object it automatically becomes highlighted with a box, as shown in Figure 10.20.

- **Move Object**: Allows you to move the selected object in three directions—X, Y, and Z. You can move the object by using the arrow

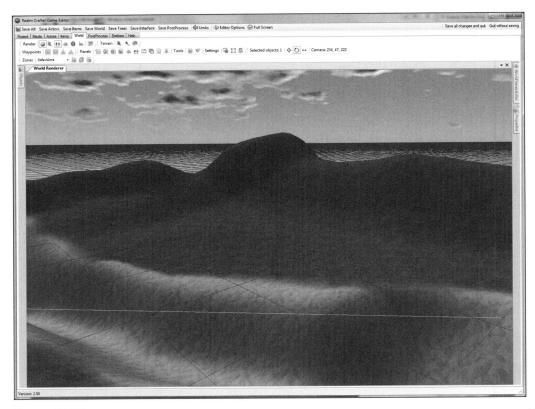

Figure 10.16
The default world with Scenery and Trees switched off.

Figure 10.17
The Terrain group's icons.

keys or clicking the mouse button and holding while dragging on the red, blue, or green arrows shown in Figure 10.21.

■ **Rotate**: Allows you to rotate the object in a particular angle or direction.

■ **Scale Object**: Allows you to make an object larger or smaller, using the mouse to click on the up arrow while dragging upward to increase the size, and dragging downward to reduce the size of the object.

■ **Camera**: Displays the current camera coordinates within the game world.

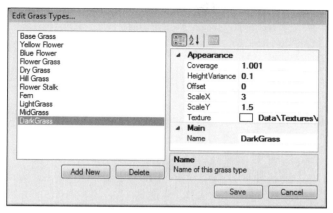

Figure 10.18
The Edit Grass Types dialog box.

Figure 10.19
The Selected Objects icons close-up.

Figure 10.20
An object that has been selected within the World Renderer.

Figure 10.21
The move arrows allow you to drag objects to a new location.

Zones Icons

You can see a close-up of the Zones icons in Figure 10.22. The Zones group consists of the following objects:

Figure 10.22
A close-up of the Zone icons.

- **Zone Selection**: You can select from a number of zones to display in the World Renderer. By default there are three zones. The first is a default test zone, and the other two are for character creation.
- **New Zone**: Create a new zone.

- **Duplicate Zone**: Duplicate an existing zone. This is very useful if you have an area that is very similar. You can then modify it to make it look different. This is useful if you have a forest area that will change into a desert zone, you can duplicate the forest zone and then modify it so that it goes from one type of terrain to another, rather than having to generate the forest from scratch.

- **Delete Zone**: Deletes the currently selected zone from the list.

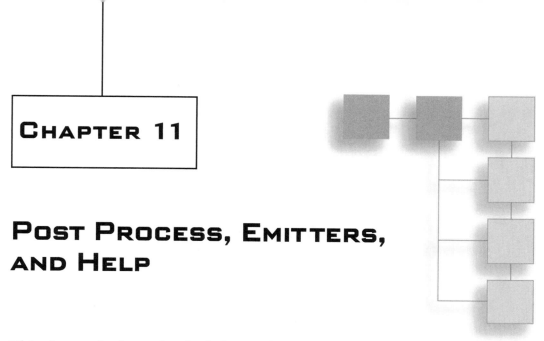

CHAPTER 11

POST PROCESS, EMITTERS, AND HELP

This chapter looks at the final three tabs available in the Realm Crafter Game Editor before introducing you to further features and techniques. These three tabs are as follows:

- **Post Process**: Post process is the method of applying graphical effects to your world after it has been created.

- **Emitters**: Emitters are the same as particles, which is a common term for graphical effects; these are very popular in today's modern games.

- **Help**: Realm Crafter has a built-in help program that allows you to view information about how to use the product.

THE POST PROCESS TAB

You may have heard of the term post process(ing) before; it's very commonly used in film making, but also used regularly in modern games. It is the process of adding special effects at the end of what has been made. With computer games, this usually means adding graphical effects to the generated game or world.

You can see the Post Process tab with the effect enabled in the world in Figure 11.1. Notice that there is a visible difference in the zone when post processing is disabled, as shown in Figure 11.2.

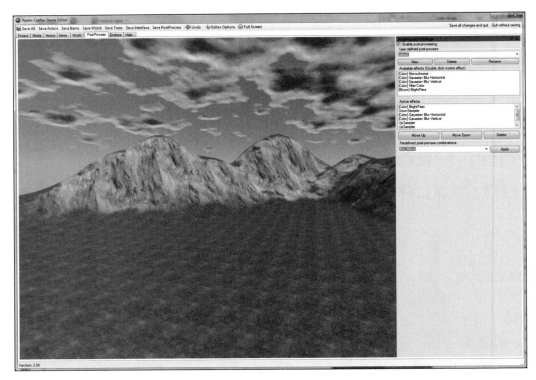

Figure 11.1
The Post Process tab with post processing enabled.

Note

The effect in print may not be as evident as when viewing it on a computer monitor. Be sure to check these post-processing effects on your version of Realm Crafter to get the full effect.

In the PostProcess Manager there are a number of options, defined as follows:

- **Enable post processing**: Enabled by default, this checkbox will apply any post-processing effects that have been configured into your MMO.

- **User-defined post process**: This provides an edit box for you to enter the name of your own user-defined post-processing settings.

- **New button**: Creates a user-defined post-process setting.

- **Delete button**: Deletes a user-defined post-process setting.

- **Rename button**: Renames a user-defined post-process setting.

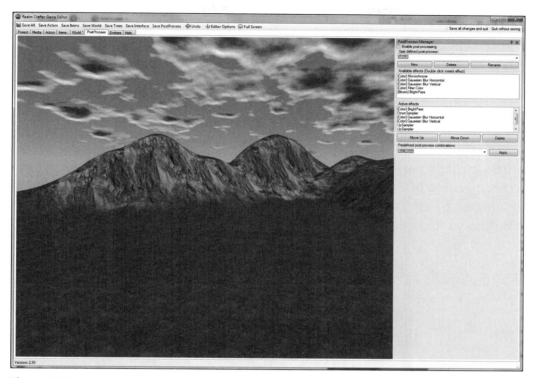

Figure 11.2
The zone without post processing.

- **Available effects**: The effects that you are able to choose from and apply to your zone.

- **Active effects**: The effects currently being applied to your zone.

- **Move up button**: Moves an effect higher in the list of active effects. The order of your effects defines the final post-processing effect.

- **Move down button**: Moves an effect lower in the list of active effects.

- **Delete button:** Deletes a particular effect currently applied to your zone.

- **Predefined post-process combinations**: There are three predefined post-process combinations that you can select and apply to your zone. One adds monochrome, another creates a red color effect, and one adds bloom.

- **Apply button**: Applies the predefined post-process combination.

Note

Bloom is a common post-processing effect used in modern computer games that creates bright light around a particular object or area. Bloom is a common effect used when you turn in the direction of the sun, for example.

THE EMITTERS TAB

Emitters create a particle effect that is "emitted" from another object. Examples of emitters could be blood splatter when hitting an NPC, the water effect from a fountain, or the effect displayed when your character casts a spell. You can see the Emitters tab in Figure 11.3.

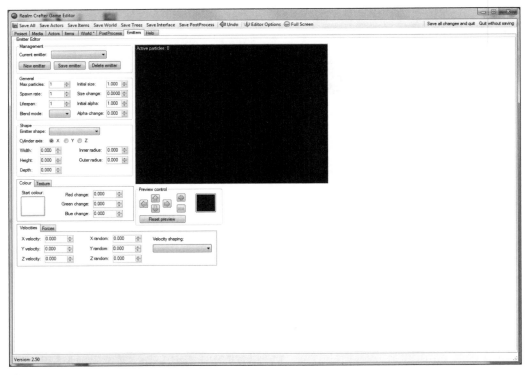

Figure 11.3
The Emitters tab.

The following options are available in the Emitters tab:

- **Current emitter**: Displays the current emitter in the preview window and provides the number of particles that the current emitter is using. You can see an example of the Blood emitter in Figure 11.4.

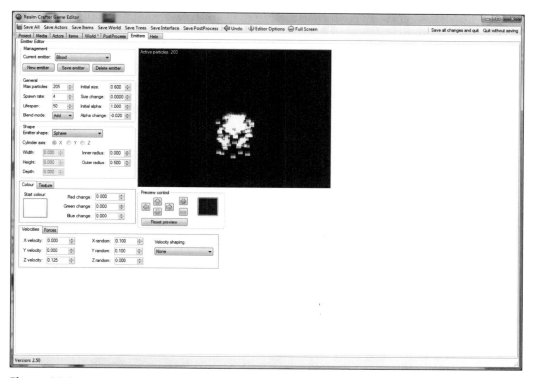

Figure 11.4
The blood emitter.

- **New emitter**: Creates a new emitter. You will be asked to enter a name for the emitter.
- **Save emitter**: Saves the emitter so that it can be used configured further at a later time.
- **Delete emitter**: Delete the currently selected emitter.

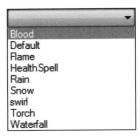

Figure 11.5
The standard available emitters.

Click on the Current Emitter drop-down box to view the current defaults that are available, as shown in Figure 11.5:

- **Blood**: Can be used to show that a character or player has been wounded.

- **Default**: A default emitter that you can use to create alternative emitters. This is a very simple effect that provides a small number of particles in the middle of the screen ready to have their properties changed.

- **Flame**: Useful for candles and other flame-based lights.

- **HealthSpell**: An example of an emitter for a spell. When creating a spell, normally you want some amazing special effect to take place, like a set of sparks flying from the player's hands.

- **Rain**: Weather-based rain example.

- **Snow**: Weather-based snow example.

- **Swirl**: A swirl effect that shows you how to create emitters that have movement.

- **Torch**: Useful for torch effects; very similar to the flame emitter but using a different set of textures to create a different effect.

- **Waterfall**: When creating an area in the world that represents water flowing, the waterfall effect is very useful for displaying water splashing.

The General area of the Emitters tab contains options for changing various properties of your emitters, as follows:

- **Max particles**: The maximum particles that the emitter will use. Increasing this figure does not necessarily display more particles on-screen, this will depend on what other options you configure (such as spawn rate and lifespan).

- **Spawn rate**: The rate that the particles will be created. The higher the number, the closer the emitter will be to using the maximum particles. The higher the spawn rate, the more particles are displayed onscreen.

- **Lifespan**: How long the particle will live. The lower the number, the shorter the lifespan (which means they exist onscreen for a set period of time before disappearing).

- **Initial size**: The initial size of the particle.

- **Size change**: The size that you want the particle to change. Making this figure higher will give the particle a zoom out effect.

- **Initial alpha**: The initial alpha value that will be used for the particle; the value ranges from 0 to 1. A value of 0 means that the particle is transparent while a value of 1 means it will be displayed without any transparency.

- **Blend mode**: Defines how the colors within the particles will be blended. There are three options available—Normal, Multiple, and Add. Normal displays the original texture; Multiple takes pixels from the top and bottom of the image and merges them together; Add adds the values of the pixels and displays the resulting value.

- **Alpha change**: This determines the amount of transparency change over time.

Note

The more particles on-screen, the more PC performance your game will require. In many cases, you can get the same effect by using fewer particles which means your game will perform better. Be sure to test the use of particles in this way to find the best effect/performance ratio for your game.

The Shape area of the Emitters tab consists of items that allow you to change the shape that the emitter creates. This is useful when you want to create an emitter with a particular special effect. For example, when you are creating water spray from a fountain or water is being blown in the wind in a particular direction.

- **Emitter shape**: The shape that you want the initial emitter to be; you can select sphere, cylinder, or box.

- **Cylinder axis**: What axis will the shape be placed on—X, Y, or Z.

- **Width**: The width of the shape.

- **Height**: The height of the shape.

- **Depth**: The depth of the shape.

- **Inner radius**: The size of the inner radius of the shape.

- **Outer radius**: The size of the outer radius of the shape.

Note

Not all shape options are available for all shapes.

The Colour and Texture tabs of the Emitters tab allow you to configure the starting color of the particles, the RGB color change, and which texture you want to use. You can see the Colour and the Texture tabs in Figure 11.6.

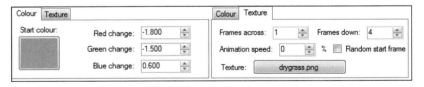

Figure 11.6
The Colour and Texture tabs.

The Texture tab in Figure 11.6 allows you to specify a texture and use a particular animation frame to generate the look of the emitter. You can also randomize the starting frame; this will pick a random animation frame to start from.

A texture allows you to change precisely the look of the emitter, so rather than using a single RGB color change, you can apply multiple colors from a single texture object. This might be useful if you wanted to create a rainbow effect, for example.

The Velocities and Forces tabs can be seen in Figure 11.7. These tabs allow you to change the direction of the emitter at a particular X, Y, and Z direction, or randomly. Changing the direction of emitters in this way can help achieve a more realistic effect.

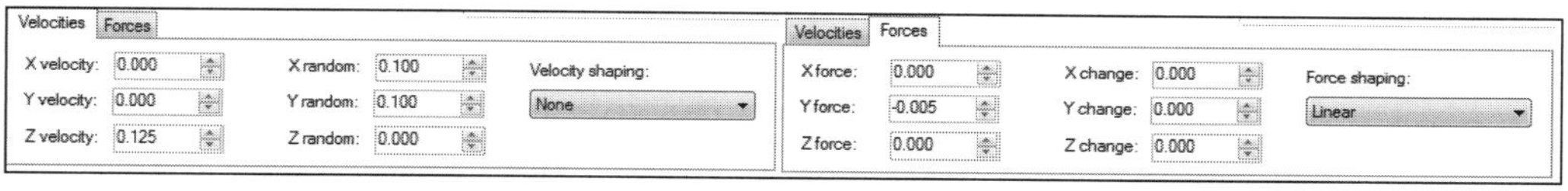

Figure 11.7
Velocities and Forces tabs.

In the Velocities tab there is an option to change the velocity shape:

- **None**: No velocity shaping.
- **Shaped**: Spawns the particles randomly in a shape (based on the selected emitter shape).
- **Strictly shaped**: Spawns the particles in a precise shape (based on the selected emitter shape).

In the Forces tab there is a Force Shaping drop-down box with the following options:

- **Linear**: Forces the shaping to use a linear path.
- **Spherical**: Forces the shaping to use a spherical shape.

The final feature of the Emitters screen is the preview control. This allows you to move up, down, left, or right of the created emitter. You can also zoom in or out in order to get a closer look at the color, shape, and texture of the emitter. You also have the option of changing the background color, which by default is black.

THE REALM CRAFTER HELP TAB

When using a product like Realm Crafter, you may need to refer to the product's Help file. The final tab in the Realm Crafter Game Editor is the Help tab, and from there you can access information about the product.

As well as reading and consulting this book for information, I recommend using the Help tab or the Realm Crafter user forums for the latest information about the latest patches and features.

Note

At the time of this writing the Help Section of Realm Crafter was incomplete; you should use the Realm Crafter forums for help if the Help tab isn't functional.

You can see an example of the Help file in Figure 11.8.

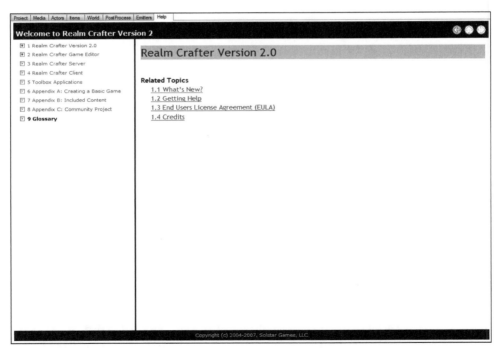

Figure 11.8
The Help tab.

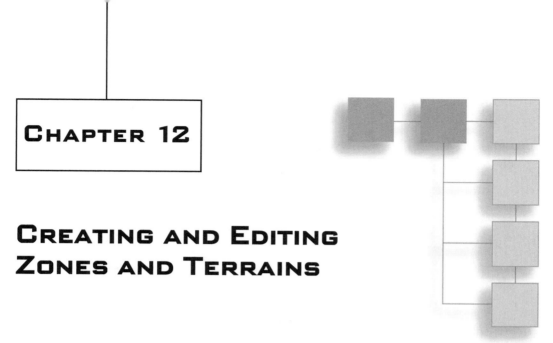

CHAPTER 12

CREATING AND EDITING ZONES AND TERRAINS

This chapter helps you discover how to create your own area in a game world called a *zone*. You will learn how to create a landscape (terrain) for that zone using a simple but extremely effective feature called *heightmaps*. You will then learn how to take your basic landscape and make it more interesting by covering it with grass and textures.

CREATING A NEW ZONE

A *zone* is an area within an MMO game world that can be used to separate a particular in-game region or separate areas based on weather or topography. So you could have a city mapped into a single zone or use a zone to contain a particular weather or terrain feature, such as a desert or mountain world. It is common to have topographies overlapping each other; an area starts off as generally flat and then becomes mountainous as players move to the edge of the zone.

Depending on the size of your game world, you may also have a game region located in more than one zone. Zones can be spread across servers. If you have a particular city that is in one zone only, you may find that many users visit the same location, which could create performance issues.

There are a number of zones already created in Realm Crafter. For this example, you'll create a new zone called Test.

1. Start Realm Crafter and launch a project (any project is fine as long as you don't mind editing it).

2. The Realm Crafter Game Editor will load. Select the World tab.

3. You should see a blank editor, which also displays a set of lines. These lines display the horizon of the world, as shown in Figure 12.1.

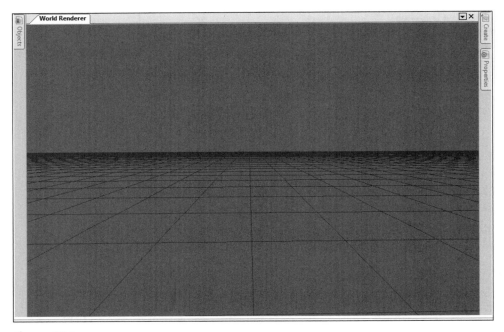

Figure 12.1
The blank world editor.

4. There are two ways to create a new zone. You can click on the New Zone button or you can right-click on the blank world editor. Select one of the methods to bring up the dialog box shown in Figure 12.2.

Figure 12.2
The Create Zone dialog box.

5. Type the name of your new zone; this example uses the name *Test*. Click on Accept once you are happy with the text that you have inputted.

The word *Test* will appear in the Zones drop-down box and will be automatically selected.

You have now created your first zone, although there is currently nothing populating it. In the next section of the book, therefore, you learn how to create a landscape in your new zone.

CREATING A TERRAIN

Now that you've created a test zone, you can learn to populate it with a *terrain*, which is the landmass of the world.

To start the process of creating a terrain for your zone, you use the Import Terrain option from the Terrain group of icons from the button toolbar. This option brings up the Import dialog box, shown in Figure 12.3.

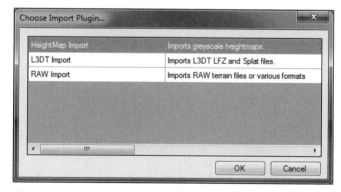

Figure 12.3
The Choose Import Plugin dialog box.

There are a number of ways of creating a terrain, as follows:

- **HeightMap**: A terrain based on a graphical image; these are very popular in the games industry for quickly creating a terrain from a 2D image.

- **L3DT**: A terrain-editing tool which stands for Large 3D Terrain Generator.

- **RAW**: You can use RAW data files that contain your terrain information. You must understand how the RAW file was constructed to be able to import such files into the editor. For more information about RAW image files, consult the Wiki web page: http://en.wikipedia.org/wiki/Image_file_formats.

When selecting any of the three options you will see another dialog box that requires additional information, as shown in Figure 12.4 for heightmaps, in Figure 12.5 for the L3DT format, and in Figure 12.6 for the RAW format.

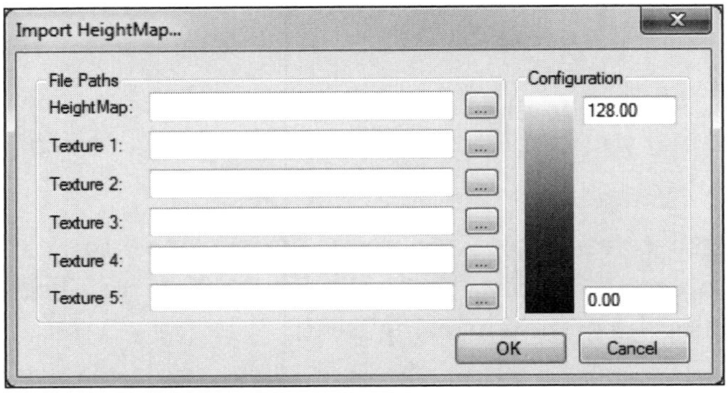

Figure 12.4
Import HeightMap dialog box.

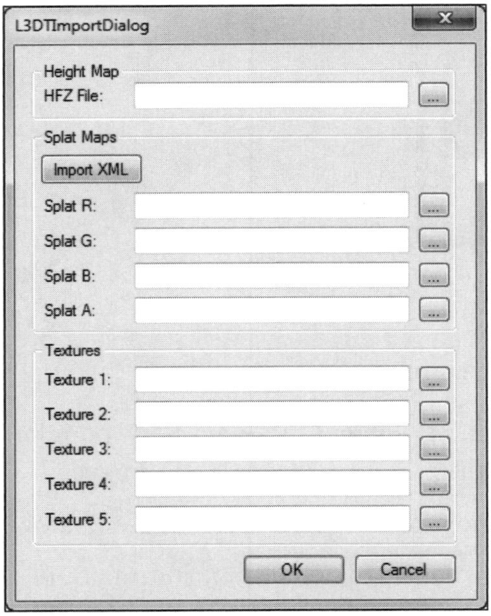

Figure 12.5
L3DT import dialog box.

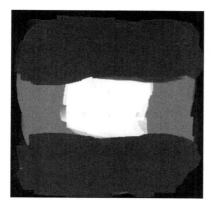

Figure 12.6
Import RAW File dialog box.

CREATING A HEIGHTMAP

Heightmaps are a very quick and easy way to create a game's landscape. Many games use this technique to generate a world's terrain rather than needing a 3D artist to spend a lot of time and effort creating a terrain manually. The artist will create an image that contains shades of grey or the colors black and white in an art package such as Microsoft Paint or Adobe Photoshop. If the image contains the color white, this means that the terrain is extremely high, whereas the color black means it's at ground level. The relevant shade of grey will define at what height the terrain will be generated; the darker the grey, the lower the terrain.

You can see a simple heightmap example in Figures 12.7 and 12.8.

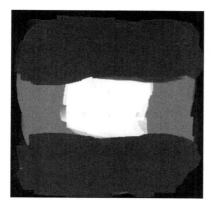

Figure 12.7
An example heightmap.

Figure 12.8
The result of the heightmap from Figure 12.7 in the World tab.

The heightmap in Figure 12.7 will generate a weird landscape, but this is just so you can see the effects that the different colors have on the game's terrain. The center of the heightmap consists of the color white, so this will be the highest part of the terrain, whereas the two strips of grey are dark, and will be much lower. There are two smaller strips of grey that will be higher than the two larger dark grey strips but lower than the white square. This simple heightmap generates the terrain shown in Figure 12.8.

Importing a Heightmap

Heightmaps are the perfect way to create terrain for games quickly and easily, but they also allow you to try out different combinations. If they don't work, you can quickly edit the image and reimport the file to see the changes you have made. This quick iteration is what makes heightmaps a common feature of games made today.

To follow this example you will need an already created heightmap. You can download an example heightmap from the following website address: www. makeamazing.com/heightmap.png.

Before you can import your heightmap, you will need to have a zone selected. Previously in this chapter you created a zone called Test; ensure that this

Test zone is selected in the Zone drop-down box before you begin the import process.

1. Click on the Import Terrain button from the button toolbar; the Choose Import Plug-in window will appear (as shown previously in Figure 12.3).

2. Select HeightMap Import and click the OK button.

3. You will then see the Import HeightMap dialog box, as shown previously in Figure 12.4. Click on the choose file icon to the right of the Height-Map text, which is shown with three dots on the button.

4. An Open dialog box will appear. Browse to the folder that contains your downloaded heightmap, select the file, and then click the Open button.

5. The Import HeightMap dialog box will now contain the path and file-name of the heightmap. You can change the range of the heightmap by amending the values under Configuration.

6. Click the OK button to import the image.

The new world will be imported. You can see the heightmap in Figure 12.9 and its corresponding shape in the World Renderer in Figure 12.10.

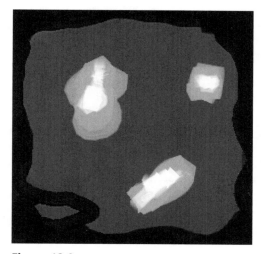

Figure 12.9
A heightmap shaped like an island.

Figure 12.10
The heightmap shown in the World Renderer.

Note

Heightmaps must be in the power of 2 and square in size, which means they must be 64x64, 128x128, 256x256, 512x512, or 1024x1024 in size. This is a requirement of Realm Crafter and not keeping to these file sizes will mean that the import of the file will fail. You should check the size of the heightmap in your chosen paint package, such as MS Paint, Photoshop, and so on, before importing.

Note

The world that you create may not look perfect, but you can then use the World Terrain Editor to modify it. The aim of the heightmap is to get the right shape and structure of your world quickly. You can fine-tune its look once you have a world shape that you are happy with.

USING THE WORLD TERRAIN EDITOR

Realm Crafter contains a tool that allows you to directly edit a zone's terrain. Once you have imported a terrain, you then have the opportunity to tweak it. You are also able to place items in the terrain and color it.

Editor Mode

The Editor Mode is a panel that allows you to access a number of features in order to edit the terrain. To access the Editor Mode, you need to switch it on from the toolbar. From the panels group, select Terrain Editor. Selecting the Terrain Editor option will display the panel shown in Figure 12.11.

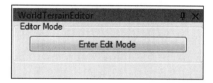

Figure 12.11
The Terrain Editor.

You may want to click on the Auto Hide pin (the thumbtack icon) to prevent the window from hiding itself automatically.

You might find that the Select One Terrain for Editing button (in the WorldTerrainEditor panel's Editor Mode section) is grayed out and you are not able to select it. If this is the case, you need to click on the Objects panel on the left side of the screen and ensure that the Terrain object is selected.

Once the button is available, click on it to display the Editor Mode features shown in Figure 12.12.

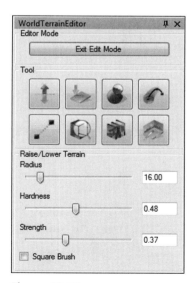

Figure 12.12
The Editor Mode features.

There is a selection of eight tools, starting from the top left, working across and then onto the second row, that consist of the following items:

- **Raise/Lower:** Raises or lowers the terrain, useful for creating hills, dips, or mountains.

- **Fix Terrain Height:** Fixes the terrain at a particular height. This tool allows you to move the terrain up and down. You can import a flat terrain and then use this option to sculpture it. Another common method is to import a terrain that is all the same height and then use this option to create a canyon.

- **Smooth:** When creating terrains, some of the terrain will look very uneven, especially when you're dealing with different heights. These "jaggies" can make your terrain look graphically poor. The Smooth tool will take the two different heights and smooth them out by reducing the angle of terrain.

- **Erosion:** Erodes the terrain, as if water has been running through the zone. This is useful for creating rivers.

- **Ramp:** Creates a raised ramp/platform, useful for creating a terrain-based bridge or crossing between two separate areas. To use this tool, select the first and second points of the ramp and the software will draw the connection between the two.

- **Paint Holes:** Removes a section of the terrain. Can be used to create a hole in the terrain where other objects can be placed, such as a cave.

- **Paint:** Paints the terrain a particular color.

- **Paint Grass:** Places a selection of grass objects onto the terrain.

Many of the options have the ability to change the size of the brush or change the brush from a circle to a square.

Editor Mode Examples

In this section of the chapter, you'll see a number of Editor Mode options and learn how to generate a zone using a basic terrain model. You will start off with a heightmap that consists of a 64x64 black square, which will create a flat terrain.

1. Create a black 64x64 square in a paint package and then import it into the game. This will create a flat, low terrain.

2. Click on the Enter Edit Mode button to reveal the various options.

3. Select Fix Terrain Height. You can see the extra options in Figure 12.13.

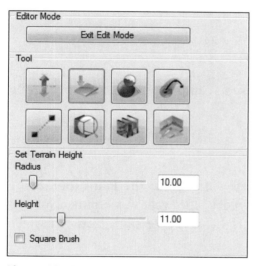

Figure 12.13
The additional options available for Fix Terrain Height.

4. Amend the radius so that you have a larger drawing area and reduce the height to 32.

5. Once you have drawn a large area, you can then reduce the height to around 7 and use it on one part of your image to create a canyon effect.

6. In my example I've also created a path from the canyon to another area, as shown in Figure 12.14.

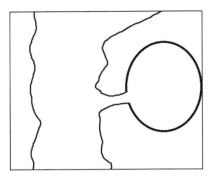

Figure 12.14
The area created using the Fix Terrain Height option.

Now that you have a basic, colorless terrain, you can paint some color onto it by following these steps:

1. Select the Paint tool. You will now see a number of settings, as shown in Figure 12.15.

   By default a number of colors have been assigned to the Paint tool, and so you could paint your terrain, red, green, blue, yellow, or pink. Not necessarily the colors that would look right in this terrain. You can assign a texture to these default items.

2. Double-click on the red Default0 option. This will bring up the Choose Texture dialog box as shown in Figure 12.16.

3. Find the Terrain option and then select 0.png.

4. Follow the same process for Default1, 2, and 3. Your texture box should now look like Figure 12.17.

5. You can now select a texture and paint it onto the terrain.

Because you have assigned the textures using the Editor Mode program, you can also use the AutoTexture feature from the Terrain toolbar. If you decide to use the AutoTexture option instead, you quickly set textures to particular terrain heights. You can see the auto terrain texture in Figure 12.18. Within the tool you are able to set at which height the system will apply the selected texture.

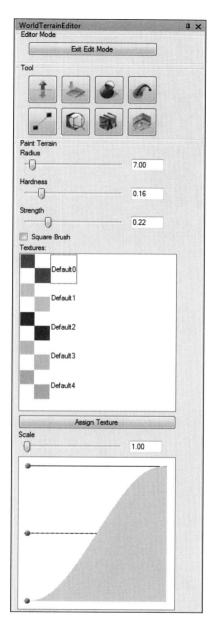

Figure 12.15
The Paint Tool option.

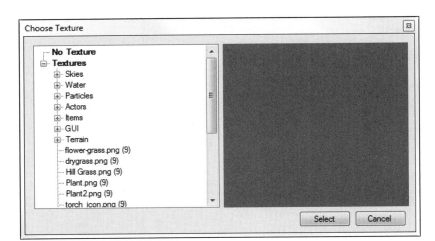

Figure 12.16
The Choose Texture dialog box.

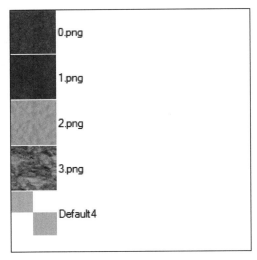

Figure 12.17
The textures in place for the Paint tool.

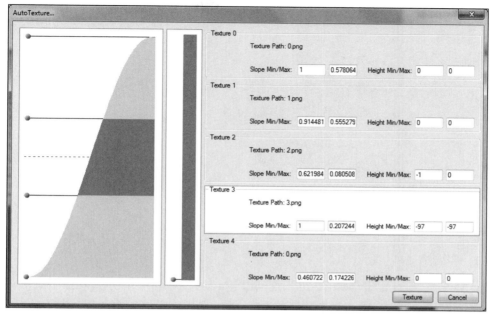

Figure 12.18
The AutoTexture dialog box.

Note

The scale option allows you to make the texture larger or smaller, which can have a dramatic effect on the end result of your terrain. Be sure to experiment with changing the scale to see what kind of result it creates.

Once you have applied some color to your terrain, you might want to smooth out any edges to your world, such as steep inclines. To do this, select the Smooth tool from the Terrain Editor and use it across the rough areas.

Now that the terrain is smooth, you are ready to apply some grass and other objects to the landscape to make it more interesting. Select the Paint Grass tool from the Terrain Editor. You will see a number of unassigned textures as shown in Figure 12.19.

1. Select an Unassigned item and then click on the Assign button.

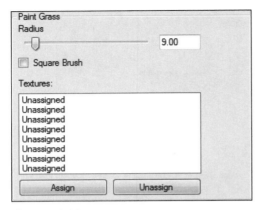

Figure 12.19
The Paint Grass tool.

2. The Select a Grass Type dialog box will appear, as shown in Figure 12.20. Select the required grass type and click Save. This example shows the use of the Dry Grass option.

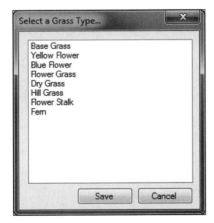

Figure 12.20
The Select a Grass Type dialog box.

3. Ensure you zoom into the terrain, and then click on the terrain to place the grass item.

You can see an example of the finished terrain in Figure 12.21. Using a combination of different textures, terrain heights, and grass objects, you can create quite an effective-looking landscape quickly and easily.

Figure 12.21
The final created landscape for the Test zone.

CHAPTER 13

THE CREATE PANEL

The Create panel allows developers to set up various systems, objects, and features within a game, such as a terrain, an emitter, or an NPC path (waypoint). On selecting the Create option from the Panels group, you will see the drop-down box in Figure 13.1. In Figure 13.2, you can see all of the options that you can choose from.

The options available are:

- **Zone**: Allows you to create a new zone.

- **Scenery object**: Allows you to place a scenery object, such as plant, tree, house, and so on.

- **Terrain**: Creates a base-level terrain tile that you can then use to generate your landscape. This is the same as creating a blank heightmap using an image.

- **Emitter**: Places an emitter, such as a waterfall or fire effect. In some cases, you may want to place an emitter on another object such as fireplace, candle holder, or water feature.

- **Water area**: Creates an area that will contain water.

- **Collision box**: Creates a zone that can check for player collision and therefore prevent players from entering that particular area.

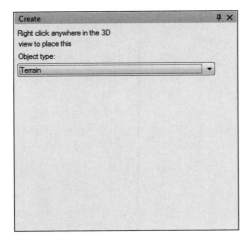

Figure 13.1
The Create panel with a drop-down selection box.

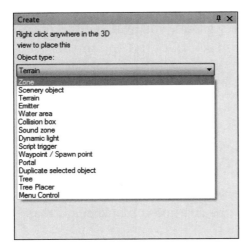

Figure 13.2
The available options in the Create drop-down box.

- **Sound zone**: When a player walks into a particular area, a sound can be played.

- **Dynamic light**: Creates a light source that can change.

- **Script trigger**: Triggers a particular script when a player enters a particular area.

- **Waypoint/Spawn point**: Creates an NPC waypoint such as a patrol route or creates a spawn point. This is where a player or NPC will appear.

- **Portal**: Allows a player transfer to another area. A portal is a way of linking zones together.

- **Duplicate selected objected**: Creates a copy of a particular object.

- **Tree**: Allows you to place a tree directly in the zone.

- **Tree placer**: Creates a zone to place multiple trees, rather than needing to place them individually.

- **Menu control**: Allows you to use a zone as a menu background.

The following sections of this chapter cover each of these options in more detail.

Note

Most of these items have additional properties that can be configured via the Properties dialog box. These can be accessed once you have created the object within your world via the Properties tab on the right corner of the World Renderer window.

PLACING A SCENERY OBJECT

A *scenery object* is any object that you add to your zone to make a scene. Think of a movie set, where you have the actors and the stage, but you don't have any objects for them to interact with. These objects could be buildings, a TV set, or small objects such as cups, radios, chairs, and grass. You have already seen how to place grass objects in Chapter 12, but you may want to place them individually in specific cases.

1. Select Scenery Object from the Create panel's drop-down menu.

   You will then be presented with the additional options shown in Figure 13.3.

2. Click on the Mesh Filename button.

3. Find the relevant mesh object that you want to apply and click on the Select button. For this example, I selected the treasure chest object, which you can see in Figure 13.4.

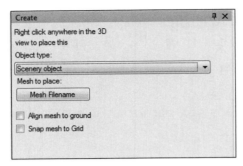

Figure 13.3
The Scenery Object properties.

Figure 13.4
The treasure chest scenery object on some terrain.

You could also have checked the checkbox items before inserting the mesh. These checkboxes do the following:

- **Align Mesh to Ground**: Aligns the scenery object to the ground.

- **Snap Mesh to Grid**: Aligns the scenery object to the grid.

If your ground is higher than your mesh you may find the object will appear partly in the ground or underground, depending on the height of the terrain. In most cases, it is prudent to check the Align Mesh to the Ground option. The chests that appear in the default project were placed using the Align Mesh to Ground option.

CREATING A TERRAIN

Rather than using a heightmap to create your terrain, you have Realm Crafter create one for you.

Note

> If you ask Realm Crafter to create your terrain map it will only create the size of the area, but it will be flat without any terrain variation.

1. Create a new zone using the Zones option or changing the Create type to Zone and right-clicking in the World Renderer window.

2. Type the name of the new zone. In this example, I use Test2.

3. You will have a blank zone. Change the object type in the Create dialog box to Terrain. Right-click on the World Renderer screen.

4. A dialog box will appear asking you which size terrain you want to create, as shown in Figure 13.5. The sizes are to the power of 2. Click on the Create button once you have decided on the terrain size.

Figure 13.5
Create Terrain dialog box.

CREATING AN EMITTER

When you have created your emitters using the Emitters tab, you may want to place them within the world. You can use the Create tab to place your chosen emitter onto the rendered world.

Upon selecting the Object type to be emitter, you will then see a drop-down box with the emitters available to you, as shown in Figure 13.6. You can see the properties selected for this object in Figure 13.7.

Right-click on the world to place your selected emitter.

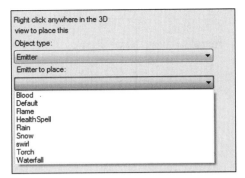

Figure 13.6
Placing an emitter onto the world.

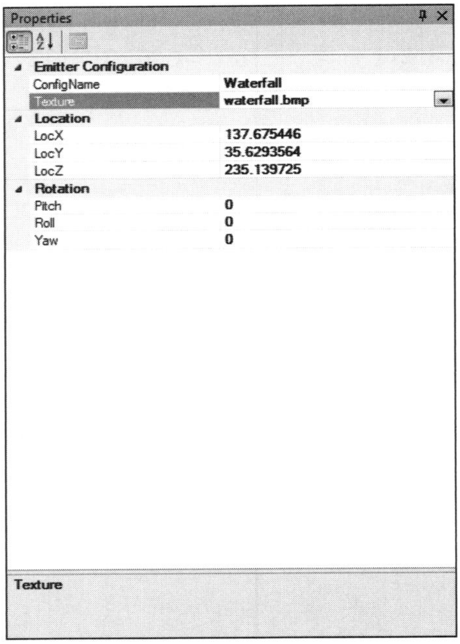

Figure 13.7
The properties of the waterfall emitter.

CREATING A WATER AREA

You can create areas that contain water, such as streams, rivers, and seas. These provide a welcome change of scenery to any game that you might have. Some benefits of having a water area in your MMOs are as follows:

- **Skills**: Water can provide your players with ways of learning new skills, such as fishing or pearl diving. Players could also have swimming skills that they could upgrade; if this skill is something that players need to train to improve, it could also provide areas where only those with a higher skill level can reach.

- **Barriers**: If you decide that players cannot swim or cross water in your game, you can use water as a barrier.

- **Border**: You can use water as a way of separating different areas.

- **Player's attention**: You can use terrain and objects to push the player in a particular direction. This is a common trick used in today's games—they use landscape items such as hills and mountains and objects such as paths, fences, and birds circling in the distance to direct a player's attention in a certain direction. You can use water effects in the same manner. Using the landscape, a river/stream, and some objects you can make a player move in a particular direction.

Note

Even though you are making an MMO, you might be wondering why you should be trying to push players in a particular direction. There are many different levels of players in the world; some will need more help than others. This is certainly true of new players who will not know your game very well. One failing some modern MMOs have is not making the game easy enough for the player to understand early on within the first few levels. Hard games like this can lead to lots of questions in the chat rooms and forums. If players get frustrated, they will move onto the next MMO or game. It's also a useful technique to give hints to players (of any experience level) that something is going on in a particular direction. If players see something interesting or intriguing in the distance, they are more likely to enjoy the game than when just randomly walking around.

To add a water effect, you need to follow these steps:

1. Select Water Area from the Create list.

2. Choose a texture to use for the water. You can see the create menu in Figure 13.8. Select the texture, and then right-click on the world to place a yellow box, which will contain the texture. You can see an example of a placed box in Figure 13.9, next to a river in the default level.

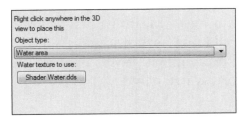

Figure 13.8
The Create menu for a water area.

Figure 13.9
A water area box placed on the World Renderer.

3. Now you need to specify a ShaderFX, which is the special effect that will be placed on the texture to give it a water effect. You have two to select from in the properties of the water area object. You can see the properties of the river placed within the default level in Figure 13.10.

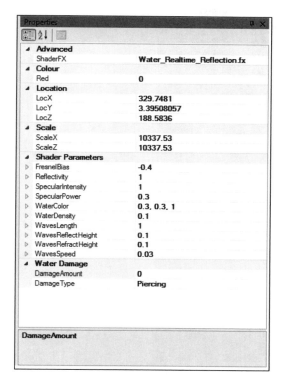

Figure 13.10
River properties.

It's quite easy to create a water-based area and fill it with water. In Figure 13.9 you can see a river, which is effectively a ditch cut out in the terrain; a water area is then placed at a certain level to fill the ditch. You can also raise and lower the water to create different effects; you could flood the whole valley by just moving the water upwards, an effect that's shown in Figure 13.11.

USING SOUND ZONES

A Sound zone is a common type of trigger object in games. When players enter a particular area, a sound file will play. You may want to vary the sounds played in a particular area, such as cricket sounds or bird song. In a horror game, the Sound zones might include a bloody curdling scream, footsteps, or heavy breathing.

Figure 13.11
The same valley with the river, now flooded.

From the Create panel, change the object type to Sound Zone and then right-click on the World Renderer to set the zone. You can see an example of a Sound zone in Figure 13.12.

Using Dynamic Light

The Dynamic Light option allows you to place a light effect that you have already generated. To place a dynamic light you will need to have already created a light effect, you may remember that under the Edit Light functions was a light flicker object. Since this is already created, this is the only option that you will be able to specify from the dynamic light properties.

1. Select Dynamic Light from the Create panel drop-down box.

2. Right-click on the World Renderer to create the dynamic light source, as shown in Figure 13.13.

Figure 13.12
The Sound zone placed within the world.

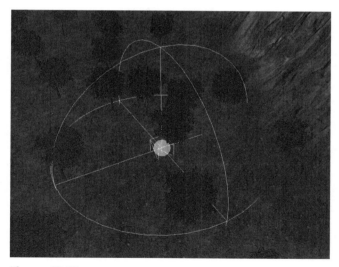

Figure 13.13
The dynamic light placed within the world.

3. In Figure 13.14, you can see the properties to configure the light source. The most important option is the LightFunction, which is where you can select the available light objects.

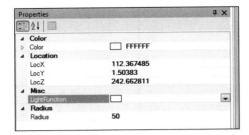

Figure 13.14
The properties of the dynamic light object type.

USING SCRIPT TRIGGERS

A script trigger is used to trigger a script that you have written when a player enters a particular area. Most of the default triggers won't be of much use to you so you will have to create your own.

The only property you will be interested in for the Script Trigger is the script filename as shown in Figure 13.15.

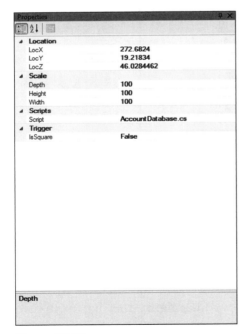

Figure 13.15
The properties of the Script Trigger object.

All scripts are written in C#, so you will need to understand how to program before you can make your own scripts. You can find out more about scripting in Chapters 14 and 15.

Note

Sometimes users create their own scripts and upload them for other developers to use them. Visit the Realm Crafter forums at www.realmcrafter.com to see if there are any new scripts that you could use within your own MMO.

WAYPOINT/SPAWN POINT

The waypoint/spawn point will allow you to configure two particular situations within your games:

- **Waypoint**: This is a location that a person moves to, very much like a navigational system in the car that provides a point for you to drive to. You can connect two points to create a simple route.

- **Spawn Point**: Creates a location where you can spawn (create) a particular set of enemies or creatures.

All games have some form of waypoint or spawning system. For example, *Call of Duty* spawns enemies on a regular basis. In fact, most FPS (First Person Shooter) games have a level where you are defending a base or point on the map from wave upon wave of enemy soldiers. Because game engines are limited to the memory in the PC/consoles, rather than creating and placing all enemies in one go (which would be very costly in terms of memory usage and the performance of the game), the game will create groups of enemies in a particular location (usually out of sight from the player). Once one wave has been destroyed, another wave will be sent, giving the players the illusion they are in a firefight with many groups of soldiers.

In MMOs, spawn points are used to replace NPCs when they have been killed. There are many players in an MMO game and if spawning wasn't used, very soon the game would have no more enemies left to fight against. In an MMO there's usually a quest where you have to kill an enemy boss. This could be a dragon, crime boss, or troll, for example. If this character was never respawned after dying, no one else would be able to complete the quest.

In all MMOs, you will have enemies that walk around the map rather than stay in one location. This is to make sure the enemies look like they are realistically patrolling an area, rather than standing still waiting for the players to come to them. It provides a bigger challenge, as the players have to anticipate where the enemies will walk. This is especially the case when players are at a lower level and want to get past the enemies without getting involved in combat.

Follow these steps to create the waypoints and spawn points:

1. To create the spawn point, click on the drop-down box in the Create panel and select Waypoint/Spawn point.

2. Right-click anywhere on the World Renderer to place a spawn point flag.

3. Now that you have created your spawn point, you can access its properties. First, ensure it is selected (you will see a yellow box around it, as shown in Figure 13.16). Then access the properties box. You can find the properties box on the right panel.

Figure 13.16
The spawn point flag with the selection box.

You can see the properties box in Figure 13.17.

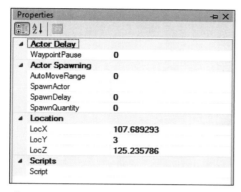

Figure 13.17
The spawn point properties box.

Some of the key properties are:

- **SpawnActor**: The actor that you want to spawn, such as Lizard folk.

- **SpawnQuantity**: The amount of lizard folk that you want to spawn.

- **Script**: The script that you want to run when the spawn point is activated.

To create a waypoint, you need to choose Waypoint/Spawn point from the Create panel. Then right-click somewhere within the zone. Now that you have two points, you can join them together.

1. Click on the first flag; this will enable the waypoint icons in the toolbar.

2. Click on the Waypoint A icon, and then click on the second flag. This will create a connection between the two flags, as shown in Figure 13.18.

CREATING PORTALS

A *portal* is a connection between zones/worlds within your game. When players enter a portal, you will want them to appear in another location. You need to place portals carefully, so that it's not a shock to the player when they are transported to another area.

Figure 13.18
Waypoint between two points.

To create a portal between two areas you will need an exit portal and an entry portal. The exit portal can also become the entry portal if the player is coming from a different direction, for example:

- Zone 1 Portal A leads to Zone 2 Portal B
- Zone 2 Portal B leads to Zone 1 Portal A

When selecting Portal as the object type from the Create panel, you have the following options:

- **Portal name:** The name of the portal.
- **Linked zone:** The zone that this portal is linked to; the drop-down box lists all zones that have been generated.
- **Linked portal name:** The name of the portal that the newly created portal should link to.

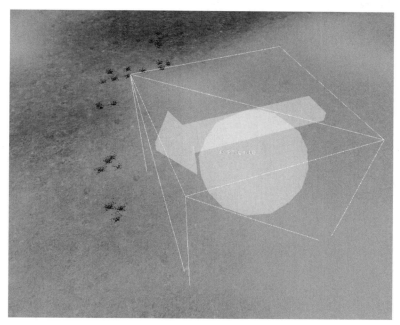

Figure 13.19
The portal object.

When you right-click on the World Renderer to place your portal, this will generate the portal area. Note the arrow in Figure 13.19; this is the direction that the player will appear from.

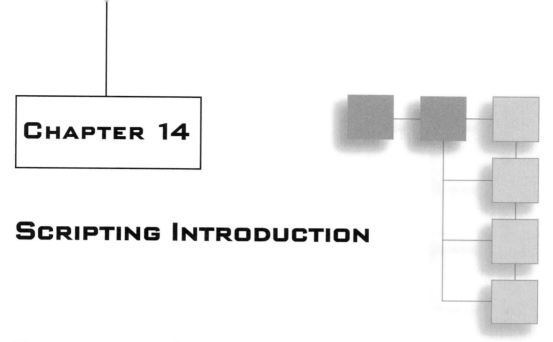

CHAPTER 14

SCRIPTING INTRODUCTION

Many game-creation tools use a graphical editor to place objects but also contain a scripting language or programming language to allow the game's creator to create the logic. Realm Crafter uses the C# (pronounced "C-sharp") language to create its game logic.

WHAT IS A PROGRAMMING LANGUAGE?

Programming languages have been around for many years, and have allowed savvy computer users to create their own computer programs that perform a particular function. Programmers could write instructions on a line per line basis and have the computer interpret them and perform a particular reaction. This program would only work on the computer that was used to write the code. In other cases programmers would compile the program into a format that they could then save to tape or disc, which could then be run on any other computer system.

Early programming languages such as BASIC, COBOL, PASCAL, and Assembly had different uses and complexity. Some were used in home computers, whereas others were popular in businesses. Not all computers were able to run all languages, and each had its own set of instructions that required the programmer to know special syntax to get it to work correctly.

BASIC (Beginners All Purpose Symbolic Instruction Code) was one of the first mass-market home user programming languages. From the early eight-bit computers such as Spectrum and Commodore Vic 20, BASIC allowed many people to make their own games and educational or business software. It helped start the concept of the home programmer, whereby someone sitting at home in front of his own computer could create a program and then sell it. Of course in those days there was no Internet and so everything had to be placed on a physical media such as a cassette tape. As technology changed and Windows-based operating systems became the main focus for many developers, programming languages were required to compile into particular formats that could be run on any computer, such as the Windows EXE (executable) format.

Note

A *compiler* is a process whereby the programming application takes the computer instructions (code) and generates a file that can run on any computer, regardless of the tools or platform installed.

Over the last few years, some programming languages have become popular while others have disappeared, or found small niche markets. Some languages are better at doing a particular task, and others will work only on a particular operating system.

Some programming languages that are in use today:

- **C++:** The descendant of C, which is an early programming language from the 1970s. Various companies created their own versions of C and C++, such as Microsoft and Borland. Today Microsoft's Visual C++ is considered the standard for programming on a Windows computer. Microsoft also allows you to download and install a free version of Visual Studio, so that you can learn the programming syntax.

- **C#:** C# was created by Microsoft. It's not as fast as C++, but is used commonly in GUI-based applications and tools as well as in the games engine XNA from Microsoft.

- **Java:** Developed by Sun Microsystems, Java's main benefit is that once you have installed the Java platform files on your operating system, you can run any Java code. This means that code that you write is not dependant on the particular platform. Unlike C#, which will only run on Windows,

Java runs on Windows, Linux, and other platforms. Java is not generally used to make games, unless the games are for the mobile platforms.

There are many other programming languages and text-based systems that people use in gaming, including LUA, Flash Script, and XML. The game tool you are using determines whether these items are available.

PROGRAMMING CONCEPTS AND TERMINOLOGY

This book is not meant to teach C# programming, but to give you an introduction to MMO creation and using the Realm Crafter tool. If you require more help in programming, you should look specifically at books dedicated to C# programming.

A good starting point can be found in the following:

- *Visual C# Game Programming for Teens* by Jonathan S. Harbour
- *Beginning C# Game Programming, 1st Edition*, by Ron Penton

This section of the book covers a number of programming concepts and terminology to give you an idea of the things that you will be dealing with when using the Script Editor. It is not meant to be a detailed guide or to teach you how to program in C#, but should serve as background information to allow you to go and find further information.

Examples and Help

In addition to the books mentioned previously, there is a large amount of help that you can get from the Internet. The Realm Crafter site is a good source of information, as is the Microsoft website at:

http://msdn.microsoft.com/library/aa288436.aspx

Within Visual C#, you can create many different types of applications, from console programs (which run in a command prompt) to applications that appear in an application window. Figure 14.1 shows a common example given in most programming books, called the Hello World example. This program prints the text "Hello, World!" in a program—in this case, in a command prompt window.

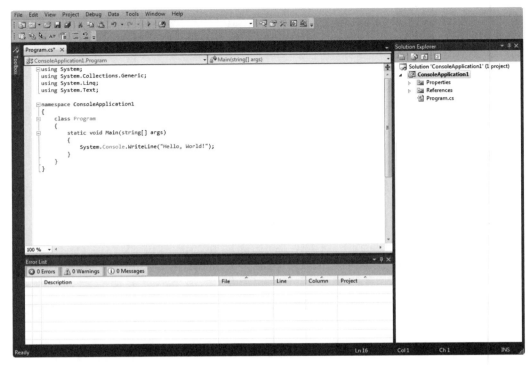

Figure 14.1
A Visual Studio simple project example.

Understanding Variables

A *variable* is a value that can change. This can be a text value or a numeric value. If you think about any type of situation in a game, you can probably come up with some values that change in the course of running it. Some examples are:

- **Currency**: A player earns more money and then spends it.

- **Time**: The time in a game world is ever changing.

- **Items in an inventory**: Players will have a changing number of items in their inventories at any point.

- **Health**: The amount of health a player has.

- **Score**: The current score that the player has achieved in a game.

- **Age**: The age of a person, which changes from year to year.

- **Playing time**: The amount of time that a person has played a level, the game today, or the total time.

In C# and in other languages, you have to tell the computer what variables you want to create. The computer will then create a space in memory to store any values that it might hold. You can also place values in those variables. To do this in C#, you can program the following:

```
int score;
int score = 42;
int health;
int totalInventory;
string name;
name = "Jason";
```

The first example uses the keyword `int` to create a variable called `score` (you will learn about keywords shortly). Elsewhere in the program, you could then use `score` within the code. The second example automatically assigns the value 42 to the score. The third and fourth examples have again just told the computer that you are creating two memory slots for `health` and `totalInventory` with an `int` keyword.

The example `string name;` tells the computer that you want to reserve a space in memory for a string variable called `name`. The next line tells the computer to put the value `"Jason"` into the string variable called `name`.

Notice that you need to complete the lines using a semicolon. This tells the programming language that the line is complete. This is very important because programming languages need to know when a particular set of instructions has finished. Code can be quite long; in some cases, it may run over a number of lines.

You can see some of these examples in code in Figure 14.2.

Note

In Figure 14.2, you will notice that there is a green line under the words `score` and `name`. This is because the variables have been declared and their values set, but the variables are not used anywhere in the application. You can ignore this for the purpose of the example here.

```
using System;
using System.Collections.Generic;
using System.Linq;
using System.Text;

namespace ConsoleApplication1
{
    class Program
    {
        static void Main(string[] args)
        {
            System.Console.WriteLine("Hello, World!");
            int score = 42;
            string name;
            name = "jason";

        }
    }
}
```

Figure 14.2
Examples of variables.

Understanding Constants

Constants are values that stay the same through the course of a program. If you take a moment to consider things in real life, you can probably come up with some quite easily. Here are some real-life and programming constants:

- **The player's name**: The name of the player, in most cases, is unlikely to change.

- **NI number**: National Insurance/security number. Or any type of number given to you by the government, such as a driving license number or social security number.

- **Bank account number**: The account number for your bank.

- **Conversion value**: Perhaps you want to convert grams into ounces, or stones into pounds. You would store the values that you want to convert by.

Some of these constants may change at some point in a person's lifetime; for example, you might want to change your bank, but programmers use constants in a game when they know that the value won't change. So if you know the player won't change their account number while playing as this particular character, you can make the value a constant.

Creating a constant is a similar process to creating a variable. You use the keyword const followed by the type (which will be discussed shortly) and the constant name.

```
const int valuesmy;
const string firstname;
const int value = 34;
```

The first example sets up a constant int (number) value called valuesmy. The second example sets up a string (text) called firstname. Finally, the third example sets the value 34 as a constant named value.

Understanding Keywords

There are two types of keywords in C#, reserved and contextual. *Reserved* words are keywords that you cannot use as variables. These are words that are known to C# and have a particular use. *Contextual* keywords are words that are used in particular circumstances, but can be used at other times.

You have already seen three keywords being used in the previous examples— int, string, and const. When I say that the words are reserved, this means that the programming language knows that these two words are special and it needs to treat them in a particular way. You can't create an int variable as follows:

```
int int;
```

This is because you can't use the reserved word int as a variable name. There are a large number of keywords that you shouldn't use; for more information consult the C# documentation.

Understanding Data Types

The previous examples used int, const, and string. These are special keywords that define the type of item that follows the word. For example, the word int means that the variable after it is of type integer, which means the value that will be stored in this variable can be between –2,147,483,648 and 2,147,483,647. A const is a value that never changes, such as a player's birthday or real name. A string data type, on the other hand, is a number of characters that form a word or sentence.

There are a large number of different data types in C#. You should consult online documentation for a complete list, but Figure 14.3 contains some of the most common data types.

C# Type	Details
bool	Booleans represent true or false values.
char	Stores a Unicode character.
decimal	Stores a decimal number with up to 28-29 digits.
double	Stores a floating point number up to 15-16 digits.
float	Stores a floating point number with precision up to 7 digits.
int	Stores an integer (whole) number.
long	Stores large numbers from −9,223,372,036,854,775,808 to +9,223,372,036,854,775,808

Figure 14.3
A list of common data types.

Understanding Arrays

Arrays are a way of storing and retrieving large amounts of data in an organized format. They are very efficient for storing data for many reasons. They can store both numbers and text.

It's best to think of arrays as sets of boxes on the floor all connected, or as a number of bookshelves where you can store your items (data). Each slot can store particular information that you can quickly retrieve at a later stage.

Figures 14.4, 14.5, and 14.6 show several conceptual views of arrays.

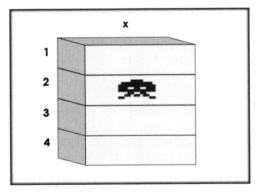

Figure 14.4
A conceptual image of a single dimension array.

In C#, you have to declare the structure of the array before you can use it. To do this, you do the following:

```
int[] salary = new int [5];
```

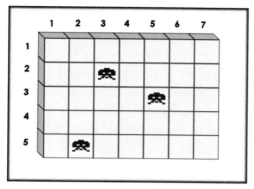

Figure 14.5
A conceptual image of a two-dimensional array.

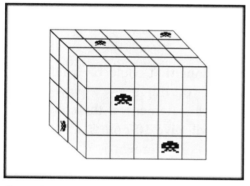

Figure 14.6
A conceptual image of a three-dimensional array.

This declaration will create an int-based array with five array slots assigned to the array named salary. By default, all slots are set to 0.

Understanding Decisions

Making a decision is important in programming. You might want to determine what value a user has typed in at the keyboard or what their favorite weapon is in a game. To do this, you need to be able to make decisions based on information you have been given. To make such decisions in code, you can use the following:

- **If:** If something is true, do something (such as add two values, remove health, and so on).

▪ **If-else:** If something is true, do something; if it's not true, do something else. You can see an example structure of the if-else command in Figure 14.7. Decisions are being made all the time in a computer game. For example, consider a scenario where a player is moving toward some enemies. If the player is within a certain distance of the enemies, the creatures will attack. If the player is outside this range, the creatures will continue to ignore the player. That is just one simple example of when you may have if and if-else logic running within your game.

```
if (expression)
    statement1
[else
    statement2]
```

Figure 14.7
An example structure of the if-else command from the Microsoft MSDN site.

▪ **Switch:** Allows you to use a number of options that could be true, and then run code specifically for an answer. So you might ask a player for her favorite color, for example. In the switch statement, if the color is red, you will give 5 points, if it's blue you will give 10 points, and if it's yellow you will add 15 points. The switch case statement is very good at assigning code to a particular response. You can also assign a default "if none of the switch case is true, use the code contained in this section" option. You can see an example of the switch structure in Figure 14.8.

```
int caseSwitch = 1;
switch (caseSwitch)
{
    case 1:
        Console.WriteLine("Case 1");
        break;
    case 2:
        Console.WriteLine("Case 2");
        break;
    default:
        Console.WriteLine("Default case");
        break;
}
```

Figure 14.8
An example structure of the switch case from the Microsoft MSDN site.

Understanding Loops

You will often need to instruct the program/game to do the same thing several times in a row, which is called a loop and is very useful when you want to draw some items on-screen or do something that is repetitive. It is also a lot easier to write a loop to do this rather than to write the lines of code separately without a loop. As an example, perhaps you were trying to make a crossword game and had to display a 17x17 grid of pictures on-screen to represent the crossword puzzle boxes. There are two ways you could achieve this effect. You could write a large number of lines of code to represent each row of boxes or you could use a loop, which would achieve the same result in a few lines of code. Hopefully from that example you will understand the power of loops in programming. Not only do loops simplify your code, they also keep you from having to write as much to achieve the same result. You will also find that reducing your code makes your program more efficient, which means in the long run it might take up less space and run faster. More importantly though, the less code you have to write the easier and quicker it is to debug your program.

There are different ways of creating loops. You can use the keywords `do`, `for`, `foreach`, `in`, and `while`. While is a very common keyword used for looping. It basically tells the program, while a statement is true keep running the loop, when it's not true stop running the loop.

Hopefully this chapter has whetted your appetite for more information about the C# programming language and about scripting in general. I recommend that you take a look at the resources online at the Realm Crafter site (see www. realmcrafter.com) or at the Visual C# site mentioned earlier in the chapter. Learning C# is a big step if you have not programmed before, but will be extremely helpful in getting your MMO up and running.

CHAPTER 15

USING THE SCRIPT EDITOR

The Script Editor is a powerful built-in programming tool that allows you to write or amend C# code. It has a similar feel to the Visual Studio interface, so if you have used that before you will feel right at home. This chapter looks at the main interface of the Script Editor, and also helps you create a simple code example that will give you a little more knowledge of the scripting system and creation process.

TOURING THE SCRIPT EDITOR

To access the Script Editor, you must be in the World Renderer tab. In the toolbar options, click on the Script Editor button as shown in Figure 15.1. Once you do so, you will see the Script Editor appear as an extra tab on the World Renderer window, as shown in Figure 15.2.

Within Figure 15.2, you can see the basic layout of the Script Editor:

- **Text Menu:** A number of options are available from the Text menu, such as opening, closing, and printing a file.
- **Button Menu:** Quick buttons to common tasks, such as redo/undo code changes, saving, and printing.
- **Project Explorer:** Shows all of the code projects that you can access. There are a number of default projects that already exist.
- **Code Area:** This is where the code for the game projects appears.

Figure 15.1
The Script Editor button.

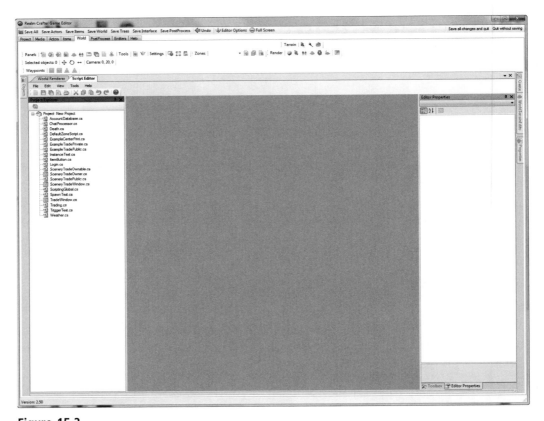

Figure 15.2
The Script Editor tab in the World tab.

- **Editor Properties:** Displays properties for any dialog box-based projects. There is also a toolbox tab that allows you to place windows-based objects within a dialog box.

Note

A dialog box is an application or game window that conveys information to the users. This could be a login box or a box asking the players if they want to quit the game.

Text Menu

You can see the main Text menu entries in Figure 15.3.

Figure 15.3
The Text Menu options.

The File option contains the following options, as shown in Figure 15.4.

Figure 15.4
The File menu.

- **New:** Creates a new project. You can create a code project or a dialog box project.
- **Save:** Saves the current opened project.
- **Save All:** Saves all of the opened projects.
- **Print Preview:** Allows you to preview your code before printing it.
- **Print:** Prints the currently selected code page.
- **Close:** Closes the currently selected code page.
- **Close All:** Closes all code pages.

The Edit option contains the following options, as shown in Figure 15.5.

Figure 15.5
The Edit menu options.

- **Undo:** If you have made a change that you want to revert, you can use the Undo option.

- **Redo:** If you have deleted a change and want to reapply it, you can use the Redo option. The Redo option also works if you have just used the Undo menu option.

- **Cut:** Removes any selected text code and places it in the Windows clipboard.

- **Copy:** Makes a copy of the selected text code and places it on the Windows clipboard.

- **Paste:** Takes any code that is currently on the Windows clipboard and places it into the code window.

- **Select All:** Highlights all of the text in the code window.

- **Find and Replace:** Finds a particular piece of text and replaces it with another piece of text or number.

- **Incremental Search:** Searches for a particular term incrementally. This is very useful if you want to find all examples of a particular variable or number within your code.

- **Go To:** Goes to a particular line number within your code sheet.

- **Comments:** Removes or adds comments to your code. *Comments* are lines of text that are used in the code to remind you what a particular piece of code does. Comments are ignored by the system when it creates your code. Comments are created by typing a double forward slash, such as //.

- **Bookmarks:** A *bookmark* is a link to a particular point in the code that you want to mark as important. At any point, you can select the bookmark and jump to that line in the code.

- **Advanced:** Provides three options to set up various settings for the code screen, such as indentation guides (displays dotted lines to show you how far a set of characters has been indented) and whitespace (displays any tabs as white spaces or full stops). Finally, the Highlight Current Line option displays the line as yellow.

The View menu option contains the following features, as shown in Figure 15.6.

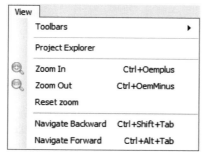

Figure 15.6
The View menu.

- **Toolbars:** Switches the toolbars on and off.
- **Project Explorer:** Enables the Project Explorer.
- **Zoom In:** Zooms in on the code view screen.
- **Zoom out:** Zooms out on the code view screen.
- **Reset Zoom:** Resets the zoom to its original setting.

- **Navigate Backward:** If you have multiple code view tabs open, this option navigates backward between them.

- **Navigate Forward:** If you have multiple code view tabs open, this option navigates forward between them.

The Tools menu contains a single option called Snippets, this allows you to store (save) a selection of code that you find useful for pasting into the editor later on. This option is currently not available within Realm Crafter.

There are no options within the Help menu. The Help menu will launch a help system that provides you with more information about programming in Realm Crafter.

Toolbar Options

The toolbar options are as follows from left to right, and are shown in Figure 15.7:

Figure 15.7
The Script Editor toolbar.

- **New:** Creates a new script.
- **Save:** Saves the currently selected script file.
- **Save All:** Saves all script files.
- **Print Preview:** Previews what the script will look like on paper if it were printed.
- **Print:** Prints the current code view page.
- **Cut:** Removes any selected code and places it into the Windows clipboard.
- **Copy:** Copies any selected code and places it into the Windows clipboard.
- **Paste:** Pastes any code that is currently in the Windows clipboard.
- **Undo:** Undoes any changes that you have made.
- **Redo:** Repeats any changes that you have made.
- **Help:** Displays the Help file.

Project Explorer

On the left side of the Script Editor is the Project Explorer. The Project Explorer displays all of the projects available within Realm Crafter. You can see a list of default projects in Figure 15.8.

Figure 15.8
The Project Explorer.

Within this list are two types of projects. You will see a selection of files with an icon that displays the text C#; this is a code file that contains instructions to perform a particular function. You will also see a second icon that looks like a dialog box; these are code files that create dialog boxes. You'll learn to create a dialog box shortly.

There is a set of pre-defined projects already available in the Project Explorer, and these projects have the following uses:

- **AccountDatabase:** Handles the logging in, creating, and saving of user account information.

- **ChatProcessor:** Script that allows players to communicate with one another in the chat window.

- **Death:** The script that handles the player's death, death animation, and how the player respawns within the game world.

- **DefaultZoneScript:** This is the default script that handles the time/day/seasons for a zone.

- **ExampleCenterPrint:** Example code on how to display text at the top center of the player's screen.

- **ExampleTradePrivate:** Example code to show how to advise the player that a particular chest is private.

- **ExampleTradePublic:** Example code to show how to advise the player that a particular chest is publically accessible.

- **InstanceTest:** Example code to show how to handle creating an instance.

- **ItemButton:** Used in inventory and spell windows.

- **Login:** Handles the player's login. By default, it creates a player with a torch item within his hand.

- **SceneryTradeOwnable:** Example code used to handle the chest opening in the example game.

- **SceneryTradeOwner:** Example code used to handle the chest opening in the example game.

- **SceneryTradePublic:** Example code used to handle the chest opening in the example game. Public allows anyone to access the chest.

- **SceneryTradeWindow:** Example code used to handle the chest opening in the example game.

- **ScriptingGlobal:** The main startup script in the game.

- **SpawnTest:** Example code to show how to spawn a character.

- **TradeWindow:** The default script to handle the look of the trade window that is used when two players transfer goods.

- **Trading:** The default script to handle the trading of items between players and characters.

- **TriggerTest:** Example code to show how to trigger a particular event.
- **Weather:** Code to handle the weather effects in the game.

All in-game scripts are stored in the following directory:

C:\Program Files\Solstar Games\Realm Crafter 2\Projects\New Project\Data \Server Data\Scripts

Code Area

The code area is where you edit, update, and create new code to improve your MMO. Coding may seem a little daunting at first, but it gives you the power to create additional features without needing to wait for someone else to code them. You can also find other users who might generate code for other tasks that you can use within your own games.

If you double-click on any of the projects, a code page will appear, as shown in Figure 15.9.

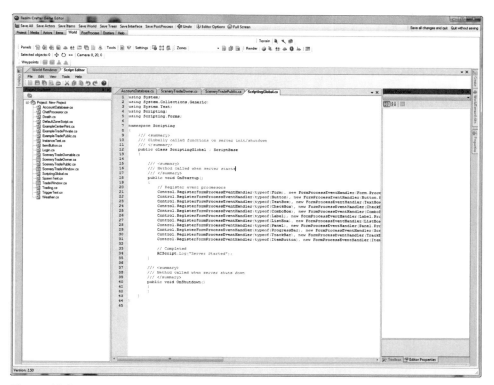

Figure 15.9
The code page.

CREATING A DIALOG BOX

Within the Realm Crafter Script Editor, you can create a script and dialog boxes. This section shows you how to create your own dialog box.

Ensure you are on the World Renderer tab and that the Script Editor is loaded. Then, follow these steps:

1. Click on the New button. A New Script dialog box appears.

2. From the Script Type drop-down menu, click on User Form, as shown in Figure 15.10.

Figure 15.10
The New Script dialog box.

3. Type in the name for the script. This example uses NewTest as the name. Click on the OK button.

4. You should now see the NewTest.cs file appear in the Project Explorer. If you were to double-click on it, you would see the code behind the dialog box. This isn't of much use to you unless you are an experienced programmer who prefers to create dialog boxes in code view.

5. The dialog box should automatically appear in the code area; if it doesn't, right-click on the NewTest.cs file and select View Designer, as shown in Figure 15.11.

6. You will now see a blank dialog box, as shown in Figure 15.12. If you click on the dialog box you will see its properties appear in the Editor Properties window on the right side of the application window, as shown in Figure 15.13.

Figure 15.11
The Script designer option.

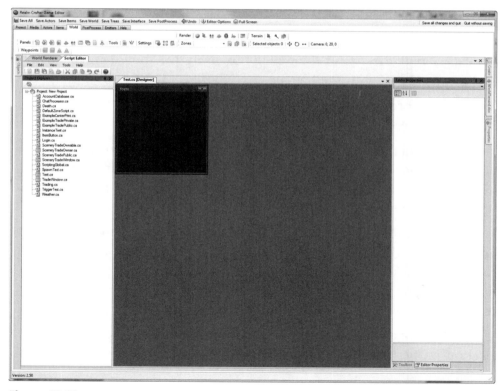

Figure 15.12
A blank dialog box.

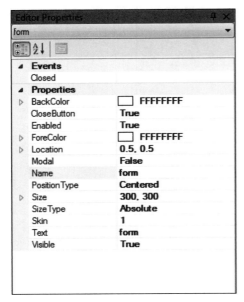

Figure 15.13
The properties for the blank dialog box.

7. You can change the size of the dialog box using the mouse cursor or by typing some values into the Size property box.

8. If you want to remove the ability for the user to close the dialog box, you can change the CloseButton's value to False.

9. You can see that the dialog box's header currently reads "form." This example changes the header to Book Test. Type your text into the Text field in the Editor Properties dialog box. Once you press Return, it will automatically update.

10. You need to add an image to the dialog box. To do this, you need to access the toolbox tab at the bottom-left side of the Editor Properties dialog box. Click on this to display all possible dialog box options as shown in Figure 15.14. To add an image, you need the Panel item. Drag and drop the Panel item onto your dialog box.

11. You will now have access to properties for this panel. Click on the Location property and type **0, 0** and press Return.

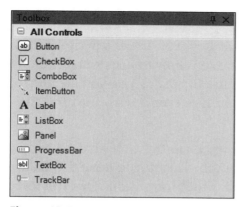

Figure 15.14
The Toolbox.

12. Resize the item so that it fits into the dialog box space.

13. Select the Image option and type the name for the image, this must also include the full path to that particular image. This example uses the RC. jpg file that is located in the following folder: C:\Program Files\Solstar Games\Realm Crafter 2\Data\RC.jpg.

14. Drag and drop a progress bar on to the screen. Place it and resize it.

15. Drop a button onto the screen and place it under the progress bar.

16. In the button properties under text, type the text **Move to Zone**. You can see an example of this dialog box in Figure 15.15.

Figure 15.15
The dialog box with the Move to Zone button added.

SCRIPT EDITOR EXAMPLE

In this section of the book, you'll take a look at how you use the Script Editor and you'll also create a simple example that you can follow to help you feel more comfortable with how the system works. You'll use the dialog box you created to warp the player to another zone when typing in the term /**twarp** into the chat window.

You have created a dialog box, and you need to create the code that responds when the player clicks on the Move to Zone button. Ensure you have the dialog box on-screen and then double-click on the Move to Zone button. This will take you into the code for this dialog box, and also place you where the code is activated when the player presses the button, as shown in Figure 15.16.

```
1   using System;
2   using System.Collections.Generic;
3   using System.Text;
4   using Scripting.Forms;
5   using Scripting;
6
7   namespace UserScripts
8   {
9       /// <summary>
10      /// Enter description here
11      /// </summary>
12      public partial class NewTest : Form
13      {
14
15
16          public NewTest()
17          {
18              InitializeComponent();
19
20          }
21
22          private void button1_Click(object sender, FormEventArgs e)
23          {
24
25          }
26
27      }
28  }
29
```

Figure 15.16
The code in Newtest.cs.

I have added some code that will activate the code to warp the player after a set amount of time has passed, as shown in Figure 15.17.

Once the code has been entered for this dialog box, you then need to initiate the dialog box when the player enters /**twarp** into the chat window. As all chat

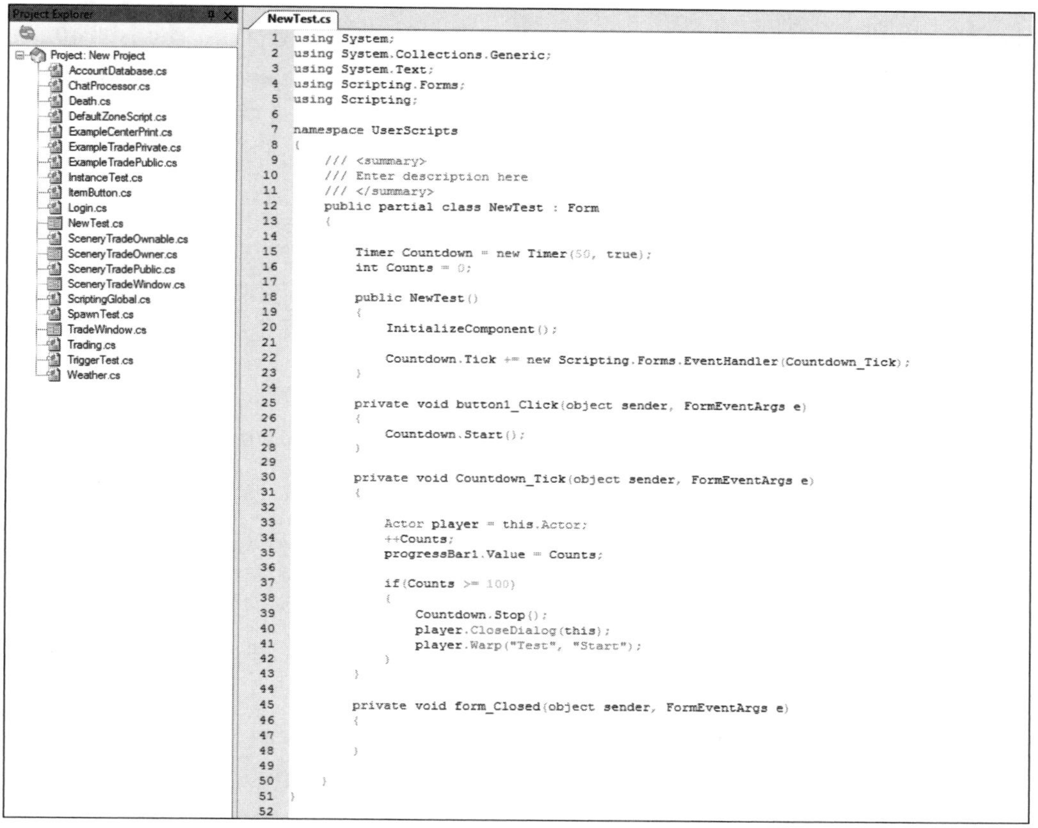

Figure 15.17
The code block that activates when the player clicks on the button.

functions are contained within the ChatProcessor.cs file, you must double-click on the file in the Project Explorer to bring up the code.

You are now in the ChatProcessor file, but before you add any code, you need to tell this file that you are going to be using the namespace UserScripts. Without this code, the script won't run. You can see this extra line of code in Figure 15.18.

```
1   using System;
2   using System.Collections.Generic;
3   using System.Text;
4   using System.Text.RegularExpressions;
5   using UserScripts;
6
```

Figure 15.18
The UserScripts line required to access the code.

Now you need to change the warping code and replace it with your own. You are looking for the line that activates a bit of code when the player uses warp; this can be seen in Figure 15.19. Select this line and delete the code.

```
78          else if (command.Equals("twarp", StringComparison.CurrentCultureIgnoreCase))
79          {
80              actor.Warp(data, "Start");
81          }
```

Figure 15.19
The code that requires deleting.

Replace the code shown in Figure 15.19 with the code shown in Figure 15.20.

```
79          else if (command.Equals("twarp", StringComparison.CurrentCultureIgnoreCase))
80          {
81
82              NewTest TestForm = new NewTest();
83              actor.CreateDialog(TestForm);
84
85          }
```

Figure 15.20
The new code you are using to warp.

Note

You can find the original example of this code on YouTube written by Jared Belkus at http://www. youtube.com/user/jbelkus123#p/u/3/OICpDwZwKGE. Check it out to see how it all flows and to get more guidance if you're having problems getting it to work.

Once you have entered all of this code, you can test that you haven't made any mistakes by running the test server. If all of your servers come online, your code is working correctly, as shown in Figure 15.21.

Run your game. When you enter the world, you will need to enter the chat window, so type **/twarp** and you will immediately see the dialog box appear on-screen. Click on the button and it will begin to transport you to your new zone.

Congratulations, you have successfully created your first C# script and implemented it within your MMO.

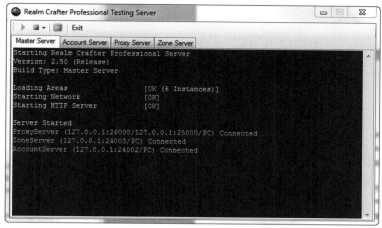

Figure 15.21
The Server dialog box showing that all of the servers are running successfully.

If you are having trouble with the code, you can review it here:

```
NewTest.cs
using System;
using System.Collections.Generic;
using System.Text;
using Scripting.Forms;
using Scripting;

namespace UserScripts
{
    /// <summary>
    /// Enter description here
    /// </summary>
    public partial class NewTest : Form
    {

        Timer Countdown = new Timer(50, true);
        int Counts = 0;

        public NewTest()
        {
            InitializeComponent();
```

```
        Countdown.Tick += new Scripting.Forms.EventHandler(Countdown_Tick);
    }

    private void button1_Click(object sender, FormEventArgs e)
    {
        Countdown.Start();
    }

 private void Countdown_Tick(object sender, FormEventArgs e)
{

    Actor player = this.Actor;
    ++Counts;
    progressBar1.Value = Counts;

    if(Counts >= 100)
    {
        Countdown.Stop();
        player.CloseDialog(this);
        player.Warp("Test", "Test_Enter");
    }
  }

    private void form_Closed(object sender, FormEventArgs e)
    {

    }

  }
}
```

Here is ChatProcessor.cs (the code change in the else if statement for twarp):

```
else if (command.Equals("twarp", StringComparison.CurrentCultureIgnoreCase))
        {

        NewTest TestForm = new NewTest();
        actor.CreateDialog(TestForm);

        }
```

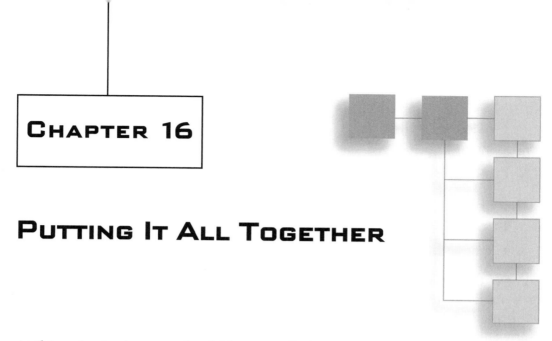

CHAPTER 16

PUTTING IT ALL TOGETHER

At this point in time you should be generally happy with the overall idea of what an MMO consists of, and how to get around the Realm Crafter tool to start putting your game together. This chapter explores all of the tasks that you need to follow to get your game up and running.

Note

You may also want to read Chapter 18 before starting on your MMO as it contains useful information about various content and websites that will be useful in making your game.

Here are the main considerations that you should be looking at when making your MMO:

- Concept and idea
- Scope and target audience
- Budget and time frame
- Servers and equipment
- Planning
- Team and outsourcing
- Design and story

- Prototyping
- Script building
- Content creation
- Quest creation
- Testing
- Release
- Continual improvement

Some of these processes you may just think about, whereas others you may want to write down (such as a planning or scope document) or even draw (such as your design and creature ideas). Doing so will give you a clearer picture of what you want to create and ultimately how you will create it.

Note

Some of the items listed for consideration may take place at the same time or over a long period of time, or can be part of the same process. For example, you may want to combine equipment, budget, timeframe, scope, and concept all into one process. The list is not exhaustive and is meant to give you an idea of the concepts you should be thinking about.

Note

It's often very useful to look at what happens in the real world of MMOs to see how it might help you make a better MMO. This is always a useful exercise, even if you don't have a $50-million budget. You may only be making an MMO in your spare time, or hoping to get a small group of people who will pay you for continual development, but looking at how other people approach making a game can provide you with useful information.

CONCEPT AND IDEA

Chapter 3 talked about coming up with an MMO idea. It's essential that the first thing you think about is what kind of MMO you want to make. Of course, there are some other considerations that you will use at the same time as deciding what to make, such as the scope of the project (its size), the budget that you have available to you, and of course the time frame. All of these have a direct link to the type of game that you want to make.

Note

Please look at Chapter 3 for more information with how to come up with your idea.

SCOPE AND TARGET AUDIENCE

The scope of your MMO will consist of a number of considerations, including the number of users that will access your service and their average age. Before you start designing your MMO, you should write a scope document, which will contain information on the user base, costs, equipment needs, and the audience you want to target.

If you are making an 18-rated MMO, it's possible that the number of users will be significantly less than if you were targeting an MMO for younger users (this is not always the case, but this will depend on the market you are targeting). Some say that people who are older have better access to funds to pay for games. A younger audience is less likely to be able to pay for subscriptions and value items.

This isn't always the case, however. If the parents of the children believe the game to be suitable and reliable, they will pay for access for their children. Many child-friendly MMOs are very successful because the parents trust the content and payment systems provided by those companies.

The scope of your project will also depend on how much money you intend to spend on the project. This should also be based on the research that you should carry out on the number of users who will access your game and how often they will spend money. You will also need to take into account any hardware/access and staff costs (if any). Even if you are making an MMO for fun, you may want to set up some aspect of payment system, and you may rely on these payments to finance the services to allow it to run, so you should invest some time in working out how many people/payments you will need to ensure you can continue to run the game. There is no point in spending 12 months making a game only to find you cannot afford to actually run it once you've finished it.

Once you know the scope of your project (whether it takes one month to make or three years), and how many users you intend to have, as well as the income expectations, you have a good idea of what is possible. Of course, even the best projections can lead to miscalculations and errors. There have been cases where

MMOs have had $100 million invested in them only to find that after a few months of running they were closed down. In the world of MMOs these days, unless you have a very well known IP and a game with a lot of depth, no MMO will be able to garner that level of success with that kind of budget.

This is why free-to-play is a tempting prospect for games companies. But for an individual or a group of indie game developers trying to make a fun game, free-to-play may not seem initially like a good idea, because how will you get people to pay for your game? A larger user base that plays the game for free doesn't make anyone any money, but when you add payable items and upgrades, it can work out to be financially better than a smaller user base who is paying a monthly subscription. If you are making your MMO on a very small scale, asking for donations can help a little but obviously if no one visits your website or pays, it won't help you get very far. If you are also small scale, its unlikely that people may pay for upgradable items, especially if your game is very much in the early stages of development and you have already released it.

You might find it helpful to look at how things are done in the commercial world, as this can give you ideas, or warnings about what you should or shouldn't do when making your own game. For example, it's quite common for a commercial MMO to start out with high figures as it's released, yet as soon as the initial subscription is over (usually 30 days when buying the game), the numbers drop considerably. If you are making an MMO for your friends, this really isn't a problem. If you are intending to make a larger game and hoping to make enough money to continue development, then it is. Over a short time, players will get far along in your game and then will probably go off somewhere else (especially as there are many free-to-play quality MMOs available). This is true of bigger budget MMOs. There are so many available these days, people download a game, play it for a while, and then move onto the next MMO that's released.

There are stories of hardcore MMO players getting to the maximum level cap of commercial MMO games within a few days or weeks of it being released. These are obviously a small number of the people who play an MMO, but these are also the people who are more likely to stay with an MMO over a long period of time.

One of the biggest issues facing commercial MMOs is that because they are so expensive and take so long to create, when they are released, they are not as complete as they should be and will take another 6 to 12 months to get to the point where they have enough content and are bug free for the majority of players. Unfortunately, in the commercial world a lot of these players may have already moved on to another game and you may not be able to get them back. It's important to consider getting a small group of testers or friends to play an early zone first and get it as content complete as possible before moving onto the next area.

All of this information should be contained in your scope document, which is a basic plan for how you intend to make the game and finance it. This will be useful for anyone who you get to help with your MMO, as it shows that you have an idea of how you intend to make it successful.

BUDGET AND TIME FRAME

Making a game can cost a lot of money. If you are making a game in your spare time, you might consider the time and effort, the late nights, and weekends to be free. Some people consider this the "cost" of making a game. Some people look at the cost of making a game only in terms of what money they spend on it; for example, paying a friend to make a logo for your website, or money used to purchase some sound effects.

In some cases, you can make a game for the PC-based platform, especially if you can program, as you can use free programs such as Visual Studio to make your game. If you want to make something more specialized or for a particular platform, you might want to use middleware and there are obvious costs to that—buying the tool to make the game, for example.

So when considering your budget, take into account the following:

- **Assets:** Art (2D and 3D), sound, and music.
- **Website:** Website hosting and domain costs.
- **Servers and other equipment:** What will you run the server on; how will other users access it.
- **Staff:** This might be your friends working on it for free or you might be paying people based on the success of your game.

These items would probably be detailed in your scope document or at least noted so you have an idea of your costs. This also gives you a good indication of the monthly cost of running a game. MMOs in the commercial world cost tens or even hundreds of thousands of dollars to run every month. There is a cost for the amount of staff running them and the amount of servers required to allow large numbers of players to play at the same time. Of course, if you are making a small game these things won't be a big consideration, but if you know what your outgoings will be for a small start-up, such as a webhost, a server, and the software. You can then work out what number of users (if any) you will need to keep those services running. In a worse case scenario, if you have no users, what would be the cost of running the system. This is essential bottom line number that is important to know if you are making an MMO with limited resources, as it may take you a while before you have enough content to get users playing it, so for a while you may have no or very few users. If you cannot run the equipment and pay for the webhost, you may be better off creating your MMO locally on your PC and getting your friends to test it until you are in a position to release it properly. At least making this budget estimate will allow you to figure out how you need to proceed.

You may want to consider how much time and effort you want to put into making your MMO, as this will have a big impact on the financial cost as well as the time it takes to make it. Many indie game creators underestimate the amount of time it will take to make a game. If you are honest with yourself at the beginning about how long the project will take, there is a better chance you will complete it. If you think a game will take one month to make and it takes two years, the majority of people trying to make that underestimated project are likely to give up. Understanding what you need to do and how long it will take are very important for both the developer's sanity and for completing a project.

SERVERS AND EQUIPMENT

This fits in nicely with the scope of the project, the budget, and the overall understanding of your user base. If you are aiming your MMO at a few family and friends, you might be able to get away with running your game on your PC and getting them to connect over your DSL connection. If you are looking at the next level up, where you want tens or hundreds of people to access your game, you might need dedicated server hardware and hosting. The great thing with Realm Crafter is that you can start off small, locally on your PC, and move up when you have the content in place.

Note

One of the benefits of having the client download the client software is that you can pass a lot of the effort from the server to the client's PC. Content such as graphics and sound will be stored locally, while movement, position, and saved information will be saved on the server. This means that less bandwidth is required to run the game, which in turn should mean lower costs.

PLANNING

You can't make an MMO without some serious planning. As you can imagine, making something as complex as a normal game requires detailed plans. However, if you are making an online game that even a few people can play, it still requires a good deal of planning to ensure it gets made, but also contains the right feature set that the players will want.

There are a few different times when planning is very important:

- **Pre-production:** Before the game is made, you need to consider what plans you have in place to make the actual game. These plans should detail who is working on the game and which areas they will be responsible for. You should break down each "task" that will need to be handled by someone and consider how long it will take, how difficult the task is, and what skills the person who takes on the task will need (do they need to be a C# programmer, for example). Once you have done this planning, you will have an idea of your potential start and finish dates.

- **In-production:** Things never go according to plan, so while you are making your MMO, make sure you keep your plan up-to-date and change any details and timescales as the game evolves. For example, if you decide to add a new feature, this will need to be detailed and planned. If one of the people who is helping you with the game becomes ill, you will also need to modify your plan so that your timescale is reflecting the lack of work on a particular feature.

- **Post-production:** Once the game has been completed, there may be other ongoing tasks that you need to consider and plan for, such as regular server maintenance (many MMO systems require routine maintenance and reboots to ensure they run smoothly), fixes to the game, and content updates.

Team and Outsourcing

You may need other people to help you complete your MMO. These could be friends, people you pay, or people who volunteer.

It would be possible to create certain types of small MMOs on your own, but the work and effort required would be quite large. So it is very likely that you'll recruit other people to help you out. This doesn't mean you will employ a team of people to work on your MMO, but you might decide to get people to do certain aspects of the work that you are unable to complete, such as the music or 3D creation.

Outsourcing means using other people (contractors) or companies to complete various aspects of your game, which in most cases means payment. You should ensure any costs associated with outsourcing are included in your budget.

Note

Chapter 18 covers more about the types of team members that you might need when making an MMO.

Design and Story

MMOs are usually very large, contain lots of content, and have a lot of quests that contain aspects of the game story.

Before you start making any physical part of your MMO, such as coding or creating graphics, you should complete the design and story. As an MMO is usually quite complex, starting on the graphics and code before you have an idea of the story would probably mean going back and redoing a lot of the content once you have completed the design. You'll lose time, effort, and potentially money. So it's essential you write at least a draft copy of the design and story before you start. It's very common for the game design to evolve while you are making it, because ideas and problems will appear that you didn't think about in the original design. This is quite normal and nothing to worry about.

The story of an MMO can be quite complex. Not only must you develop the initial story, you also have to take the players through the ongoing story as they complete the quests available to them. Not all quests will necessarily contain something that will move the game world story forward, but they do need to reference areas, people, and events that are taking place. Because of that, the story can become difficult to write, and it's easy to make errors in the story's arc.

When writing a long story that contains many characters and many story arcs, it is easy to make a mistake. These can be wide-ranging errors, such as talking about an event that didn't happen or a character that doesn't exist. An example of this is that many years ago, I decided to write some sample chapters of a fiction book. In one chapter, I talked about the main character's dead uncle, but by the time I got to another chapter, I had mistakenly written that the uncle was alive and had been kidnapped. When writing large amounts of content, such mistakes are common.

Consider planning how the story of your game will work. This should involve writing and planning some of the following in detail:

- **World:** General information about the world in which your game is set. This could include how the world came to be, for example "after the great war, a new world order begun to emerge from the ashes."

- **Timeframes:** When is the game set and what is special about this particular timeframe. For example, "is it 2050 and computers have become self aware," or "we are living in 1,050 and the poor are being treated like slaves." Knowing about your time period can set up many story elements for your game.

- **Characters:** The main characters in the story, along with their backgrounds. You will also need to write some backgrounds on the lesser characters within your games, even if it's just a paragraph or two.

- **Factions:** What groups exist in the game, and how do they get on with each other. Even in a game idea like *Zombie Invasion* there could be different sets of humans working for and against each other.

- **Places:** What are the key places that the players will visit. This could be the major cities or locations within a city. MMOs break their worlds into named zones and then named areas within zones. I like the method that is used in the game *Fallout 3,* where smaller but just as interesting locations are defined, such as the truck stop, the park, someone's house, and so on. It's up to you how much you define your world, but the more interesting and well-defined the world, the better the game.

- **Past events:** A game world generally doesn't just appear, it has a past, a history. This history can explain why things are like they are today and why certain factions don't like each other. Telling this history is not easy; some games build on the game's history as they release further versions, whereas others releases large amounts of written material to tell the story.

- **Future events:** Having knowledge of what is going to happen in the future is very important in a game. You may not be initially thinking about the future as you are creating your MMO, but as an MMO creator you will need to be creating additional content. This might mean events taking place that you didn't originally plan for. Creating a game timeline (a list of events from the past, today, and in the future) is a good way of planning where your game might go next.

- **Animal bestiary:** Creating a list of creatures and animals for your game is a very important step in its design, but also for helping you create an interesting world. You can also use the bestiary to help create a list of creatures that you use to design/model the game as well as to help write the back-story. For example, if you decide you will have a river troll in your game, consider why it exists, where it lives, and what it eats. All of these questions will be important when you begin to place these objects in the game world and decide their faction rating (if they should attack the players or not).

PROTOTYPING

Prototyping is creating something to see if it will work. This could be a simple game mechanic to a particular screen or level in the game. Prototyping is very useful as it allows you to test small parts of your game without needing to make it all first and then suddenly realize that what you designed isn't actually going to work.

With your MMO you should be continually creating prototypes to see if the various aspects of your game work and work well together.

SCRIPT BUILDING

One thing is certain when creating an MMO and it's true in Realm Crafter also, and that is you will need to build many scripts. These scripts will range from improved inventory systems to chat and battle routines. There are some basic scripts provided with Realm Crafter, but to get the game you really want, you have to make your own.

You should handle script building very much as part of the game design process. First you should be identifying how your MMO is going to work as part of the design, then you write the scripts. It is also useful to create prototype scripts for the more complex features so you can see how they work before spending a lot of time programming them.

CONTENT CREATION

When I talk about content creation, I mean 3D models, sounds, textures, and other items used in the game. Content creation is a big task for anyone making a game, but even more so if you are making an MMO. You will find as you are making your MMO that you won't have all of the content in place all of the time. For example, you may have created your terrain and have started putting down the odd 3D model, but you may find that you don't have enough buildings or content within the buildings to complete an area. The other problem is that unless you have all of the content in place you don't know how the area will perform. Most games use placeholder objects or textures while they make the game and wait for their content to come online. They can get on with making the game rather than having to delay their work while they wait for content to appear. Content usually is delivered over a long period of time, and so it's a lot more efficient to use placeholder content.

Note

Chapter 18 covers providers of third-party content such as 3D models and music.

QUEST CREATION

MMOs can contain hundreds of quests; some of these quests might be very short, whereas others might be chained quests. Chained quests are all part of the same quest, but typically require the players to go to another area, or meet another character.

As you can imagine, making a few hundred quests and chained quests can take a lot of time. When making quests, you should be utilizing the game design, story, and character information you have generated previously.

You must also ensure that your quests take into consideration the areas players might visit and what level those quests are. Many MMOs color-code the quests so the players know if they are at the right level, such as red (the player has no chance of succeeding on their own), yellow (there is a chance they might succeed), and green (the player should be able to handle this quest).

TESTING

What with large areas, many quests, and different factions, testing an MMO is not an easy prospect. The testing process should start as early as possible in the game's life. If you are working in a small team, you should be looking at generating only one or two zones at a time. Of course, you will have the designs for the other areas and how they will be connected, but you should limit the amount of zones that you have available. Otherwise, you will end up with too much area to cover and won't be able to test them all effectively.

Starter zones are always a good place to begin, because many of the initial quests are limited to a very small area in the zone, so that you can introduce the players to the basic concepts. Get this completed as early as possible and you can then begin to follow the players through further zones to ensure it all works correctly.

Note

When making a game, it is very easy to miss game-breaking issues such as problematic controls and confusing game-play mechanics. This is because as a developer you get too close to the game; you are playing it perhaps daily and no longer see any problems. Mainly this is because you know how the game works and you know how to navigate the issues. It is important to get people who don't know much about your game to play it, as they will give you much better feedback than those people who know how the game works.

RELEASE

Once you have created your game and tested it, you are ready for the game's release. The size of your potential user base determines what you need to have in place. If you are making this for a few friends and family, you don't necessarily need a website or lots of online information about the game.

If you are making a more professional game, you need to consider creating a website that contains information about your game, its history, and instructions on how to play. You may need a website designer to help you generate a quality website or you might be able to make one yourself using products such as Dreamweaver.

You will also need to consider the payment side of your system, and whether people can pay via PayPal or using other methods.

Once you have released your game, it's very important to ensure that you keep your players up-to-date on what is happening in the game on a regular basis. If you have server downtime, you should definitely be telling your users about when the servers will go down and when they will be available again.

Note

More information about the role of a website designer can be found in Chapter 18.

CONTINUAL IMPROVEMENT

Many games, once written, have only the odd update or patch, and that's it. This is because the game creator needs to move onto another project. MMOs don't follow the normal game convention. Once they have been created, they need constant improvement to ensure that players keep coming back and playing. These changes might be fixes to the balancing of the game (because one particular faction or character type might be more powerful than others). This rebalancing takes place throughout the life of the MMO. There is also the need to create new stories and quests and more importantly new areas. MMOs are always looking at regular content to ensure those players who play the game a lot will always have something new. You should ensure you have a plan for new content and use the story data that you have already written (history, current and future events) as the basis for your new content.

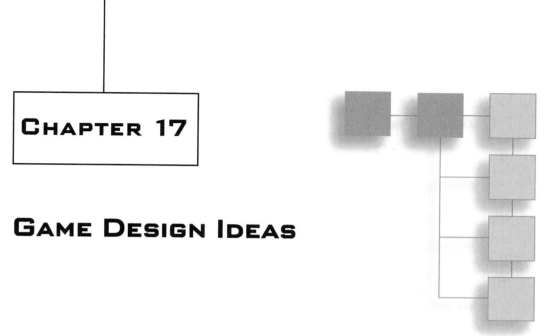

CHAPTER 17

GAME DESIGN IDEAS

This chapter details different MMO ideas that you can use or build upon for your own MMOs. The list isn't exhaustive, but should give you a good set of ideas to begin your MMO adventure. It also discusses some of the possible ideas behind the games, and how you can easily introduce the MMO concept into any game idea.

Note

These are just examples that are meant to spark ideas. They are not fully fledged ideas, but a starting point for you to take and build upon.

The following sections list ideas for some MMOs that you could make with some additional background information.

VICTORIANS

Story: It's 1888, London England. Crime is at an all-time high, the streets are crowded with thieves, and the police are struggling to maintain order. There have been a number of recent riots from groups trying to push their political aims. The government has called in the army to restore order.

You are just starting out your career. Can you make it to the top, or will you end up on the prison ships heading for a far-off land? Welcome to the world of the Victorians.

Background: Victorian England and more specifically Victorian London was an extremely interesting place, both for emerging technology and crime. It was also a time of great upheaval with many people moving from Britain and emigrating to Australia, America, and Canada.

England was a powerhouse across the globe and had claim to many different colonies across the world. This means that London was a hub of activity and the connection point to travel through to various parts of the world. But as it was the central hub for many parts of the world, there was political and social unrest. Some of these themes and historical items would play nicely in an MMO, especially from a background and story point of view.

In Victorians, you have the chance of playing one of a number of character types:

- **Soldier:** You are a trained soldier whose main skills are in combat.
- **Policeman:** You are a policeman, working for London's famous Scotland Yard.
- **Criminal:** You are a petty thief working in London's back streets.

The aim of the game is to move up in fame and fortune and become rich and successful. The character you choose to play will determine the types of skills that you will have available to use, such as solving crimes, committing crimes, or helping the government restore order in the city.

Victorian London has been depicted many times in many films and books, such as:

- *Jack the Ripper*
- *The Strange Case of Dr. Jekyll and Mr. Hyde*
- *The Invisible Man*

MEDIEVAL WARS

Story: You knew it was a setup; you knew you should have taken some of your home guard with you in case of trouble. But you didn't and you nearly paid the ultimate price, your life.

Having found a transcript of a local lord's plot to overthrow the king, you decided to pass this vital information on to the king. Little did you know that the message was intercepted by the traitorous Edmond, the king's key advisor. Two days after passing on this information you were handed a note to meet the king at an old abandoned stone circle. You went expecting to see the king, but were instead ambushed and left for dead. Somehow you will get your revenge, but you cannot go home, and you have no money. Can you save the king in time?

Background: Another time in history that's pretty interesting and has already been used in many MMOs is that of medieval times. Many MMOs don't use it directly as a point of reference (history) but take many of its concepts and build it within their old game world/history.

In Medieval Wars, you take the role of a character in one of the great Medieval European countries. Your initial aim is to try to raise funds and make acquaintances to start building a force that can take out those who want to remove the king. You are taken in by a local farm, where you are given help and a job. You know that you cannot initially tell anyone about your plight as you don't know whom to trust.

There are lots of sources of inspiration for a medieval-based game, in TV programs, books, and films such as the following.

TV:

- *Robin Hood*
- *Robin of Sherwood*
- *Cadfael*
- *Merlin*
- *Horrible Histories*

Movies:

- *Robin Hood* (many different versions)
- *Kingdom of Heaven*
- *A Knight's Tale*
- *First Knight*

Games:

- *Lords of the Realm*
- *Castles*
- *Elder Scrolls: Skyrim*
- *Assassin's Creed*

KNIGHTS OF OLD

Story: You were destined to be king, son of Harold, and rightful heir to the throne of England. But your father is murdered and Edward has announced himself King. You escape the guards that are sent to kill you and escape to the Forest of Dean with a few loyal subjects.

You can no longer be known as the future king, but you are determined to take back what is rightfully yours and avenge your father's death.

Background: Using part of the story of Robin Hood with a twist (that you are meant to be king). English medieval history is full of tales and stories that can provide interesting quests and challenges for any medieval-based MMO. You could also make an MMO based on the *Robin Hood* story.

The great thing about the *Robin Hood* story is that you have a place to start (in a secluded location), where you can slowly open up the story as the player levels up. Starting the players in a forest in a small hidden camp is a great way of giving the players a sense of trouble and allowing you to give them easy initial tasks. Perhaps they need to get firewood, or provide food as the followers in the camp are starving. Medieval people were generally poorly fed and famine was a common issue. These types of quests can give a better sense to the game and be truthful to the time frame, which makes for a more convincing game.

You can use the same inspirations as the Medieval Wars concept.

SPACE FLIGHT

Story: The Earth is dying. Overpopulation, deforestation, lack of resources, and pollution are slowly bringing the planet to its knees. It has been decided by the Planet Council that we need to look beyond our own planet for new resources and technology and to create colonies to help populate other planets.

The Council has already begun setting up population centers on nearby planets such as the Moon and Mars. Further bases are coming online.

You are at launch site Alpha 1. This is the staging area for travel to the outer reaches of the universe.

Background: A simple idea can grow into a very complex and useful game mechanic. From this story, we have already established that the planet has no more resources, and that the Earth Council is opening up new planets and locations. These two concepts provide the core mechanics for the MMO as well as a reason to be doing certain things within the game. You now have a reason for collecting resources, resource management, and item creation. This gives the players a reason to play the game, but also a good reason why they will need to do the things that many consider "grinding" in MMOs, such as mining or collecting 20 arrows, and so on. Giving the players a background as to why they need to do something is very important in preventing them from getting bored.

As the Council is in charge of the routes in the game, you can have a reason why a place is not yet navigable within the game. It's very much a game-play technique as seen in normal AAA games such as *Grand Theft Auto*. For example, you are in a city and you can get half way over a bridge but it's currently closed for repair. On the radio the player is being told that the repair is ongoing and they will open it up shortly. This is providing the players with knowledge of the game world and they know that at some point they will be able to travel to the next area. This is a useful concept to use for MMOs. The players can see that in the future they can travel to another location, but you must ensure that the players are aware (via news or reports) that this location is going to open up sooner or later. This gives the players incentive to keep moving their characters forward to see what is on the other side of that bridge, or in the Space Flight game idea, what is behind the next space travel route.

The spaceport can be the starting location for the game, and provide some simple straightforward quests such as getting the relevant papers and equipment before transferring to the Moon base. You could also get the players to reach a particular training level and skill. "All people leaving Earth must be suitably trained and equipped before leaving for the Moon."

As with all MMOs, you need an issue or challenge to the main story of the game. It may be that not everyone agrees with the Council, and that a number of underground groups have been established to fight the Council. There may be other groups that are peaceful that disagree with the way the Council is handling the whole situation. ("Why travel across the universe when we should be solving the problems we have on our planet?") These groups and factions could have their own bases around the map, whereas some locations may be accessible only if players can infiltrate a particular group.

Finally, don't forget that in space you can make up the rules. Consider alien species and other creatures that the players could meet when going to a new planet.

Following are some resources that have aliens, space, or the need to collect resources.

TV:

- *Space 1999*
- *Babylon 5*
- *Star Trek*
- *Blake's 7*
- *Space: Above and Beyond*
- *Farscape*
- *Firefly*
- *Battlestar Galactica*
- *Invaders*
- *V*
- *Alien Nation*
- *Earth: Final Conflict*
- *Earth 2*
- *Lost in Space*

Movies:

- *Contact*
- *Total Recall*
- Any of the *Aliens* or *Predator* films
- *Star Trek*
- *Lost in Space*

Games:

- *Red Faction*
- *Command and Conquer*
- *Elite*
- *Freelancer*
- *X-COM*

PIRATES AND TRADERS

Story: Welcome weary traveler to the port town of Port Royal! Here, you can make your fortune or die in obscurity. All is possible for a young sea dog like yourself. Want to make your fortune as a pirate? This is a great place to try your luck. What about a sailor or soldier for one of the many countries fighting for control of these islands? Or if you are of the peaceful kind you can see how successful you can be as a trader, selling your wares to anyone who is interested.

Background: Even though sea piracy is still happening in small areas around the world, it was a very common problem in the 1600s, especially in the Caribbean. The great thing about a setting like piracy in the Caribbean is that there are many different stories from real life that you can get inspiration from. Port Royal, for example, was a place that pirates used to go to (and were initially welcomed) and spend their money. Thousands of people are living and working on a very small area, with taverns and traders and merchants. All of this provides a rich tapestry in which to build your game world. The other nice fact is that small islands with tightly packed buildings make the game world easy to navigate to begin with.

Games:

- *Pirates*
- *Port Royale*

Films:

- *The Bounty*
- *Pirates of the Caribbean*
- *Master and Commander*

Nuclear Fallout

Story: It was inevitable; too many countries had their own nuclear arsenals. We don't know who launched first and at this point in time we don't really care, all we know is that the world has changed.

Cellar 7 was one of the first places that people appeared at when the first bombs dropped. An old fallout shelter that had been scheduled for destruction, the majority of its services were still in place, such as an underground water source and food creation areas.

That was 500 years ago and pockets of humans have been living underground across the world since that fateful day. The human race has adapted and changed to meet these challenges, but overcrowding, worsening conditions, and a lack of food has meant that many have asked the question—when are we sending people above?

The time has come to start sending people above to investigate the world and see if it can be repopulated.

Background: With some games you can take a situation that hopefully will never occur, add in radiation, chemical spill or experiment and a period of time, and you can change the whole basis of the world that we know. This allows you to continue to include things that the players know well, but also allows you the creative license to make changes for the benefit of the game. The game *Fallout 3* is a perfect example—you can still see buildings and goods, but there are giant ants, strange creatures, and 1960s-based goods.

Games:

- *Fallout 3*
- *Rage*
- *Metro 2033*

TV:

- *Jericho*

Movies:

- *WarGames*

DUNGEON WALKER

Story: Atlantia is a dangerous place, filled with thieves and mercenaries doing the bidding of the dark lords. But there is no place more dangerous than the dungeons of the Underground. Some say they span for hundreds of miles, while others say they are unending.

There are stories that some of the dungeons are paved with gold, and that there are rubies and jewels the size of a person's hand. Just one ruby would make you rich.

Every year hundreds of people enter the dungeons in search of their fortune; many do not return. Those that do recall stories of giant beasts, foul traps, and dark dangerous passageways. Welcome to the Underground.

Background: Nearly every fantasy-based MMO has some form of dungeon that the players visit, so why not create a game with a core story about the dungeons that exist under the cities and towns above them? Considering most games make you visit a dungeon, it seems sensible that they should play a bigger story part in the game. Of course to ensure there is depth to the MMO, you still have towns and cities above ground with alliances and factions.

Different factions would own or run different parts of the dungeon; the dungeon could contain various traps and an underground city. You could also introduce the players to this world either as someone who lives/works in the dungeon or as someone who is intending to enter it. If they are someone who is about to enter the beginner's dungeon, you could have a training ground where they have to pass a number of quests before they get the royal seal to enter the guarded entrance.

Inspiration for this idea comes from a book I read when I was a child years ago, called *Deathtrap Dungeon* by Ian Livingston, which was part of the *Fighting Fantasy* group of books. These books would be read initially like a normal book, but at the end of every major paragraph was a set of choices. Based on your choices, you would be given a page number/paragraph to read, where the next part of the story would be revealed.

Books:

- *Fighting Fantasy* (such as *Deathtrap Dungeon*)

Games:

- *Dungeon Keeper*
- *Dungeons & Dragons*

Robot Empires

Story: We made robots to help automate the building of cars and equipment, and we then took the next step by giving them basic intelligence so they could follow simple instructions. Finally, we gave them the ability to think for themselves. This was our biggest mistake.

It's been five years since the first attacks, and they are becoming more frequent by the day. The world's governments have decreed that robots are now outlawed and are to be destroyed on sight.

Background: This can be on Earth or some fictional location. From a story point of view, it's not that farfetched to think that in the future we will be able to build intelligent robots that can follow instructions. In fact, we already have robots that clean and build things based on a set of instructions. So creating a story based on something that already exists that will improve in the future is a great way of building a game that links very well in today's modern world. As previously discussed, if you create a game that feels that it could or might happen and has some link to the society today that people recognize, gamers are a lot happier with the concept.

The game could allow the players to take the role of a robot or a human character. There could also be groups of robots that have decided that they do not want to attack humans and want peace; these could be elements of a robot resistance (much like the resistance in the TV show *V*, in which not all the aliens want to destroy humanity).

Movies:

- *Terminator* series
- *Screamers*
- *I, Robot*

TV:

- *Terminator: The Sarah Connor Chronicles*
- *V* (original and new TV series)

Note

I have suggested *V* as a show that is worth watching to get ideas for Robot Empires. *V* is a show about aliens and humans, in which the aliens want to use the humans for resources. There are no robots, but this doesn't mean one story doesn't contain elements that are useful to your game. Always investigate ideas that are linked to your game idea; in this case it's the alien resistance that wants to help the humans, which would work perfectly well in the Robot Empires game. Don't think that you have to watch just cop shows to get ideas to put into a cop-based MMO; look further afield than that if you want to make a good game.

PLAGUE

Story: It started as a small cough, and within 24 hours they were dead. A combination of bird and swine flu resulted in an illness that was more deadly than the bubonic plague. With international travel and large population centers, it wasn't long before all corners of the world were feeling its effects. It seemed there was a 5% chance of immunity, and while many of the world's services fell apart, the survivors were having their own problems, dealing with a lack of food and rioting from those yet to get infected.

Background: Although the subject matter may not be to everyone's liking, disaster stories and stories of survival generally make for interesting games. It creates a set of challenges for the players that can become the core game-play mechanics to the game.

Looking for food or goods, building items to survive, or navigating problems with the terrain—these all provide a challenge for the player. The concept of plague can easily be interchangeable with zombies, alien invasion, or any other type of major disaster.

Games:

- *Dead Rising*
- *Alone in the Dark*
- *Alan Wake*
- *Resident Evil*

TV:

- *The Stand*
- *The Walking Dead*

Films:

- *2012*
- *Armageddon*
- *Deep Impact*
- *Mad Max*
- *The Day After Tomorrow*
- *Volcano*

ROMANS AND GLADIATORS

Story: You are the slave Octavius; your owner Gaius owes a debt to Titus and has offered you as payment. Titus accepts and decides you are to be a gladiator fighting to earn him some money.

No one expects you to last very long, but if you win your matches you may yet win your reward of freedom.

Background: Players could start out in a gladiatorial training camp, not necessarily in a major city. Much like in the film *Gladiator* you could start the players in some backwater town. You could also start the game before the player becomes a gladiator, to allow the player the chance to explore a town and take part in a number of introduction quests before the main story arc takes place.

Roman history is fascinating, with lots of intrigue, wars, political unrest, and stories of betrayal. There are many stories that can be utilized as part of your own game. Of course, you always need to be careful when using history within your games. Although with something as long ago as Roman times, you are unlikely to offend someone if you change the facts or story.

With Romans and Gladiators you can take advantage of what an amazing spectacle living in a Roman town or city would be. You can also make use of all of the different tribes and countries that fought against the Romans as the factions in the game.

Movies:

- *Gladiator*

Games:

- *Caesar*
- *CivCity: Rome*

TV:

- *Spartacus*
- *Rome*

ALIENS VS. WORLD

Story: It happened so fast. One minute we were following our normal routines, and the next alien ships landed millions of troops. The aliens took no prisoners and began shooting as soon as they appeared. That was six months ago. Now the human resistance fights on, while billions are enslaved. It's time to fight back.

Background: Alien invasions provide two key things to an MMO. The first thing is the threat that the players must face. The second is an unknown quantity, as the aliens are fictional beings in a real-world setting, so they provide you with the creative license to make any type of alien that you want. You also have the opportunity to create many alien species, rather than just one. The TV show *V* took this one step further and had another alien species that were at war with the invading aliens.

Movies:

- *Independence Day*
- *Contact*
- *War of the Worlds*
- *Invasion of the Body Snatchers*
- *Mars Attacks!*
- *Terminator* series

TV:

- *The Day of the Triffids*
- *V*
- *Terminator: The Sarah Connor Chronicles*

Games:

- *X-COM*

FASHION ELITE

Story: You are starting from the bottom of the career ladder, and you want to be a rising star in fashion. You want to be Fashion Elite.

Background: Not all games must have a deep story to hold the player's attention. It all depends on the type of game you are creating and the audience you are aiming for. For example, if you are making a game for kids, you may want it to have a more straightforward and less complicated story if it fits your game. Don't misunderstand this statement though—kids can enjoy stories that have depth when playing their MMOs. Games such as *RuneScape* have many stories and adventures that the player can really enjoy and talk about to their friends. It is just not always the case that an MMO background story has to be complex. As long as the game has depth of game play, that is probably the key to a game's success. In Fashion Elite the basic premise to the story could be very simple. You start out at the bottom of the career ladder at the local fashion business. But in your spare time you are working on your own designs, which are stolen by an unscrupulous boss, and you are subsequently fired. The fashion business has just launched your stolen designs to market and has become an overnight sensation. Your job is to start your own fashion business and compete with this evil corporation while trying to get your designs back.

This game still maps to the concept of an MMO. The designs for an outfit could be the items you can create; you can collect things such as thread and materials. Depending on your training you could make certain items. Games such as this rely more on the social aspect of gaming rather than the need to fight creatures. So rating someone else's outfits, getting awards, and seeing/showing off outfits would be the key focus.

TV:

- *Project Runway*
- *Project Catwalk*
- *America's Next Top Model*
- *The Network*

Note

Even though some of these ideas touch on real places, you can change them to anything you like, perhaps something local or even fictional. These are just ideas for you to think about.

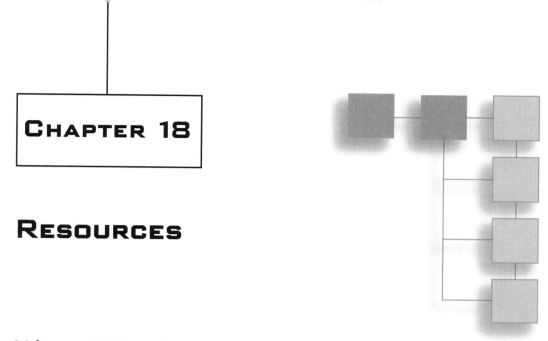

CHAPTER 18

RESOURCES

Making an MMO is a big task, and though you can start off small and build up the size of your game over time, you might want further help or resources to help you get there quicker. The type of help you need depends on your skill set and the other resources you have available, such as programming, design, or artistic talents. It may also depend on how much money you have; if you are making your game cheaply, you may not be able to pay for items or resources. On the other hand if you do have some money in your budget, you may be able to get things done quicker.

This chapter takes a look at which skills you need for yourself or your team members, great resources to access, and how to accelerate your MMO creations.

SKILLS AND TEAM MEMBERS

Games require people with many different skills and it is an unfortunate fact that most of us don't have all of the skills that are required to make a game on our own. (Although, depending on the type of game you are making, this may not necessarily be true. For example, if you are using a drag-and-drop game creation system such as Multimedia Fusion, you may be able to make a game from start to finish without any help.) With an MMO, there is no easy way to do every aspect of the game yourself in most cases. Making something in 2D is totally different from making something in 3D, with its tens, hundreds, or thousands of users.

There are many roles that are required to create an MMO, and you may find that you can fill some of these easily, while you struggle with others. The following list will give you an idea of the kind of skills that are needed in the creation and management of an MMO. Some of these skills you might not have, but as you scale your game upwards, you might find you need some of these additional skills to help push your game to the next level.

- **Designer:** The designer is the person who sets the overall theme of the game, generates the core ideas, and designs how it will generally work. The designer needs to come up with a general plot theme; he or she can do this independently or use a story writer, or a combination of both. The designer will create a multitude of material that documents the fine details of how the game will play. All through the game's creation, the designer will continue to have input on how things work, or should work, or how things might change if a particular feature is not working as expected. It is most likely that you are the designer of the MMO; you may be doing this process alone or with a friend.

- **Story Writer:** Even though you might have a theme for the MMO, you still need the idea to be expanded. MMOs require a lot of back-story. A back-story is the history of a character, the setting, and related events, all which give the game a level of depth that is essential if you are making a good MMO. The designer might create the basics, and then the story writer takes the basic plot and expands upon the back-story and develops the characters' details. For example, in the zombie concept used in this book, you might explain who the sheriff is and his history with the people he meets. The main issue for MMOs is how you introduce this information to the players so that they can understand better the game world they are living/playing in. In many games, this might take the form of an introduction video(s), cut scenes, narration, or other game-play features that focus the player's attention on a particular text. You may find that the writer and designer are the same people.

- **UI (User Interface) Artist:** This is the players' HUD (Heads Up Display), menu options, and any graphics that the players see in-game that allow them to play the game. UI artists have a particular set of skills that allows them to understand what works well with the game genre, and allows the player to navigate the UI successfully. UI Artists usually work closely with designers to ensure that the game design is reflected to the player.

- **Model Artist:** A model is the graphical 3D content that makes up an MMO. A model could be represented in game by many different things, such as a building, an animal, a human, a table, or a piece of furniture or household item. Some model artists might have particular skills, and may only be able to create certain model types. This is one of the harder skills to fill in the role of an independent MMO, but it is also time-consuming. You will read about alternatives to this later in this chapter.

- **Website Designer:** If you are making an MMO initially for your friends to play together, you can almost immediately cross this off your list of required skills. If you are making an MMO that people will pay for, this is an essential part of your game. An MMO website needs to contain information such as how to get started on the game, how to create an account, the price (if any) of the game, and information about the game world. You will also need basic introductions about how to complete the main tasks in a game, such as how to trade, communicate, where to store goods that you collect, and so on. It's surprising how little information some MMOs give about playing the game, and are so complex that all you see from new players are lots of questions in the chat window asking how to complete what should be a simple task or something that should be mentioned in the documentation. One of the best approaches to documentation that I've seen is for *Ultima Online*. The guides are extensive and contain a lot of information to get a player started quickly in the game. Unfortunately, many MMOs ever since that game have not been as successful at following that example.

- **Sound Designer:** Creating an atmospheric game is something that can make a game feel more realistic, scary, or accurate, depending on the type of game. Horror games need good sound to make the player feel that anything could happen around the next corner, whereas First Person Shooters need to use realistic gunfire and loading sounds to make the players feel they are right in the middle of the action.

MMOs have an extremely wide range of sound requirements, from birds chirping, to footsteps, to hitting/attacking sounds.

▪ **Music Creator/Designer:** Many MMOs use music as a way of welcoming players to a new area or region. For example, in *World of Warcraft,* you might hear a triumphant music score when visiting your home city. There are other times you might want to use music, such as during game loading, at the menu screens, or when players are travelling between areas.

▪ **Mission Creator:** The mission creator is the person who generates missions for the game. He or she may be someone who actually writes the mission scope or follows a brief from the designer.

▪ **Mission Designer:** This could be the same person as the Mission Creator or the Game Designer, but the mission designer's job is to create as many high-quality missions (quests) as possible. These missions should be based on the story of the game, helping to unfold parts of the story as the players progress through the missions. For example, in the Zombie Invasion MMO example, you could have a number of missions to rescue particular characters from the town where the game is situated. This would allow you to provide more details about the characters. The mission designer might be using background information provided by the storywriter.

▪ **World/Level Editor:** The world/level editor is the person who generates the world that the players move around. This can include placing small objects around a particular area or building or creating the landscape in a zone. In some games, the terrain is randomly generated and then modified using a terrain map and then the Level Editor will modify this world to suit the design. The World/Level Editor's job is actually quite important, and will provide the users with visual cues so that early on the players know which direction they should be travelling. The Level Editor's job is also key in ensuring the game world is realistic and believable. Even when it's a cartoon-based MMO, you still need to make that believable for the type of game you are creating.

▪ **Video Editor:** There are a number of places where video is essential within an MMO. This could be the CGI video at the start of the game, which introduces you to the game world, or in game videos used on the website for promotional purposes. You can even have videos while the players are travelling between worlds, or for set pieces/instances in the game. Most MMOs will have at least the intro video and game-play videos on their websites, unfortunately not many have further in-game videos to help tell the story to the players. This is a great shame as it's a fantastic way of continuing to tell the story of the game and is much easier for the players to understand than using lots of text. The only downside to doing this is the time and cost to implement it, which is why many MMOs have not gone down this route in-game.

- **QA:** Quality Assurance, or game testers, are an extremely important aspect of any game. They are the people who will test various parts of your game over and over again. They will test the game in many ways to ensure that they can replicate what the users would do. Unfortunately, MMOs are notoriously difficult to test. Unlike a linear game, where you pretty much know where the players will go and what they are likely to do, an MMO has so much depth that it can be difficult to replicate everything players could do within the game; in fact, it's generally impossible. When looking for testers, it is usually better to get people to help who were not involved in the game's development, as they can usually find bugs that someone developing the game might easily miss.

- **Customer Services:** If you are thinking of creating an MMO where money will change hands, you should have someone (or a collection of people) who will look after customer queries. This might include dealing with payment creating or payment issues, such as someone not getting a particular service that they have paid for.

- **Events Manager:** Once an MMO is up and running, that isn't the end of the game-creation process, unlike traditional games where you can make a game, sell it, and not make any more content for it (ignoring *DLC* in this instance). An MMO requires constant maintenance and, more importantly, new features. MMO players are more likely to invest more time and effort into a game over a period of time, and if you want to keep these players coming back, you need to consider creating or setting up new content and, in this case, events.

An *event* is something that happens on a regular basis in MMOs—it could be a collection of events that happen at particular times, such as the Christmas holiday or Valentine's day. Or they can happen more often such as weekly or monthly battles or social gatherings. An events manager will coordinate these events and ensure the user base is made aware of when they are happening. This might be with posts on a forum or website, or messages in game.

■ **Programmers:** To create an MMO, you need a programmer. You can do quite a lot of the ground work with Realm Crafter, but to really create a game that has the features you need, you need to be able to program in C#. You might be able to utilize some scripts that other users have donated to the Realm Crafter community, but in most cases you will need a person or group of people who can program.

■ **Tools Programmers:** When you are creating games, you will need special tools to get the most out of your development. This could be a tool that converts a specific graphic type you are using to the required format needed by Realm Crafter, or a tool to access the user database. Although creating tools to aid your MMO development will take longer to initially get started, you will find in the long run that the designers and mission creators will be able to create content quicker.

Useful Websites

This section of the book details some useful websites that you might want to consider looking at; this is a selection of sites that will help you get your MMO up and running quicker.

Sites for 3D Content

An MMO needs 3D models, such as characters, buildings, and world dressing objects. Dressing objects (commonly known as props) are those that make a world look believable. If you had a game set in modern times, it wouldn't be very realistic if your environment didn't have objects that are available in the real world such as TVs, mobile phones, cars (stationary or moving), cups, plates, chairs, and other day to day items. If the game is set in medieval times, it could be a suit of armor, wooden utensils, and cloth-based materials such as flags.

Of course, creating your own 3D content could take a while, and in some cases it would be quicker and easier to get content from elsewhere. There are many sites online that allow access to 3D models for a small charge, and can allow you to build up your scene more quickly, rather than having to wait for your own models to be created.

Turbo Squid

Turbo Squid has been a place to get 3D models and textures for a number of years. They have a wide range of professional and semi-professional models available for purchase. They have a large database of objects in a variety of file formats.

Some of the object categories that are available are as follows:

- Architecture, such as houses, tower blocks, and shopping malls.
- Cars, such as sports cars, police cars, and utility vehicles.
- Electronics, such as TVs, radios, and microwave cookers.
- Furnishings, such as chairs, tables, and lights.
- People, such as soldiers, medics, and business people.
- Transport, such as planes, trains, and bicycles.

You can find out more about Turbo Squid at www.turbosquid.com.

Falling Pixel

Falling Pixel is another site that contains a large amount of 3D content in an easy, searchable form. Some of the subjects they cover are as follows:

- Aircraft, such as fighter planes and bi-planes.
- Anatomy, such as brains, eyes, and skeletons.
- Military vehicles, soldiers, and weapons.
- Musical instruments such as piano, guitars, and drums.
- Plants and other flora, such as trees, flowers, and cornfields.

You can find out more about Falling Pixel at www.fallingpixel.com.

Daz3D

Daz3D is another long-standing 3D content provider, and they also provide 3D creation software, so having 3D content is a perfect fit and a single place for content and tools.

Because Daz3D also creates a number of 3D packages, their content is also more suited to their products, but you can find things such as:

- 3D figures/characters.
- Animals, such as dogs, cats, dragons, and mythical creatures.
- Clothing that would appear on their characters, such as T-shirts, skirts, and trousers.
- Hair shapes, styles, and colors.
- Scenes and props, such as household appliances, TVs, tables.
- Motions and poses, such as a sportsman posing while throwing a football.

Daz3D's content is structured around its terrain- and character-based 3D programs, which is extremely useful when creating MMO games.

You can find out more about Daz3D at http://www.daz3d.com.

There is also a link called Game Ready Content; this is content that has all the necessary parts included that will work in a number of game programs. You should check all relevant details before purchasing to make sure that it will work in Realm Crafter.

Note
___
> You should read the license terms of any models/websites where you purchase content, as some items will not allow you to use their 3D models in commercial programs or games.

Sound and Music Websites

You already know how important using sound and music is within a game, how it can set the scene at the start of a zone, or give the players an indication of how dangerous (or pleasant) a particular area that they have just entered is.

When using music and sound within your game, it is very important that you only use royalty-free content, or write and create your own. If you decide to use royalty-free music, you must ensure that you read any usage requirements of that content before you purchase and download it. Some content is not allowed in games or commercial projects. If you have any concerns or questions, you should contact the publisher in the first instance. If you don't get the answer you were hoping for (or don't get any answer), you are best to move on and find another site that can meet your requirements. There are many music and graphics websites that sell content, so if one doesn't work for you, then don't worry, there are many others that you can look at.

Here are some websites that you can look at for reference:

- Royalty Free Music: www.royaltyfreemusic.com
- Media Music Now: www.mediamusicnow.co.uk
- The Music Baker: www.musicbakery.com

N o t e

Don't be tempted to use copyrighted music or graphics as placeholders in your games as a test. In other words, if you are thinking you want a song at the start of the game, but have yet to find anything suitable, do not be tempted to put your favorite pop band's song in as a temporary measure. When working in any game of the size of an MMO, it is quite easy to forget that you have added that content, and it's possible that you might not remove the content before the game's release. To ensure that this never happens (and that you don't get into a lot of trouble), don't add content that isn't yours to use within your game.

Gaming Websites

If you want to be serious about making games, you should be prepared to read, learn, and practice the necessary skills. You should play lots of games that are in the same genre that you want to make, you should read as many gaming magazines as you can afford to purchase, and finally you should visit as many gaming websites as possible to give you an idea of what the press and also the gamers are saying about particular games. Making games is a job and requires skills like any type of employment.

Here is a list of some of the websites that I recommend that you visit from time to time.

- **Eurogamer**: This is a European website that posts a lot of information and details about games. This includes reviews, game-play videos (including the first 15 minutes of some games), and technical analysis. You can find out more about Eurogamer at www.eurogamer.net.

- **IGN**: The IGN site covers gaming as well as movies and TV shows. There is an extensive amount of content available to view, including reviews, videos, guides, and cheat guides. You can find out more about IGN at www.ign.com.

- **GameSpot**: GameSpot is another gaming website, with a similar type of news and review content as IGN and Eurogamer. What I like about this site is the "most popular" board, which shows which titles are getting the most visits/views. You can find out more about GameSpot at www.gamespot.com.

- **GameTrailers**: GameTrailers is a gaming website, but consists mostly of game trailers and videos, and so is a great resource for looking at game-play and game trailer content. They also have a wide range of interview-based videos that discuss gaming. You can find out more about GameTrailers at www.gametrailers.com.

Useful Books

Books like the one you are reading now can really help you fast-track into learning a product or skill, rather than getting lost or taking a while to fully understand a product's interface or a particular coding syntax. In this section of the chapter, you'll look at some reference material that could help you learn the skills that you need to make the best game possible.

Programming Books

As you are now aware, in order to use Realm Crafter you will need to learn C# (or know someone who can program in it). Here are some useful books that you should consider reading to further your knowledge about programming and C# in general.

Microsoft Visual C# 2005 Express Edition – Programming for the Absolute Beginner 1e
Aneesha Bakharia

ISBN-13: 9781592008186
ISBN-10: 1592008186

Although this book is based on an older version of Visual C# Express, it is written in an easy and clear language, and is a great way to get an idea of the basics of programming in the language.

Visual C# Game Programming for Teens 1e
Jonathan S. Harbour, The University of Advancing Technology

ISBN-13: 9781435458482
ISBN-10: 1435458486

Even if you are not a teen, the Teens books are a great way of getting into the basics of a subject and will certainly give you an easier start to the subject matter.

XNA Game Studio 4.0 for Xbox 360 Developers 1e
Jonathan S. Harbour, The University of Advancing Technology

ISBN-13: 9781584505372
ISBN-10: 1584505370

Even though XNA is a programming platform from Microsoft to get games onto the Windows 7 and Xbox platforms, XNA uses C#. So why not learn C# for Realm Crafter while learning about XNA development? The great thing about programming in something like C# is that you can learn more than one skill, which can be used elsewhere.

Game Design Books

Although this book has touched on various aspects of the games creation process, there is a lot to learn about the subject of good game design. In fact, this is one subject area that you will probably continue to learn about throughout your game-making life. Here are some books to check out:

Game Design for Teens 1e
Les Pardew, Alpine Studios
Scott Pugh
Eric Nunamaker
Brent L. Iverson, University of Texas, Austin
Ross Wolfley

ISBN-13: 9781592004966
ISBN-10: 1592004962

This is another teens book that I recommend even if you are not a teen. Especially if you don't have that much experience in making or designing games. You can learn a great deal from these books.

Game Creation for Teens 1e
Jason Darby

ISBN-13: 9781598635003
ISBN-10: 159863500X

In this book you will learn a 2D game creation system that uses drag and drop and a simple, yet powerful event-based system to code the games. The book contains information on how to design a set of simple games and is a great place to get more general information about games creation.

Going to War: Creating Computer War Games 1e
Jason Darby

ISBN-13: 9781598635669
ISBN-10: 1598635662

This is another one of my books that focuses on making war games. This book gives details on how you break down your idea (in this case a tabletop/top-down-based war game) and come up with ideas to create it. Although it's directed at people who want to make war games, the suggestions for thinking of themes, features of a game are valid for any type of genre. If you can design one type of game, you have the basic skills to start making a different type.

Challenges for Game Designers 1e
Brenda Brathwaite
Ian Schreiber

ISBN-13: 9781584505808
ISBN-10: 158450580X

You may want to practice being a game designer without needing to actually create a game on the computer, or challenge your skills and hone your talents before typing away at a computer. This book provides you with a set of design challenge exercises to get those brain cells working overtime.

USEFUL TOOLS

The tools you use in making, designing, and publishing your MMO (or any other games) will depend on your budget and products. Here is a list of handy products that you should consider:

- **Excel:** Microsoft Excel is a spreadsheet application that allows you to place items into row and columns. Excel is very useful in game design/creation and is used extensively for storing data. From the point of view of making an MMO, it's a very useful tool for listing quests, items, and character attributes. There are alternatives to Excel if you cannot afford to use this product, such as Open Office.

- **Post It Notes:** These can be the paper type or the ones that you download an application for and place on your desktop. When you are creating games, you will have ideas at any time, and it's a good idea to write them down. Many a good idea can be forgotten in the rush to do something else. Many writers even have a notepad next to their bed so they can write something down after having a dream or nightmare. Sometimes you might not even be at home or in front of a computer, so this presents a small challenge to make sure you don't forget. But even mobile phones have a way of storing data such as emails or task notes.

- **Word/Wordpad**: You can use Word (or the free Wordpad) to create your stories or game information. You might also want to create your game documentation and help in this software. If you are going to distribute it to users via your website, you might want to convert it to Adobe Acrobat format first. It is easier to use Excel if you intend on creating content that will be used in-game, but Word is much more useful if you want to document your game-design information.

- **Mind-Mapping Software:** Mind-mapping software is used when brainstorming a game idea or concept. You can find free or paid for mind-mapping software via the Internet. If you think of a tree root, it has many branches; this is what a mind map looks like. Using a mind map, you can connect ideas. It can be the whole game or parts of the game. For example, you could create a tree for a particular game feature such as weapons, or for characters of a particular type, such as zombies. You can find a free mind-mapping tool at http://freemind .sourceforge.net/wiki/index.php/Main_Page.

Note

The site links provided in this chapter are for reference only; we cannot be held responsible for any transactions, usage, downloaded files, or links provided by these sites.

INDEX